Encountering Difference

Encountering Difference
Diasporic Traces, Creolizing Spaces

Robin Cohen and Olivia Sheringham

polity

First published in 2016 by Polity Press

Polity Press
65 Bridge Street
Cambridge CB2 1UR, UK

Polity Press
350 Main Street
Malden, MA 02148, USA

ISBN-13: 978-1-5095-0879-2
ISBN-13: 978-1-5095-0880-8(pb)

A catalogue record for this book is available from the British Library.

Library of Congress Cataloging-in-Publication Data

Names: Cohen, Robin, 1944- author. | Sheringham, Olivia, 1981- author.
Title: Encountering difference : diasporic traces, creolizing spaces / Robin Cohen, Olivia Sheringham.
Description: Cambridge, UK ; Malden, MA : Polity Press, 2016. | Includes bibliographical references and index.
Identifiers: LCCN 2015042065| ISBN 9781509508792 (hardback : alk. paper) | ISBN 9781509508808 (pbk. : alk. paper)
Subjects: LCSH: Cultural fusion. | Assimilation (Sociology) | Emigration and immigration--Social aspects.
Classification: LCC HM1272 .C64 2016 | DDC 306|-dc23 LC record available at http://lccn.loc.gov/2015042065

Typeset in 10.5 on 12 pt Sabon by
Servis Filmsetting Ltd, Stockport, Cheshire
Printed and bound in the UK by CPI Group (UK) Ltd, Croydon, CR0 4YY

For further information on Polity, visit our website:
politybooks.com

Contents

Acknowledgements

Robin Cohen wishes to thank research participants and friends in Cape Verde, Mauritius, Louisiana and Guadeloupe, including Maria Cândida Gonçalves, Vijaya Teelock, Lindsey Collen, Ram Seegobin, Robbie and Catherine Stephen, Arnaud Carpooran, C. Le Cartier, J. F. Lafleur, Rosebelle Boswell, Loran Medea, Sheila Richmond, Mary Gehman, Susan Dollar, Peter Gregory, Monique Bouyer, Terrence Mosley, Mary Wernet, Kathe Hambrick-Jackson, David I. Beriss, Michael S. Martin, Julien Merion and Rose-Lee Raqui.

Olivia Sheringham wishes to thank all her research participants and friends in Martinique, Guadeloupe and Cape Verde, including Richard and Sally Price, Dominique Aurelia, Paulo Athanèse, Patricia Donatien, Pascale Lavanaire, Gerry L'Etang, Gilles Alexandre, Roberte Verdan, Roger de Jaham, Patrick Chamoiseau, Christiane Emmanuel, Suzanne Laurent and Barbara Colombe in Martinique; Gerard Delver, Fred Reno, Léna Blou, Rose-Lee Raqui, Emmanuel Ibéné, Alijah, Carole, Nicole de Surmont, Julien Merion and Bernard Phipps in Martinique and Guadeloupe; and Josina Freitas, João Fortes, Manuel Lima Fortes, Tambla Almeida, Margarida Martins, Moacyr Rodrigues, Celeste Fortes, Manu Cabral, Kiki Lima and Jorge Martins in Cape Verde.

Interviews in French and Portuguese were conducted by Olivia Sheringham in Martinique and Cape Verde. (She has provided her own translations.) Interviews in Mauritius and Louisiana were conducted by Robin Cohen. To minimize the number of endnotes, we have simply indicated in the text that the source of information is an interview. Where appropriate, individuals have been identified by name.

On a personal note Olivia would like to thank Emma Klinefelter and James and Leo Cattell, while Robin likewise extends his thanks to Selina Molteno Cohen and Jason Cohen. He gives a special 'thank you' to Paola Toninato, his co-editor on *The Creolization Reader* (2010).

Both authors wish to thank the Leverhulme Trust for funding this research (Grant number F/08/000/H) and the Oxford Diasporas Programme (http://www.migration.ox.ac.uk/odp/). Zoe Falk, Claire Fletcher, Jenny Peebles and Sally Kingsborough provided administrative and editorial support to us and to the programme at large. Colleagues who provided critiques and support include Josh de Wind, Khachig Tölölyan, Steve Vertovec, Ian Goldin, Nick Van Hear, Peggy Levitt, Jørgen Carling, Ralph Grillo, Denis Constant Martin and Edgar Pieterse. We particularly profited from Thomas Hylland Eriksen's detailed reading of the manuscript.

We wish to acknowledge that some of the material in chapter 7 is reproduced from an article published in *Ethnic and Racial Studies*, February 2016.

A Note on Usage

'Creole(s)' (with a capital letter) refers to a person or people who are so identified by others or self-identify using that description.

When it appears in lower case, 'creole' is used adjectively, as in 'a creole language' or 'creole food'.

The popular language in Cape Verde is 'Krioulu', which in Martinique is 'Kréyol'. 'Krio' is widely spoken in Sierra Leone, while the majority of people in Mauritius speak 'Kreol'.

Framing the Question: A Preamble

Jamaican-born Stuart Hall, who died in 2014, was one of Britain's most perceptive and revered public intellectuals. Asked to define the key issue of the twenty-first century, he responded as follows:

> How are people from different cultures, different backgrounds, with different languages, different religious beliefs, produced by different and highly uneven histories, but who find themselves either directly connected because they've got to make a life together in the same place, or digitally connected because they occupy the same symbolic worlds – how are they to make some sort of common life together without retreating into warring tribes, eating one another, or insisting that other people must look exactly like you, behave exactly like you, think exactly like you?[1]

This book addresses Stuart Hall's question. It is, of course, all too easy to list the countless examples of conflict between different ethnicities, nationalities and religions. News bulletins are replete with militant demands for ethnic exclusivity, minority-language education, religious orthodoxy and territorial separatism. Think, for example, of the conflicts between Kosovars and Serbs in the Balkans, Hutu and Tutsi in Rwanda, Christians and Muslims in

Lebanon, Jews and Palestinians in the Middle East, Tamils and Sinhalese in Sri Lanka, Protestants and Catholics in Northern Ireland, Alawi, other Shias and Sunni in Syria or Russians and Ukrainians in eastern Ukraine. Instead of focusing on the many forms of ethnic and religious conflict, the potency of which we do not contest, this book is centred on how, when and where people of diverse heritages meet and converge, and why understanding this more positive outcome might be important for the future of humankind.

We decided to pursue a number of complementary strategies. We reasoned that new social identities arise at the formative moment of meeting (when initial stereotypes are generated), identities that become modified as encounters deepen and become more multifaceted. Social actors bring to these 'thicker' encounters what they cannot let go from their pasts and what they need to absorb, or want to embrace, from their present situations and contexts. This line of thinking induced us to develop and refine three seminal concepts – social identity formation, diaspora and creolization, all of which we delineate in chapter 1.

We also noticed a decided lack of compelling historical explanations with which to situate the beginnings of cultural difference. Was difference, as some religious accounts suggest, a result of God's will – an act of divine punishment for humankind's effrontery in seeking to reach for celestial power and understanding? (The story of the Tower of Babel exemplifies this narrative.) Did difference arise as a result of genetic mutation, migration and the differential adaptation to new environments, an inference that might be derived from a Darwinian starting point? Were differences simply inevitable, a sort of instinctual heterophobia driven by mutual distrust or terror as people who looked and acted differently, or spoke mutually unintelligible languages, encountered each other for the first time? In chapter 2 we look in some detail at these initial contacts between disparate peoples and show how cultural boundaries were imagined, constructed and transgressed.

Having addressed our problem conceptually and historically, we thought it indispensable to complement 'the when' with 'the where'. Initial encounters between strangers, essentially driven by trade and exploration, later gave way to the production of tropical commodities, the expansion of industrial production and (now) to the globalization of finance and services. As we argue in chapter 3, particular contact zones (islands and plantations, port cities and 'super-diverse cities') embody these shifts in the political economy and provide the main sites, the creolizing spaces, in which emergent societies, shared social practices and new identities emerge.

Subsequent chapters provide empirical descriptions and comparative analysis of cultural encounter and convergence. Using arresting and instructive examples from original fieldwork, we show how diasporic resources are evoked and new social identities emerge, sometimes only in embryonic form. In chapter 4, we focus on language and music. Next, we consider how the celebration of carnival (chapter 5) and the construction and reconstruction of heritage (chapter 6) provoke a complex interplay between new and old identities, between diaspora and creolization. In chapter 7, we analyse how conflicting tugs of identity are 'marked' in terms of representation, cultural theory and political loyalties.

We conclude the book by indicating the way in which our account illuminates how people learn to live with difference, which is, as Stuart Hall's prescient remarks signalled, surely one of the most challenging issues of our day (chapter 8).

1

Shaping the Tools: Three Concepts

Social identity is the first of our three organizing concepts (the others being diaspora and creolization). It is a relatively recent construct in mainstream social sciences, yet now seems to be of ubiquitous concern. This stronger need to form or defend social identities is probably a reaction to the increased connectivity associated with globalization and the greater volumes and diversity of migration of all types (forced, semi-free, free, male or female, and from nearly all ethnicities, religions and nationalities). Identity construction arises among migrants, refugees and settled populations and involves assertions or reassertions of ethnicity, nationalism and religious observance as well as an embrace of more cosmopolitan possibilities. When do these manifestations of social identity result in different and contradictory trajectories? When, by contrast, do they intersect or converge?

Unlike social identity, diaspora and creolization are of much older provenance. Diaspora is an idea that ancient Greeks developed and that Jews appropriated and re-burnished for contemporary purposes. The term was conventionally deployed to represent a history of exile and dispossession, a sense of co-solidarity with other members of the dispersed group; it is associated with the development of myths of a common provenance and home, as well as determined efforts to establish or re-establish a homeland. If the term was to be generalized, the first task was to move it beyond its near exclusive usage to describe Jews (and to a lesser extent Armenians and Africans), and to transcend the trope of victimhood. This task was accomplished by social practice – as more and more groups (mainly ethnically denoted) described themselves as diasporas – and by the interventions of a number of social scientists, who liberated the notion from its old anchor points and gave it wider conceptual purchase.[1]

A contrasting form of identity formation to diaspora is the idea of creolization, our third organizing concept, which centres on cross-fertilization between different societies as they interact. One must immediately confess that this term has a remarkable plethora of near synonyms – hybridity, *métissage* (French), *mestizaje* (Spanish), *mestiçagem* (Portuguese), interculturalism, multiculturalism, multiculture, pluriculture, transculturation, cultural pluralism, syncretism and mixity. No doubt, we have missed a few besides. Without going into a detailed etymological and historical explanation of each expression, the ones we consider paralleled and complemented our intentions are briefly amplified below:

- *Hybridity* has been used in recent years, particularly in cultural studies and literature, to signify overlapping cultural traditions and the creations of 'third cultures'. Hybridity had unfortunate origins in the history of racial science and plant biology, indicating vigour combined with sterility and, in extreme versions, degeneracy, but a more positive use has now been widely accepted. One dissenting voice argues that because discussions of hybridity have become so pervasive, non-hybrid elements are 'rejected, silenced, or exterminated from cultural discourse'.[2]
- *Syncretism* is used mainly to describe the fusion or selective adoption of religious beliefs, an arena of social interaction that is discussed by us from time to time. Charles Stewart notes that syncretism was mainly used for religious mixing and refers to its 'objectionable but nevertheless instructive past. If this past can be understood, then we are in a position to consciously reappropriate syncretism'.[3]
- *Interculturalism* is perhaps the newest term to be deployed to

signify cultural convergence. Its great virtue is that it evidently transcends the segmentation implied in multiculturalism. Interculturalism has been favoured by progressive educationalists and frequently used in their rather restricted circles. However, it is gaining increasing acceptance in international agencies and the United Nations and is chosen in a valuable discussion of 'community cohesion' in Britain.[4]

Though our argument draws on all three concepts, our favoured expression is creolization, a more deep-seated idea – firmly anchored in historical experiences, scholarly use (particularly in linguistics) and popular practice. For at least five centuries there have been creole languages, self-described Creole peoples and creole/creolizing societies. We explain below how we use the term.

Social identity formation

In general, interest in social identities has increased dramatically over the past 30 years – to such a degree, indeed, that it has become a dominant theme in anthropological and sociological studies. Historically, this is surprising given that most of the grand figures in these disciplines (luminaries like Max Weber, Karl Marx, Emile Durkheim and Bronislaw Malinowski) managed perfectly well without recourse to the idea of social identity. These thinkers were not so naive as to assume that ethnicity, nation, community, class or religion ('gender' was rarely used) were fixed and unyielding social categories, but none foresaw the extent to which some identities would become so malleable. It may be that the scholars we list are too easily and conventionally chosen and that an alternative early genealogy of identity-related thought can be found in Georg Simmel, George Herbert Mead or C. H. Cooley, particularly in the latter's idea of the struggle of the marginalized minority to escape the impress of conformity dictated by the majority. This different intellectual provenance is discussed in Richard Jenkins's account of social identity. However, he also dates the paradigmatic shift more recently, declaring that 'identity became one of the unifying themes of social science in the 1990s and shows no signs of going away'.[5]

Three accounts are emblematic of this shift:

1 Erik Erikson moved the study of identity from an examination of how the ego and personality adjust over a lifespan (the traditional domain of psychology) to that of the social roles individuals are called upon to play. The idea that there might be a tension between these processes was vital to his notion of an 'identity crisis'.[6] A number of other social scientists have picked up and diffused the sociological aspects of his analysis.

2 An influential work by Peter L. Berger and Thomas Luckmann generated a conviction in social constructivism that almost became an article of religious faith among some social scientists.[7] Their work fed a radical anti-essentialism that questioned any given historical fact or material entity, let alone the contours of any group identity. In other words, representation, imagination and social action could construct, destroy or reconstruct reality itself.[8]

3 Given such a radical programme, it was perhaps a modest enough claim to suggest, as Benedict Anderson did in his famous account, that the nation was also an imagined community.[9]

Paralleling the shifts in academic thinking were changes in the real world as the axes of political mobilization shifted away from class politics to the politics of identity. A wide range of communities – ethnic, racial, gender-based or religious – proclaimed their distinctive programmes amidst an array of other voices clambering to be heard.

The outcome of these intellectual interventions and social changes was to shatter any notion of fixed social identities. The social world became a world of identity flows, boundary formation/deformation, frontier zones, blurring, uncertainty, hybridity and mixtures rather than one marked by purity, homogeneity, timelessness and bounded entities.[10] This new emphasis on fluidity resonated with many aspects of an increasingly globalized world. Improved connectivity had brought many cultures into eye contact, sometimes into collision. Increased resistance to neo-liberal versions of global capitalism reactivated old religious beliefs and new social movements alike. The more varied origins of international migrants meant that alien ways appeared not only on television screens, but also as lived realities in local communities. For radical social constructivists, this was predictable and explicable. Modernity, with its attempt to integrate differences through ideology, citizenship and the nation-state, had to yield to the ambiguous and complex world of postmodernity, where grand narratives explained nothing. Reality was reduced to radical contingency.

Following the near collapse of the global financial system in September and October 2008, the wheel turned again. For a start, nationalism has resurfaced – in an ugly xenophobic form in Russia, South Africa, Greece and Israel, and in a determined reassertion of the modernist project (which we may crudely describe as integration through citizenship) in Europe, Canada, Australia and many other places. Old-fashioned demands for protectionism and anti-foreigner sentiment have emerged from under the apparently tranquil, fluid surfaces of the transnational. Led by cynical politicians, threatened working classes and the unemployed have frequently embraced such sentiments. Even the early Obama phenomenon, which looked so promising to a world battered by the neo-conservative nostrums of unilateralism and militarism, was marked by evocations of Lincoln, a swelling patriotism in the USA and a determined attempt to reconstruct a new *unum* from the new *pluribus*.[11]

Five forms of social identity

Despite this new swirl of sometimes liquefying and sometimes congealing identities, we can condense the possible outcomes for those seeking to define or redefine their self-conceptions, or identity trajectories, in the face of the challenges arising from globalization, international migration and other rapid social changes.[12] We delineate five major forms of social identity formation, which are described below and illustrated in figure 1.1.

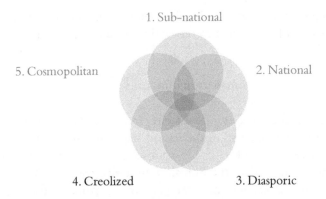

Figure 1.1   Five forms of social identity

- a reaffirmation of felt (namely socially constructed) primordial loyalties to *sub-national entities* like clan, tribe, ethnicity, locality or language group;
- a revival of *nationalism*, particularly in the wake of the break-up of the Soviet Union, the fragmentation of the Balkans, the terrorist incidents of recent years and in response to current global financial and migration crises;
- a recasting of *diasporic identities* and other supranational and transnational identities such as world religions (for example, the *ummah* or global Catholicism) and world language groups (for example, *francophonie*);
- a linking and blending with other groups through a process of *creolization and hybridization*; and
- the development of a universal spirit that transcends any particularities and simply stresses the quality of being human, namely the *cosmopolitan* possibility.

We have arranged the sequence on a spectrum from the narrowest to the broadest forms of social identity, starting at the top of figure 1.1, then moving in a clockwise direction. As the Venn diagram clarifies, the boundaries of identity formation are not mutually exclusive; synchronicity and overlapping is common. One example is that the reaffirmation of religious belief has both sub- and supra-national aspects. It is nonetheless useful to separate the main forms of social identity analytically. Let us say a little about the trajectories numbered 1, 2 and 5, before turning to our formative concepts of diaspora and creolization (numbered 3 and 4).

Sub-national identities

It is at the level of clan, tribe, ethnicity, locality or language group that significant challenges to the nation-state have arisen. To give some obvious examples of sub-national movements, *clans* are often more salient than the Somali state itself. *Tribes* remain significant units of sociality in some parts of Amazonia, Africa and the hill provinces of India. *Ethnicity*, seen either as a euphemism for tribe or as a more inclusive concept, has provided significant challenges to the nation-state in many parts of the world. Likewise, *religions* have refused to become fully subordinate to state control, have often claimed exemption from state laws (as in the cases of Mormons, Mennonites and Rastafarians) or sought to gain adherents across national frontiers. Pope John Paul's proselytizing missions in his Popemobile, the reawakening of the global Islamic *ummah* and the claims of the Vishwa Hindu Parishad are three examples. *Local* loyalties have survived two or three centuries of state centralization. Thinking merely of Europe, we need only evoke the cases of the Basques, Chechens, Welsh, Scots, Bretons and Catalans to make the point. Finally, despite the advance of the six major world languages (Mandarin, Spanish, English, Hindi/Urdu, Arabic and Portuguese), smaller *languages* have remained resilient in many places.

Nationalism

The very idea of multiculturalism (still sustained in official discourse in Australia and Canada but contested or opposed in other places) is recognition enough that the monochromatic vision promoted under the aegis of modernity has been significantly attenuated. In many places, the nineteenth-century phrase 'one space for each race' now sounds like a ridiculous claim and an absurd demand. Even the modified view of a single language, one set of public laws and norms, a shared national secular school system, a citizen army, a single exclusive citizenship and national sovereignty – all these ideal elements of nation-states have been significantly eroded.

Nonetheless, nationalism – briefly defined here as the territorial expression of a social identity – still has great allure to the many nation-peoples who do not have it. There are approximately 200 nation-states and more than 4,000 'ethno-cultural entities', members of which generally accept life in a plural society, but sometimes demand the creation of new nation-states.[13] Clearly, it is unlikely that all these claims will be fulfilled, so the frantic attempts of the newer claimants to gain recognition have accelerated. There are at least two stateless nations – Kurds and Palestinians – who show no likelihood of giving up their struggles; the Kurds, however, may benefit from the carnage of the civil wars in Syria and Iraq. Since the nineteenth century, the collapse of empires has generated nation-states; it was thus with the Ottoman, French and British empires and the pattern resurfaced with the end of the USSR. Often narrow forms of nationalism emerge, including murderous attempts to ensure social uniformity by ethnic cleansing. Establishing India and Israel created vast numbers of refugees and, albeit to a lesser extent, so too did nation-state formation in the Baltic, Balkans, Caucasus and other parts of Eurasia.

Beyond this phenomenon, the revival of nationalism has also taken place among longstanding resident groups in response to sub-national threats of secession or autonomy, or transnational threats, such as the pace of regional integration, the perils of economic and cultural globalization and the perceived threat to national distinctiveness posed by immigration – both by refugees and migrants in general. The growth of right-wing political parties in France, Italy, Greece, the Netherlands, Austria and the UK provides compelling evidence of this point. However, the growth of nationalism is not confined to these new nations or to right-wing movements. Outbursts of xenophobic violence directed against migrants and refugees have shaken precarious democracies such as South Africa, which boasts the most progressive constitution in the world. We might add to this volatile nationalist cocktail the manipulative tactics of populists such as Silvio Berlusconi in Italy or Vladimir Putin in Russia. Putin's annexation of Crimea and the continuing war in eastern Ukraine demonstrate the danger of open appeals to ethnic and national solidarity.

Cosmopolitanism

Cosmopolitanism is the most universal form of social identity in the sense that it entails the rejection or diminution of all other social categories in favour of the idea of being human.[14] It is, of course, an old idea, alluding to the openness of Athenians to outsiders in classical times. This was famously celebrated in Pericles's funeral oration. 'We throw open our city to the world,' he declaimed, 'and never by alien acts exclude foreigners from any opportunity of learning or observing, although the eyes of an enemy may occasionally profit by our liberality.'[15] As Steven Vertovec and Robin Cohen argue, the idea of cosmopolitanism has been revived as the term seems simultaneously to transcend the nation-state model, connect the local and the global, respond to the anti-essentialist turn in social science and represent complex repertoires of allegiance and identity.[16]

At first sight, the term also seems serviceable for our primary purpose – looking at when and how societies mix and merge. We were indeed tempted to deploy the idea of cosmopolitanism, but rejected it on three grounds. First, it still mainly evoked a state-led initiative or political project led from above by the intelligentsia or a political class.[17] We wanted, by contrast, an explicitly bottom-up concept. Second, it implied a normative posture – the superiority of humanism – which is attractive but flawed, for, as Stuart Hall perceived, 'the masking or disavowal of difference always involves the operation of some kind of power over "the other"'.[18] Third, we need to recognize that non-universal social identities are remarkably persistent, probably because they respond to the human need to locate temporally, spatially, genetically, psychologically, emotionally and socially. Social identities merge, converge, disappear, reappear, get flattened and reconstructed, look backwards, sideways and forwards. Cosmopolitanism captures none of these inflections, these twists and turns of social identity formation from below. To meet these objectives we turned to 'diaspora' and 'creolization'.

Diaspora

In its revisionist form, the new use of the idea of diaspora was very much part of the transnational and anti-essentialist turn in the study of social identities characteristic of the 1990s and 'twenty nough-ties'. It came to serve many functions, but, in particular, it spoke to the ways in which we could understand old minorities that had never fully integrated, and new migrants who wanted to, or had been forced to, maintain their cultural and social ties to their countries of origin. It captured and still captures a more mobile world, a world of belonging and alienation, of home and away, of political inclusion and social exclusion. Though its universality was always disputed, in a welter of studies of international migration and ethnic relations, 'diaspora' became the keyword to explain the hitherto inexplicable world of contemporary migrants (see table 1.1).

Beyond the world of social scientists, cultural, literary and postcolonial studies rapidly incorporated the idea of diaspora. For example, Chariandy argued that the concept of diaspora could be used to illuminate contemporary forms of progressive cultural politics. Although he recognized that we were still 'struggling to develop adequate terms for the profound socio-cultural dislocations resulting from modern colonialism and nation building', he found in diaspora the potential to show how 'historically disenfranchised peoples have developed tactics to challenge their subordinate status'. Diaspora studies would 'help to challenge certain calcified assumptions about ethnic, racial, and above all, national belonging and . . . forge new links between emergent critical methodologies and contemporary social justice movements'.[19]

A weighty intellectual and political agenda was thus assigned to 'diaspora' and, arguably, it was always an error to load so much onto a single concept. When the inevitable doubts set in over the utility of the concept and its increasingly profligate use,[20] the opposite danger of over-scepticism arose. We argue that diaspora continues to work as an insightful way in which to understand an important trajectory of social identity construction, one marked by incomplete subordina-tion to a single national identity, on the one hand, and a continuing

Table 1.1 Diaspora

Definition	Virtues
Diasporas display strong ethnic group consciousness sustained over a long time and based on a sense of distinctiveness.	Reflects the transnational and anti-essentialist turn in the study of social identities.
Diasporas articulate a common cultural or religious heritage and share a belief in a common fate. This heritage is shared transnationally.	Speaks to the ways in which we can understand old minorities that failed fully to integrate, and new migrants who wanted to, or had been forced to, maintain their cultural and social ties to their countries of origin.
Diasporas are marked by dispersal, often traumatically, from an original homeland to two or more foreign destinations.	Captures a world on the move, a world of belonging and alienation, of home and away, of political inclusion and social exclusion.
Additionally, or alternatively, diasporas are formed following migrants' search for work, in pursuit of trade or to further colonial ambitions.	Provides a prism through which the displacement and exodus of refugees can be viewed.

sense of belonging to an original homeland or a more loosely imagined 'home', on the other. Between the two poles of integration and attachment to homeland are many transnational practices (including remittance-giving, family visits, food preferences and sporting loyalties) that survive or thrive as 'diasporic traces'.

Creolization

In selecting creolization in preference to other related ideas, we found a concept that had deep historical resonance, not one that was simply cooked up for the sake of novelty. The expression '*crioulo*' was first deployed in the fifteenth century when Portuguese and African cultures interacted on Santiago, one of the islands of Cape Verde. It later spread across the Atlantic to the New World and many other places. Creolization is about the mixture and continuing admixture of peoples, languages and cultures. When creolization occurs, participants select particular elements from incoming or inherited cultures, endow them with meanings different from those they possessed in the original culture and then creatively merge them to create totally new varieties that supersede the prior forms (see table 1.2). Creolization thus evokes a 'here and now' sensibility that erodes old roots and stresses fresh and creative beginnings in a novel place of identification. In a diasporic consciousness, by contrast, the past provides a continuing pole of attraction and identification.

Theories of creolization are exemplary cases of polysemy; that is, they have multiple meanings, among which we mention the three most important strands:

1 The targeted use of creolization refers to cultural contact in extreme conditions of trauma, isolation and repression, notably on the islands and plantations of the Caribbean, which are seen by some scholars to be the paradigmatic case of creolization. Stephan Palmié, in particular, has perhaps been the most vociferous and articulate voice arguing for limiting the term. He is unconvinced that a theory originating in linguistics can be applied in other disciplines, which he fears will lead to a 'massive confusion of analytical tongues'. He also avers that the general use of creolization theory has become a postmodern weapon unjustly deployed, as he sees it, to attack older, and still valid anthropological theory.[21]

2 The broader use of creolization refers to the prior case of Cape Verde, and to recognized creole societies in countries as diverse as Sierra Leone, Nicaragua, the Guyanas, Cape Verde, the Caribbean islands and coastal zones on the edge of the Caribbean Sea, Réunion, Mauritius, Seychelles, Liberia and Nigeria. The substantial mixed heritage populations in Brazil, South Africa and the USA have also been re-examined through the lenses of creolization. More daringly, the diverse mix of peoples found

in contemporary cities has triggered the idea that new forms and sites of creolization are emerging. Transcending its manifestations in particular countries and settings, the Swedish social anthropologist Ulf Hannerz has provocatively suggested that we all live in a 'creolizing world'.[22]

3 The third strand of creolization theory provides a contrast between alternative outcomes of creolization. The first suggests a largely stable cultural synthesis, or 'third culture', exemplified by the francophone Caribbean expression *'créolité'* (creoleness). The second insists that creolization is a continually iterative and sometimes messy process. In particular, theorists such as Édouard Glissant maintain that creolization, in its old settings and in new 'megalopolises', is an unending 'inferno' replete with ambiguities, discontinuities, diversity and transience.[23]

Although we have been attentive to the strands in creolization theory outlined above, in this book we have focused strongly on discussions about creolized popular cultural practices (especially in food, carnivals, music and dancing), syncretic religions and creole languages. Whereas these have been studied for decades, the new understandings of creolization emerging in sociology, anthropology and the study and practice of cultural politics have permitted significant reinterpretations. Interestingly, some of the same forces employed to underwrite the concept of diaspora are also used to legitimate creolization. Mobile, transnational groups are seen to practise shared forms of social behaviour, just as diversity and international mobility have crisscrossed and sometimes deeply subverted dominant, formerly more monochromatic cultures. It is this last quality that lends credence to the notion that cultures are no longer as bounded or autonomous as they perhaps once were and that complex and asymmetrical flows have reshaped inherited social identities in new ways. While we accept that creolization had its *locus classicus* in the context of colonial settlement, imported black labour and a plantation and/or island setting, by indicating that there are other pathways or possible theatres of interaction with similar features, we argue that creolization has gained a potentially universal applicability.

Table 1.2 Creolization

Definition	Virtues
When creolization occurs, participants are required to, or freely, select elements from incoming or inherited cultures.	Mainstreams in social theory a concept that emanates from the periphery, not the core.
Social actors evolve meanings different from those they originally possessed, then create merged varieties of attitudes and behaviour that supersede prior forms.	Avoids the unfortunate biological underpinnings of the notions of 'hybridity' or 'mixed race'.
Creole societies, cultures and languages are 'structured in dominance'; that is, one culture dominates, but no culture fully disappears.	Refers to real historical, contemporary and evolving languages, societies and cultures.
In acts of resistance, new ideas, folkways and sensibilities are born.	Celebrates creativity in developing alternative languages and folkways.

Conclusion

We have framed our investigation as a response to the question, 'How do people of different heritages who find themselves in a common space forge some kind of shared sensibility?' We concede that there are other possibilities. They can wage endless war with each other – a Hobbesian nightmare of unyielding hatred, geno-cide, racism and xenophobia. They can ignore each other, living in parallel universes, sharing only the most minimal of interactions and the most restricted of common spaces. We openly express our starting point in saying that, instead of considering all possibilities, we want to focus on how people can interact with each other in more innovative and positive ways, how they can create new cultural forms and identities while drawing on older identities and collective memories.

This collective process of identity formation results in a number of possible outcomes and trajectories that we have described earlier. For the purposes of understanding how new social identities and practices emerge, we see people bringing to the interaction some level of valorization of their past identities (where they are from), just as they embrace some elements of other cultures they encounter (where they are at). Shared identities thus emerge as a combination of part recovering, part experienced and part imagined possibilities, processes that we think are usefully conceptualized through the prisms of diaspora and creolization. How these shared identities have happened historically and experientially form the remainder of this book. We have ranged far and wide in our examples, drawing on research experience and long residence in Brazil, the Caribbean, West Africa, Europe and South Africa. We have undertaken specialized fieldwork in four sites – Cape Verde, Mauritius, Martinique and Louisiana – contexts where the delicate dance between diaspora and creolization diverges and converges in significant and illustrative ways. Within each site, we have deployed secondary analysis of written material (including grey literature) in English, Portuguese, French and, where possible, a local creole language. This has been augmented by visits, interviews, participation in salient events and a study of popular culture (including dance, carnival, music, art, religion and heritage construction).

In chapter 2, we turn to the evolution and representation of difference and how intercultural communication began.

2

Exploring Difference: Early Interactions

In chapter 1 we developed our three conceptual tools – 'social identity formation', 'diaspora' and 'creolization'. However, before we can apply them, we need to understand the texture, contexts and history of cross-cultural interactions, the subjects of this chapter. In trying to assess how hosts relate to strangers, we often confront two irreconcilable views. The first proposition is that humankind has always been driven by a primordial or historically acquired sense of difference, nowadays signified by Huntington's often-quoted phrase 'a clash of civilizations'.[1] Alternatively, some suggest that human cultures are forever melding and mixing in a timeless melting pot. Instead of accepting one or other of these propositions as givens, we periodize and situate the construction of difference in early modernity, when the variety and complexity of encounters, and their representation by (largely) European thinkers, created the main lines of demarcation. At that time, difference was both delimited and significantly eroded though explorations, both literal and figurative. We suggest that, in their contemporary interactions with people from different parts of the world, long-established communities deploy sometimes overt, sometimes more covert, language and social practices developed in the early modern period. Difference is ameliorated by enlarging the capacity of human beings

of various backgrounds to talk to each other, so we also explain
how new languages (pidgins and creoles) began to emerge.

Early explanations of difference

In the beginning there was no cultural difference. Humankind,
more or less as we know it, is descended from a common set of
ancestors in Africa. Genetic and DNA research has now pinned
down one probable cradle, allegorically called the Garden of Eden,
to the Namibia–South Africa border zone. Today it is an extraordinary landscape, a wild and dramatic rock desert, with saxicolous
lichens, 60 rare grasses and minute penile plants struggling to find
the nutrients to support life. Then, 100,000 years ago, the area
sustained a genetically diverse human population, the diversity
attenuating as social groups separated and migrated north and east.
Perhaps as few as 150 people crossed the land bridge now separated
by the Red Sea to populate the rest of the world.[2]

As our ancestors moved, they faced varying climates and terrains,
and met new threats from other forms of life. They discovered new
ways of coping. They gathered food, found shelter and clothed
themselves in ways that increasingly diverged; and they evolved
new languages, folkways and religions along the way. Migration,
genetic differentiation and varying environments thus provide the
basis for the scientific understanding of phenotypical and culturally
denoted difference. Famously, Darwin ducked the issue in his *On
the Origin of Species*, published in 1859, with the exception of his
vague remark that 'light will be thrown on the origin of man and
his history'. He was clear enough that humans were one species,
while he briefly surmised that humans were likely to have evolved
in Africa. However, he said little about the origin of human differences. With his reputation established, Darwin later returned to
the issue in *The Descent of Man*, arguing that differences in mating
preferences accounted for the visible differences between native
populations in various parts of the world. Surprisingly, he suggested that sexual attraction could be more salient than natural
selection alone.[3]

Those who believe in the literal truth of the Bible advance a radically alternative explanation for human variability and cultural difference, namely that God decreed it so. This is the crucial passage from Genesis to which those steeped in the Judeo-Christian tradition turn:

Now the whole earth had one language and few words. And as men migrated from the east, they found a plain in the land of Shinar and settled there. . . . Then they said, 'Come, let us build ourselves a city, and a tower with its top in the heavens, and let us make a name for ourselves, lest we be scattered abroad upon the face of the whole earth.' And the Lord came down to see the city and the tower, which the sons of men had built. And the Lord said, 'Behold, they are one people, and they have all one language; and this is only the beginning of what they will do; and nothing that they propose to do will now be impossible for them. Come, let us go down, and there confuse their language, that they may not understand one another's speech.' . . . Therefore its name was called Babel, because there the Lord confused the language of all the earth; and from there the Lord scattered them abroad over the face of all the earth. (Genesis 11: 1–9)

There is some historical basis for the allusion to a tower reaching to the heavens – the ziggurats built from 2900 BC in the Mesopotamian valley, which took the forms of terraced step-pyramids apparently constructed for religious purposes. It is possible that the edifice in question was the ziggurat of the great temple of Marduk in Babylon. However, the biblical story is meant not as history, but as moral reprimand. It has a close resemblance to the postlapsarian story of the Edenic exile: God does not tolerate vaulting human ambition or the desire to attain too much knowledge. Any such endeavours will be met with divine retribution. The deity created incommensurate languages and cultures because, so religious argument goes, humans need to be taught humility and obedience.

In the case of Islam, the ninth-century Muslim theologian al-Tabari provided comparable accounts in his *History of the Prophets and Kings*. According to al-Tabari, the ruler Nimrod ordered a tower to be built in 'Babil'. Again, God was displeased and the common language of humankind, Syriac, was dissolved into 72 languages.[4] In his *Folk-lore in the Old Testament*, the pioneering Scottish social anthropologist, James George Frazer, noted that similarly doomed attempts to reach the firmament occur in African folklore, in Mexico, among the Karens in present-day Myanmar, the Mikirs in Assam and in the Admiralty Islands. He also lists a number of folkloric explanations for the diversity of language that do not involve towers, including the ancient Greek version that Hermes, without the sanction of Zeus, instructed humans in the use of many languages.[5]

Babylon as metaphor

All these accounts are easily dismissed as legend, folklore and myth, but they indicate pervasive, if often naive, attempts to account for the diversity of the species. Nearly all explanations of difference stress the issue of mutually unintelligible languages, with the key feature of discord surviving from the story of the tower of Babel. The etymological resemblance between 'Babel' and 'balal' (the Hebrew word for mix or confuse) has reinforced that meaning. Indeed, Babel appears in many examples of high and popular culture. Anton Rubenstein's opera *Der Thurm zu Babel* is one example. Others are the well-known paintings of the tower of Babel by M. C. Escher, Athanasius Kircher, Gustave Doré and Pieter Bruegel (figure 2.1).

To the depiction of human folly and linguistic confusion has been added the additional implication of human wickedness. This is particularly true of popular artists. For example, in Elton John's lyrics to his song, 'Tower of Babel', this is where Sodom met Gomorrah.[6] Likewise, in an imaginative contemporary interpretation, the Syrian-American sculptor Diana Al-Hadid links Babel to 9/11. According to the Saatchi gallery description, her sculptures of towers signify ideas of progress and globalism, but are 'both in legends such as the Tower of Babel, and reality, such as the horrors of the World Trade Center attacks . . . symbols of the problems of cultural difference and conflict'.[7] The poet Leonard Schwartz effects a similar association in his prose poem, 'The new Babel',

Figure 2.1   Pieter Bruegel's (1525/30–1569) depiction of the tower of Babel
Source: Wikimedia Commons, Google Art Project

providing the supplementary twist indicating the linguistic diversity contained within the monolingual use of 'Ground Zero':

> Babel of course is the fall of a Tower, followed by a vast, manipulated confusion of words.
> Babble is language's beginning, before it's a language, while it's still song.
> As Babel is both a ground and a zero, Middle English ground and Arabic zefir, cipher, Gallacized zero – let's call it Ground Zero.
> Babel is defiance of the demiurge and hubris of the heart, ziggurat aimed at suns yet unborn, inside the mouth the mouth as desire: man creates gods.
> Where before stood the North and South Phallus now yawns a smoldering Cleft, smoke subject to variable breezes.
> The smoke contains bodies; we breathe one another. Thus, Babel is Kabul. We breathe one another.[8]

Julian Temple's powerful documentary *London: The Modern Babylon* (2012) is another example of the deployment of the Babylonian analogy to understand contemporary issues. His rapid-fire collage splices Victorian and Edwardian black-and-white stills with videos from the 1980s and 1990s. As a reviewer comments:

> Violence and the mob is a subject to which Temple returns, and he is perhaps guilty of nostalgifying and romanticizing this kind of disorder. Watching this film, I began to wonder if periodic outbreaks of violence are simply the inevitable price of cramming people together . . . symptoms of the same strange, dark dysfunction that also gives us explosions of music, poetry and art.[9]

To complete the roll call we will add one final example. When Julie Bertucelli filmed her documentary of a reception class for 11–15-year-old's arriving in a Parisian suburb from 24 countries, it was, perhaps unsurprisingly, called *La Cour de Babel* (School of Babel) (2014).

Kant: the flawed cosmopolitan

Eighteenth-century European philosophers raised the possibility that cultural discord and the confusion of tongues, so characteristic of early understandings of difference, could be surmounted by discarding particularism in favour of a universal humanism. This idea was at the heart of French Republican ideals and views of Enlightenment thinkers. But perhaps no one embodies the universal more than the German philosopher Immanuel Kant (1724–1804), who has a soaring reputation as one of the most important expositors of cosmopolitanism. He indeed pinpointed some of the most pressing issues still facing humankind. The power of the nation-state should not, he thought, overwhelm the freedom of individuals. There should be a 'lawful external relation among states', a sentiment that anticipated the United Nations and the growth of international law. And, most notably from our starting point, he argued that there should be a 'cosmopolitan order' based on a 'universal civic society'. Moreover, he saw that the cosmopolitan ideal could not simply be abstracted from empirical observations of history and society but had to reach forward to other ways in which humans could construct a new moral order.[10]

For the sake of balance it should be added that these prescient and progressive ideas concealed a less savoury side. We refer to Kant's early work on geography. Harvey describes the contents of his work in this field as 'nothing short of an intellectual and political embarrassment'. He quotes such Kantian gems as 'humanity achieves its greatest perfection with the White race. The yellow Indians have somewhat less talent. The Negroes are much inferior and some of the peoples of the Americas are well below them.' Hottentots are 'dirty and smelly'; Javanese are 'thieving, conniving and servile'. People of the 'far north' resemble people of hot lands 'in their timidity, laziness, superstition and desire for strong drink'.[11]

In short, Kant's views on race are odious – an impression lent greater force by his notion that the German 'has a fortunate combination of feeling, both in that of the sublime and in that of the beautiful'. The English and French were thought only to possess half of that feeling. It is interesting that Emmanuel Eze's early exposé, *Race and the Enlightenment,* was widely taught in black studies courses, but is rarely used by Kantian scholars or cited even by Harvey, who is sympathetic to Eze's outlook. Are we imposing anachronistic notions of race onto an eighteenth-century setting? Was Kant merely reflecting the commonplace ideas of his time? This 'let out' for Kant only goes some way, as is clear in Kant's awareness of his contemporary Herder's *Ideas on the Philosophy of the History of Mankind.* Johann Gottfried Herder (1744–1803), whose arguments we discuss below, did not think it possible to classify various races by skin colour. And Herder, unlike Kant, thought each culture deserved respect and could not be considered 'inferior' or 'superior'. Kant systematically attacked Herder's views on these questions.[12] The point of this critique of Kant is not so much to disparage the poster boy of cosmopolitan ideals, but rather to confront a more general problem, namely that an appeal to universalism can mask the politics of cultural hegemony. To take one contemporary example, the outlawing of the *niqāb* (face veil) in France in 2010 was not only in conformity with the country's secular values, feminist ideals and spirit of the Enlightenment; it also conveniently played into the anti-Islamic prejudices of the electorate.

Civilization or *Kultur*

We have alluded to the crucial issue of cultural hegemony, why some cultures affirm their predominance while others appear to languish or struggle. For theorists in sociology and cultural studies, the contrasting dyad is seen as a hegemonic culture versus resistant subcultures. However, at the level of the global history of ideas, the dualism is posed quite differently, essentially as a contrast between an overarching universalism and small-scale particularism. 'Culture' became conflated with 'civilization', as Norbert Elias's two-volume history, *The Civilizing Process*, documents. In the first volume, *The History of Manners*, Elias makes a crucial distinction between the French concept of civilization and the German concept of *Kultur* (culture). The French bourgeoisie of the eighteenth century used *civilisé* to distinguish refined, courtly manners (which they sought to emulate and propagate) from crude, primitive ways. Civilization was designed to improve, modify, develop and transform simple modes of living associated with 'barbarism'. Those who opposed this civilizing mission were simply locked into irrational, backward and superstitious ways. For the heirs to the Enlightenment and the Revolution, their mission was to spread universal rights, freedom and fraternity. It is noteworthy that when Napoleon's army set out for Egypt in 1798, he successfully urged on his troops by declaring: 'Soldiers, you are undertaking a conquest with incalculable consequences for civilization.'[13] Only Rousseau dissented, elevating the freedom of 'the noble savage'. But his views were ignored or derided by those who saw culture as a shimmering star, an unquestioned universal good to which uncultured people needed to aspire by setting aside their old-fashioned and atavistic ways.

Herder's intervention

The contrast between this French Enlightenment tradition and the German Romantic thinkers could hardly be greater. Instead of being one universal civilization, *Kultur* was seen as the marker *between* societies. Fred Inglis argues that the German philosopher Herder made the key break both with Christian theology and with Enlightenment thinkers, a rupture that promoted the idea of culture as designating separate societies.[14] Instead of everyone having to move along a preordained or preferred course towards one end (effectively European Christianity or secular rationality), Herder suggested that we should celebrate 'the vital', 'seething' and 'absorbing' nature of difference. Pagan societies were 'not mere anticipations of Christianity, but brimming with their own kind of beauty and creative vivacity'. Herder's position is usefully summarized in this quotation:

> The nation . . . was individual and separate, distinguished, to Herder, by climate, education, foreign intercourse, tradition, and heredity. Providence he praised for having 'wonderfully separated nationalities not only by woods and mountains, seas and deserts, rivers and climates, but more particularly by languages, inclinations and characters'. Herder praised the tribal outlook, writing that 'the savage who loves himself, his wife and child with quiet joy and glows with limited activity of his tribe as for his own life is in my opinion a more real being than that cultivated shadow who is enraptured with the shadow of the whole species,' isolated since 'each nationality contains its centre of happiness within itself, as a bullet the centre of gravity.' With no need for comparison since 'every nation bears in itself the standard of its perfection, totally independent of all comparison with that of others' for 'do not nationalities differ in everything, in poetry, in appearance, in tastes, in usages, customs and languages? Must not religion which partakes of these also differ among the nationalities?'[15]

The Herderian legacy created a dominant mind map portraying multiple cultures that served to isolate the people of the world into hermetically sealed caged identities. Such views of rigidly delimited cultures are now routinely denounced as 'essentialist' or 'primordialist'. We, like many social scientists, are in the anti-essentialist camp. However, it is worth remembering some of the progressive elements of the multiple cultures tradition:

- With Herder, one can celebrate the sheer beauty, vitality and variety of human cultural expression. The Herderian view of culture give rise to modern nationalism, multiculturalism and anthropological understandings of culture that survived to the mid-twentieth century.[16]
- In colonial times, the insistence of some brave souls that all humanity should be valued protected forest people and isolated societies from exploitation. (This tradition survives in the support given to indigenous peoples' movements.)
- The explicit recognition that there are many ways to worship and believe provides a riposte to religious zealots who want to impose the certainty of their own faiths.
- The bland uniformity of some aspects of contemporary cultural and commercial globalization can spread like an oil slick. Appreciating other ways reminds us that there are drinks other than Coca-Cola, food other than hamburgers, clothes other than those found in a shopping mall and games other than those at the other end of a computer joystick.

With long-distance sea voyages emanating from Arabia, China and Europe, more intense and complex forms of cross-cultural contact made it increasing impossible to identify unique cultures. Societies with more or less clear edges became more permeable, with fuzzy boundaries and shared, evolving and dissolving traditions. These transformations of cultures took place in two phases. First, increasingly prolonged contact, including trade, missionary activity, imperialism and colonialism ('the modern era'); second, a step change in the volume and directions of international connectivity, including flows of ideas, goods, images, migrants, tourists and visitors (the contemporary period, or what we shall refer to as 'the global era').

Dancing and cannibal talk

In the modern era, strangers were sometimes greeted as friends or even gods; sometimes they were treated as frightening enemies who had to be exterminated or, at least, driven away. More often than not, wild stories about other societies and peoples pre-circulated actual contact. Some coastal Chinese, for example, believed that Europeans were genetically prone to constipation; this explained their corpulence. Without voluminous supplies of rhubarb to purge their bodies, so the rumour went, they would swell up and explode. From the European side, the vantage point best documented in the literature, a combination of misapprehension, denigration, fear, fascination, curiosity and mimicry marked cross-cultural contact.

In the absence of a common language, newcomers and locals had to communicate somehow. As many accounts of early encounters show, they resorted to dancing and music. Sixteenth- and seventeenth-century expeditions to North America carried complements of drummers, trumpeters and other musicians. Inuit (Eskimo) groups were induced to trade after ships' crews danced to music. In 1603, Algonquians in Massachusetts were lured by the 'homely music' of a young guitarist. They showered the musician with gifts and danced around him 'using many Savage gestures [and] singing Io, Ia, Io, Ia, Ia, Ia'.[17] Similar stories abound in other parts of the world. For example, on 29 January 1788, when a British fleet anchored at a place subsequently known as Botany Bay, one Lieutenant William Bradley had his first meeting with indigenous Australians. They were unarmed and friendly and, commented Bradley, 'these people mixed with ours and all hands danced together'. The next day 'there was another impromptu dance party'. In a later watercolour, Bradley depicted the dancing as similar to that of children, hand-in-hand, at a picnic.[18]

Another, more famous, encounter arose when the *Beagle* entered the bay in Tierra del Fuego in 1832. On board was the young naturalist Charles Darwin, who had absorbed the myth of the ferociously savage Fuegians. 'I could not have believed', wrote Darwin, 'how wide was the difference between savage and civilized man . . . the expressions of their countenances [were] distrustful, surprised and startled.' This did not, however, last for long. Competitive face pulling, singing and, again, dancing followed the unintelligible outcries. The British party initiated these antics, but the astonished Fuegians soon joined in and were quickly able to imitate the waltz. By the evening, Darwin tells us, 'we parted very good friends; which I think was fortunate, for the dancing and "sky-larking" had occasionally bordered on a trial of strength'.[19]

As Darwin's reaction indicates, just beneath the surface of these cordial meetings was apprehension. Europeans were afraid of what Ehrenreich describes as 'ecstatic ritual', moments when 'the natives would gather to dance, sing or chant to a state of exhaustion and, beyond that, sometimes trance'. The European construction of the savage, Ehrenreich continues, 'came to focus on the image of painted and bizarrely costumed bodies, drumming and dancing with wild abandon by the light of a fire'.[20] Suggestive and sensual movements particularly outraged the ships' captains, scientists and other respectable observers, though one suspects that less elevated members of the crew were not quite so repelled. For example, the botanical artist on one expedition stripped and painted his penis with charcoal to show his friendly intentions. Another empathetic observer of an African American religious service found himself swept along with the shouts, shrieks and 'expressions of ecstasy'. His own face was 'glowing' and his feet stamped as if he had been 'infected unconsciously'.[21]

What was more threatening than ecstatic ritual was the prospect of being eaten. In an often repeated caricature, natives dance by firelight, but in the middle of the fire is a European – often a missionary – being cooked alive. Two leading scholars on these encounters have largely debunked this myth. William Arens bluntly declared: 'excluding survival conditions, I have been unable to uncover adequate documentation of cannibalism as a custom in any form for any society.'[22] Likewise, Gananath Obeyesekere, who has carefully examined the likely authenticity of travellers' accounts of cannibalism particularly in Polynesia, has concluded that much of it was not cannibalism, but 'cannibal talk', that is, exaggeration, fabrication or misunderstanding. There are three main aspects to his argument. First, small strips of flesh of loved ones were indeed consumed, but these were forms of religious and sacrificial anthropophagy, resembling Aztec rituals or, indeed, the Christian Eucharist. It was an act of respect to ingest a fragment of the deity's essence. Stories of such rituals were ludicrously magnified to imply widespread flesh eating in the so-called 'cannibal islands'. Second, there are many accounts of displays of human skulls from which it was quite wrongly inferred that the bodies from which they were severed were eaten. In fact, decapitations are a common feature of early warfare and, if one is enticed by psychoanalytical arguments, are expressions of castration anxieties. Certainly, walls of skulls are often found after battles and sometimes displayed in Christian churches. (A glass case in the cathedral at Otranto, Italy, contains 813 skulls of 'martyrs' killed by an Ottoman army, but there is no indication that their bodies were eaten.) Finally, Obeyesekere recounts documented cases of Maoris holding up large animal bones and pretending to eat or lick the flesh off them. This was an apparently effective technique to frighten and warn off credulous European intruders.[23]

Even when the encounters between far-off voyagers and natives were more benevolent, they rarely constituted deep or meaningful interactions. We can assume that neither party fundamentally altered its attitudes, habits or dispositions and that an enormous gulf remained between the actors concerned. They shouted at each other, gesticulated, shared food, thumped backs, pinched skins, combed hair, sang and danced, dressed up and cavorted about. Despite the undoubted gusto shown, these displays generally remained superficial attempts to communicate and interrelate. Of course, as many tourists in far-off places will testify, one can 'get by' with signs and signals. Gulping sounds should bring you some water, pointing to the mouth while obviously masticating should prompt some food, while yawning, snoring and leaning on folded hands should produce a bed or a hammock. However, the desired result arises less from the visitors' avid study of Marcel Marceau (the celebrated mime artist) and more from the reasonable inferences made by the villagers upon whom they alight that long-distance travellers are likely to be thirsty, hungry or tired.

Early European explorers tried other means of communication; for example, they developed a quite sophisticated and extensive 'silent trade' in goods with indigenous people along the coast of West Africa. One party would proffer beads, muskets, coinage, textiles, or metal pots, a few at a time. The other would reciprocate with wood, grain, meat, palm wine, cowries or vegetable oil, again in restricted quantities. Adding to or subtracting from the pile, shaking heads or nodding, eventually created the basis for the bargain. In another unusual African case, neophyte workers developed a pictorial language when they were recruited to work in the Southern Rhodesian gold mines. Carved into trees were newly invented symbols, directed at other workers of different ethnicities, warning of brutal conditions, poor food or unsympathetic bosses.[24]

Talking to each other: the beginnings of convergence

While similar interactions sufficed for a few purposes, the lack of a common spoken language greatly impeded any more profound relationship. The creation of pidgins and creole languages was to surmount this. Cape Verde provides an instructive example. In 1462, Portuguese mariners had landed on an Atlantic island they subsequently called Santiago, one of the ten islands forming the modern-day country, Cape Verde. The name Cape Verde came from a green islet in Senegal, but it was a wildly optimistic misnomer, for most of the islands comprised dry volcanic rock. There was one important exception. In the south of Santiago, a large stream debouched into the ocean where ships could tie up and take on fresh water.

There were no indigenous inhabitants to oppose their settlement and the Portuguese captains began to dream grand dreams. They would build Cidade Velha – the first and greatest European city in the tropics – advance the righteous cause of the Church and, not least, make large sums of money by trading with the unexplored continent. If one walks around Cidade Velha today, one gets a tantalizing glimpse of these grandiose imaginings from the massive stone fort on a hill and the remains of an imposing cathedral. The dusty main square is less impressive, with a drab municipal building and bus park on one side and the Loja China (Chinese shop) on another, near a restaurant that struggles to serve any meals at all. Opposite are a museum-cum-souvenir shop and a stone monument on which happy children clamber. This, however, turns out to be a much more sinister remnant of Portuguese colonization, for it is the pillory where Fula slaves were auctioned, and beaten or killed if they refused to accept baptism. Africans had dug a yawning well in the centre of the hill fort and they showed Europeans how to line the sides with clay to prevent leakage. In the backyards of Portuguese homes and farms, Africans wove cloth strips in elaborate patterns for use as currency to underwrite the slave trade from the continent. Attempts to start first cotton and then sugar plantations failed because there was insufficient water to support such enterprises. As Europe met Africa in a thorough way for the first time, we see the development of a shared language, people and culture, all three described by the word *crioulo* (creole). We do not wish to imply a static outcome – a creolized space had emerged, but creolization continues to this day. With the burgeoning slave trade, a creolizing impulse crossed the Atlantic to the Caribbean archipelago and the American mainland, putting down new roots, thrusting out new shoots and absorbing new influences.

Africans and Europeans learnt to talk to each other in pidgins and creoles. There is a good deal of controversy over the differences between the two and over how they arose. Visitors to creole-speaking areas, and sometimes even creole speakers, often confuse pidgins with creoles, though most linguists insist there is a profound distinction between them.[25] Let us start first with how pidgins might arise. In attempting to initiate a transaction, two adults from different cultures try one word in their own languages, then another in what they think is the other's language, then use what they imagine is a mutually intelligible third language. Finally, when all these strategies have failed, a new word is invented by mutual agreement. As Donald Winford makes clear, pidgins 'arose to facilitate communication between groups of different linguistic backgrounds in restricted contexts such as trade, forced labor and other kinds of marginal contact . . . these contact varieties were highly reduced and simplified, fashioned solely for the limited purposes they served'.[26] Though the term 'pidgin' was coined in the modern era (and is a corruption of the English word 'business'), analogous simple languages, like the Mediterranean Lingua Franca, had emerged in the Middle Ages or earlier. It is not surprising that many pidgins developed at trading posts.

How then are creoles different? In his enjoyable autobiography, *Bastard Tongues*, Derek Bickerton makes the following contrast:

> *Pidgins* are often spoken slowly (about three times more slowly than creoles). They have no consistent structure and grammatical rules. They have a very limited and changing vocabulary. They are often spoken by adults. The parent languages are retained.
>
> *Creoles* are as structured as any human language; they are nearly always developed by children, not adults. They have a large and growing vocabulary that can convey a full range of emotional sensibilities, reasoning and abstract thought. They become mother tongues, at the expense of the parent languages, which diminish or disappear. Surprisingly, creoles all over the world seem to resemble one another.[27]

A complementary account of the differences between pidgins and creoles is provided by Rajend Mesthrie, who argues that pidgins are often used for 'vertical' commands, when a powerful group requires communication with a dominated group, but has little interest in reducing the social distance between them. By contrast, creoles are 'horizontal' languages that become mother tongues, or languages of intimacy. As he explains, 'creolization is in some ways the opposite of pidginization, since it is a process of expansion rather than reduction'.[28]

Starting at places where different population groups had been forced to live together, creole languages have now taken root in many parts of the world. A creole language usually refers to a European language that has been blended with a local or other imported language. However, the East African language Swahili does not have a European vocabulary and can be considered an Arab-African creole, while the creole spoken in the Andaman Islands is based on Hindi. A number of creoles have multiple root languages. For example, Hawai'ian creole, spoken throughout the islands, is a blend of English, Hawai'ian, Portuguese, Spanish, Cantonese, Ilocano, Korean, Okinawan and Japanese. Often the additions of local or other imported words are so great that, for instance, French-based creoles may be mutually incomprehensible and difficult for a native French-speaker, while creoles based on a French lexicon may be unintelligible to those using other imported lexicons like English, Dutch, Spanish or Portuguese. Creole languages took root in a tropical and subtropical belt across the world but, with migration and diffusion, are now spoken in many different countries. There are, according to one count, some 84 creole languages.

As in other languages, creoles are under a continuous process of change in response, for example, to educational policies, identity politics, social status and the migration of creole speakers to 'super-diverse' cities, where many international migrants congregate (see chapter 3). Sometimes a creole will become 'deep', as in London Jamaican, thus moving further towards its substrate (or diasporic origins); sometimes it will move in the opposite direction, to its lexifier (the language providing the dominant vocabulary). However, the general direction of travel is that, whereas a pidgin will remain simple, as a creole becomes a mother tongue it will become richer and more complex. Language, according to this theory, needs to do something quite profound. It needs to respond to a new environment, allow the full development of the human personality, express a complete range of emotions and permit the emergence of concrete and abstract reasoning. Sociolinguists are particularly interested in how children construct a new language in games, schoolyards, parks and streets.[29] The architecture of language formation, they surmise, is fabricated in the brains of young people, who build its structures from whatever fragments are to hand. This is how Bickerton puts it:

> What they build from these scraps won't be exactly the same everywhere. It can't be, because the scraps will be different in different places and they will incorporate into the new language whatever they can scavenge from the scraps – more in some places than in others. But the model into which these scraps are incorporated will reveal the same basic design wherever these children are and whoever they are, and similar structures will emerge, no matter what languages their parents spoke.[30]

Let us assume that this argument is right; if we can penetrate the mysteries of creole language formation we will have a remarkable insight into the very seedbed of human creativity. We can understand how human ingenuity can construct new from old, complexity from simplicity, and a burgeoning imagination from thriving, waning or moribund traditions. These inventive and creative possibilities inherent in creole language provide the basis for the extension of our argument to other forms of creolization (in music, dance, carnival and many other aspects of social life, which we discuss later).

Conclusion

Humankind has common origins and we still share much in terms of our genetic makeup. Some evolutionary genetic differences have, of course, taken place and are now more measurable, particularly through the analysis of Y-chromosome diversity and our new appreciation of selective interactions with Neanderthals in Eurasia. Difference is often both phenotypically evident and socially constructed through the growth of mutually unintelligible languages. Difference is expressed in many other ways, which can loosely be described as 'marking' (see chapter 7). This takes a literal form in the case of scarification (etching or branding the body), which is used to provide a visible 'social skin', a marker of a separate identity. This is often deployed when phenotypes are similar, as in a number of West African countries. Another less visible, but no less painful, marker is circumcision, which sometimes happens as a reaction to miscegenation. One historical case concerns diasporic Jews returning from their exile in Babylon who introduced the practice of male circumcision to distinguish 'pure' Jews from those who had intermarried with other ethnic groups living in ancient Judea. Differences in ornamentation, clothing, hairstyles, facial hair, headdress, dance, music and many other cultural and social practices are often deliberately adopted or fashioned to emphasize difference.

While we fully accept that there are countless processes of

cultural differentiation, our argument in this chapter is that they were rationalized, amplified and represented in three stages. First, difference was explained by religious exegesis – people were made different by the deity who exacted this outcome because of their collective effrontery. Second, difference was magnified and distorted through the variety and complexity of encounters in the modern era and their depiction by (largely) European thinkers. Third, these explanations and distortions entered and embedded themselves in dominant discursive spaces defining who is the 'self' and who 'the other'. It would be an overstatement to say that contemporary popular discussions of cultural difference are akin to cannibal talk, but we recognize some similar processes of captivation, anxiety and exaggeration in, say, European politicians' views of immigrants.

In their interactions with peoples from different parts of the world, long-established communities deploy overt, sometimes more covert, negative opinions and forms of conduct derived from the modern age of exploration. However, that period also included the beginnings of more benign forms of cultural interaction, especially the development of shared languages, creoles. Although we use creolization in a much wider sense in this book, the debates of the sociolinguists are pertinent and instructive insofar as they explicitly recognize the intricacy of and continuous reinvention of intercultural relations, and address the issue of power between those who find themselves along the many points of what is called 'the creole continuum'. This elaborated scholarship anticipates many of the key issues found in sociological and anthropological discussions of creolization, while showing many of the advantages of adopting this core idea into new contexts and paradigms. In particular, the creative, responsive, inventive capacity of creole language formation is crucial to understanding the phenomenon of how diasporic pasts are reworked and fashioned into new modes of convergence between peoples of different provenance who have been brought together by choice, chance or force.

Even in the early encounters we describe, we see how labels for the 'self' and for the 'other' were construed, how boundaries were imagined, formed and transgressed. A wholly sedentary society is very rare, but so long as settlement patterns were local and not radically disrupted, creolization remained limited. However, a far-reaching rupture occurred during the era of mercantile capitalism, when 10 million slaves were transplanted across the Atlantic, followed by 1.5 million indentured workers. The newly created plantation societies of the New World became febrile creolizing spaces, which were to generate worldwide resonances. As we explain in chapter 3, first islands and plantations, then certain ports and now 'super-diverse cities' become the major contact zones where creolizing and diasporic interactions gained their crucial expression.

3

Locating Identity Formation: Contact Zones

Two vectors of relativity are time and space. Historians emphasize the first, geographers the second. Here, we want to concentrate on the question of space in the sense of locale or site, while not ignoring temporal change. That social encounters and interactions take place are prerequisites for any social science, but as a number of social geographers emphasized, *where* they take place decisively influences their character. In short, space matters. Drawing on the work of social theorists such as Henri Lefebvre and Michel Foucault, geographers like Doreen Massey have highlighted the complex, dynamic and relational nature of space. Key to their argument is the notion that space is a social construct and thus, as Massey contends, is 'constituted through social relationships and material social practices'. Yet, she goes even further in arguing not only that space is socially constructed, but also that the social is spatially constructed. In other words, the spatial organization of society influences how it works. Accordingly, far from being the realm of stasis or a passive container of human activity (compared with the dynamic realm of the temporal), space is 'the simultaneous coexistence of social relations that cannot be conceptualized as other than dynamic'.[1]

In this chapter we are particularly concerned with investigating how space or context enables or constrains the articulation of processes and practices relating to diaspora and, more particularly, to creolization. We also consider how these concepts have developed or changed as they have migrated to new settings. Diaspora has long escaped the cage of the formerly paradigmatic case of ancient Judea, while creolization is increasingly gaining use as a concept to describe particular kinds of diversity and social interaction in many spaces. Of course, terms change as they migrate to new settings. For example, 'home' and 'homeland', so important to the core idea of diaspora, are more ambiguous notions in an age of mass travel and global connectivity. Nonetheless, 'home' has to be there even if the diasporic space has been displaced or memories have become fainter diasporic echoes, or traces, rather than constantly lived realities. Likewise, while we must be cautious in applying the word 'creolization' to intercultural relations in metropolitan contexts, it has considerable purchase provided there is clear reference to the historical settings from which it emerged and to the way in which cultural interactions are conditioned by class, gendered or racial/ethnic power. Sadly, however, such features of social life are all too common. As Françoise Vergès suggests, we can 'find echoes of the plantation in the modern world and the geopolitics of inequality'.[2] She adds elsewhere that, 'we need more studies on sites where processes of creolization might emerge (global cities, regions)' and continues, 'my hypothesis is that processes of creolization will exist alongside other processes produced by contact and conflict, such as indifferent multiculturalism, apartheid, segregation and the creation of ethnic enclaves'.[3]

We advance the view that creolization and diaspora intersect in three major contact zones – islands and plantations, port cities and contemporary 'super-diverse' cities. We borrow Mary Louise Pratt's concept of 'contact zones' as it allows us to draw both historical and spatial parallels. In Pratt's words, these zones are 'social spaces where disparate cultures meet, clash, and grapple with each other, often in highly asymmetrical relations of domination and subordination – such as colonialism and slavery, or their aftermaths as they are lived out across the globe today'.[4] The first zone, corresponding to the phase of mercantile capitalism, comprises islands and plantations where tropical products were produced by slaves or other unfree labourers. The second zone, associated with the expansion of trade and industrial capitalism, involves the enhanced movement of goods and people, which profoundly affected certain seaports. The third zone, marked by the rise of global capital, consists of cities where diverse populations have migrated, often working in the financial and service sectors.

Islands and plantations as contact zones

To quote Vergès again, 'creole cultures emerged out of two matrixes: the island and the plantation'.[5] We concur. There is something salient about both the spatiality of islands and the brutality of the plantation that made them particularly fecund spaces for the emergence of creolized identities born from different diasporic origins. Though many plantations were (in the Caribbean Sea and the Atlantic and Indian Oceans) located on islands, let us consider the latter first. Our argument is not that creolization takes place only on islands, but that the spatial characteristics of many islands have meant that one can point to a certain 'elective affinity' (to borrow Johan Goethe's phrase) between creolization, diaspora and islandness. Is there, we ask, a quality of 'islandness' that helps to explain how islanders relate to one another – how they construct their space and how, in turn, island space shapes their social relationships? An immediate difficulty presents itself: islands are by no means all similar. There are 5,675 islands larger than 10 square kilometres, most of them inhabited.[6] However, these include very big and very small ones. It seems unlikely that we could explain the social and normative order of New Guinea by virtue of that country being an island. If we are to infer that there is something different about the experience of living on an island, we have to think first in terms of a space that is relatively small, allowing continuous and perhaps intense forms of encounter between inhabitants.

There are other commonplace observations and questions that follow. The Île de la Cité is a small island certainly, but it is the very centre of Paris, supporting two metro stations, linked by majestic bridges to the rest of the city and containing the famous Notre Dame cathedral, admired by 13 million visitors each year. Merely being an island is insufficient. If we are to demonstrate that islandness is sociologically salient, we also imply some degree of remoteness and inaccessibility. That of course prompts the geographical question of how remote, and the temporal questions for how long and over what period. Often islands are bypassed, then connected or reconnected to global currents. We think that this vacillation between abandonment and insertion/reinsertion is a significant feature of islandness. As McCusker and Soares argue, 'the very seas that would appear to act as guarantors of separateness have always been conduits, facilitating movement and exchange between peoples and cultures'.[7] Indeed, such movements inform the nature of islands as spaces of colonization and oppression, laboratories for colonial projects, and exoticized spaces in which to fulfil political ambitions or personal fantasies.

We can propose other questions when defining or qualifying the special characteristics of islandness. Was the island under scrutiny ever inhabited? If inhabited, did the long-established populations resist newcomers or easily succumb to imported diseases or superior weapons? Were the newcomers ethnically homogenous or from diverse diasporic backgrounds? If from diverse backgrounds, how many cultures were represented and how distinct were they from one another? Islands are more vulnerable than landmasses to hurricanes, volcanoes, tsunamis and, now, rising sea levels. Does this enhanced susceptibility to natural disaster provide another distinguishing condition generating particular forms of social cohesion and cooperation?

David Pitt was one of the first scholars to move these rather prosaic observations into the main body of social theory, though his reflections are somewhat incomplete and underdeveloped. He notices that in 'folk sociology' islands are seen to have a cohesive social and moral order, akin to the notion of community. This is based partly on the idea and reality that islands are intermittently isolated, though surrounded by oceanic highways. Insofar as islands experience sequestration they can become, Pitt suggests, 'centres of seminal ideas' or havens of 'cultural survival'. The mixing of cultures in out-of-the-way settings, he adds, might generate 'vigorous social actions' (like cargo cults in the Pacific or Vodou in the Caribbean), a high degree of 'religious intensity' or 'creativity'. He insists that islands are never totally isolated. They are linked to the larger context (the sea) and to larger societies (the mainland). The natural boundaries of islands act to enclose and delimit social groups, but they also permit boundary crossing. Indeed, 'because boundary crossing is so important, because there are many inter-linking institutions and even a kind of hybrid vigour, [islanders] may have the potential for productive cooperation amongst them-selves and increased resistance to outside interference'.[8] Much of this reasoning evokes the idea and possibility of creolization. Though Pitt does not use the concept, one may nonetheless infer from his observations that while islandness does not cause creoli-zation, islands provide apposite settings where creolization might develop.

Another strand of social theory is to examine the sociologi-cal profile of islanders, rather than islands. Vannini, for example, depicts the social characteristics of islanders settled off British Columbia, Canada. Many of his 400 interviewees appear to be islanders by choice, having dropped out of what they called the 'rat race' on the mainland and turned their backs on urban and suburban lifestyles. In this, they are atypical islanders, whose choice of residence echoes those whom Benson and O'Reilly term 'lifestyle migrants'.[9] They resemble not at all those islanders who were dumped there by passing ships or taken by force to work in the coffee, cocoa, banana and sugar plantations located on tropi-cal islands. Despite the atypicality of Vannini's sample, he argues that the very fact of their island location provides islanders with two 'constellations' of island living that seem to be common to all islands, namely the experience of 'insulation' and 'isolation':

Insulation and isolation are two opposite sides of the same coin, as it were, the coin of islandness. Insulation refers to the more positive (as perceived by locals) dynamics occasioned by dwelling in communities that are one step removed from some of the hegemonic spatial mobili-ties practised in large cities. Isolation refers instead to the more negative (again, as perceived by locals) dynamics which originate as a result of their peripherality and marginalization. Insulation and isolation are not

only characteristics of these communities' constellations of (im)mobil-
ity but also the outcomes of the unfolding of these constellations.[10]

As mentioned, many plantations were located on islands, so the
cultural matrix of islandness was reinforced and amplified by the
brutal conditions of slave labour. The scholarly literature on what
cultural traditions survived the Middle Passage (the sea route from
West Africa to the New World) is now immense, though scholars continue to owe an immense debt to the painstaking work
of Melville J. Herskovits in documenting African customs and
practices in the New World. Equally impressive is the imaginative recreation of the social and cultural characteristics of mainland
plantations in Brazil in the classic account by Gilberto Freyre.[11]
Perhaps the easiest way of summarizing this literature is to recognize that while some African cultural practices could be retained or
rebuilt, whole original societies could not. A bottom–up 'cultural
grammar' (in drumming, dance, oral traditions, customs, religion
and languages) re-emerged, and did so with greater or lesser difficulty. Michel-Rolph Trouillot points to the variable degrees
of economic efficiency of the plantations and the differential
demographic balances (between white and black, and men and
women) both of which significantly altered the extent and level of
'cultural apartheid' between masters and slaves.[12] The bedrock of
creolization was the island and/or the plantation; the rhizomes
of creativity and resistance grew from the multiple and often unno-
ticed efforts of Africans to recover their heritage, their diasporic
traces, and learn to relate to the unfamiliar world in which they
found themselves.

The features of islands and plantations we have alluded to – of
insulation and isolation, remoteness and reconnection, repression
and boundary-crossing – produce a particular form of sociality that
is found in plantations and islands and, as we shall see, in mainland
settings where comparable characteristics develop. Seen in this
way, identities can be 'islanded' in a considerable variety of locales
– for example, in the swamps and bayous of Louisiana (see chapter
4), in the ghetto of the Venetian Republic, the self-governing
spaces of other port cities, and the ethnic enclaves of global cities,
examples of which we discuss below.

Islanded identities

We turn first to the Caribbean, which has provided one of the most important contact zones for the analysis of islanded identities and creolization. Indeed, Aisha Khan refers to the region as providing a 'master symbol' of the idea. Like Khan, we take issue with the delimiting of creolization to one specific geographical location/moment. By substituting the model for reality, it can become a 'fiction', which, as Khan argues, 'supports some of the very assumptions and approaches it is meant to dismantle'.[13] If we consider some of the convergences between the term 'island' and the concept of creolization, we can note that both words work at a number of levels. They have both been used very specifically to refer to particular spaces or to particular moments in history. Yet, they have also been used metaphorically: creolization as a metaphor for cultural change and resistance, islandness as a metaphor for remoteness, insularity or detachment. Moreover, used metaphorically, both are often adopted to denote notions of liminality or in-betweenness, and of processes that are not yet complete. Indeed, while both have been used to refer to particular, bounded processes and practices, they have also both been used to denote connectedness, openness to the world, what Glissant describes as a 'poetics of relation' (see chapter 7), a notion that is echoed in Benítez-Rojo's idea of a 'repeating island'.[14]

These semantic similarities provide some clues as to why forms of creolization are particularly striking in these oceanic spaces characterized by travelling, movement and 'routes' as opposed to 'roots' or origins. Because islands are refuges and nodal points in oceanic highways they are also salient in the articulation of creolization processes. Here the insights of the spatial theorists (outlined above), who pointed to the dynamic relationship between the social and the spatial, are illuminating. The argument is not that islands necessarily provide environments for creolization. Island space is not a blank page or tabula rasa for emergent social relations, but rather constitutive of, and deeply embedded in, those social relations that are, in the case of the Caribbean and many other postcolonial island spaces, characterized by deeply unequal relations of power. As Stuart Hall argues in his discussion of creolization, 'questions of power, as well as issues of entanglement, are always at stake'.[15]

If we take the islands of the French Caribbean – the Antilles – as an example, we can see that creolization has been highly contested. Scholars such as Richard Burton noted a tension between, on the one hand, a 'creole revivalism' and the legitimation (albeit highly contested) of creole language, culture and thought and, concurrently, processes of what he describes as 'decreolization' resulting from the continuing relationship of dependence on France (see chapter 7).[16] Yet, this is where the islandness of these French departments becomes relevant and perhaps has been, in part, responsible for the resistance to complete assimilation into French mainstream culture. On the one hand, these islands, as French 'possessions' since colonization, have seemed to represent exoticized, precious 'objects of desire' moulded by the French imagination.[17] On the other hand, while a considerable mimicry of France and French culture may mark Antillean identity, there is also little doubt that the Antilles have been exemplary examples of intense creolization, of expressions of difference and resistance to monochromatic identities and to the French assimilationist project.

In his seminal work, *The Poetics of Relation*, the Martinican writer and thinker Édouard Glissant pointed to the unpredictability and creative chaos that characterizes Caribbean identity, born out of the trauma of its history and of the plantation. He suggested that 'within the space apart that it comprised, the always multilingual and frequently multiracial tangle created inextricable knots within the web of filiations, thereby breaking the clear, linear order to which Western thought had imparted such brilliance'.[18] For Glissant, the composite, rhizomic nature of Caribbean identity, the creolized spaces that emerged out of traumatic historical experiences, present new ways of thinking about the world, a world of 'relation' (see chapter 7). In a more recent intervention, he wrote:

> Dare we suppose that there are some places that I shall call Archipelago places (in the Caribbean, in the Pacific, and in so many other areas . . .) – where such a concept of the Relative, of the open links with the Other, of what I call a *Poétique de la Relation* shades or moderates the

splendid and triumphant voice of what I call Continental thinking, the thought of systems? Most certainly, we cannot and must not propose any model, any pattern, available for all. But in such diffracted places – in these 'laboratories' of chaos, which are metaphors for our chaos-infested world – let us say that chaos is beautiful; not chaos born from hate and wars, but from the extraordinary complexity of the exchange between cultures, which may yet forge the Americans that are at last and for the first time both deeply unified and truly diversified.[19]

As the above quotation suggests, there is a sense in which creolized and archipelagic (or we might say 'islanded') identities represent an interpretation of contemporary societies. We are thus by no means arguing that creolization is *only* observable in islands.[20] We are, rather, suggesting that bringing 'islandness' into the equation can help us to identify distinctive forms of creolization and allow us to reflect on some of the processes, practices and environments through and in which creolization – both literally and metaphorically – becomes salient.

Port cities as contact zones

Much of the early discussion of port cities centred on the world of the Mediterranean – including the renowned ports of Athens, Istanbul, Genoa, Izmir, Thessaloniki, Trieste and Alexandria. These and other Mediterranean harbours exhibited significant 'concentrations of people, power and social and cultural capital'.[21] The very idea of cosmopolitanism (linking the Greek words for 'universe' and 'city') was born in Athens, and in such settings the confluence of people of diverse origins led some scholars to use the loose description 'cosmopolitan'. Such a designation should not lead to the assumption that intercultural relations in port cities were suffused with sweetness and light. To illustrate this point, we take a perhaps unexpected literary illustration, namely Shakespeare's *The Merchant of Venice*.

As historians remind us, Venice was one of the most powerful and wealthy port cities in the world, so powerful, indeed, that by the fourteenth century it outshone other European cities and rivalled many countries. Its fleet dominated the Mediterranean until the Great Council of Venice finally exceeded the Venetian Republic's reach by occupying Constantinople, Crete and parts of Greece. At its height, traders from many parts of the world were drawn to live in Venice, the Jews being allowed to settle in 1385, largely because of their usefulness as money lenders financing long-distance trade (precisely the occupation of Shakespeare's fictional character, Shylock). While being allowed to practise their religion, Jews were restricted in many ways, including having to wear a yellow circle on the left shoulder of their garments when they left their segregated space in the ghetto. The Venetian ghetto was the first so-named in the world, after a nearby 'getto', or iron foundry.[22] The term is now used to describe the segregated and disadvantaged areas of many cities.

The plot of Shakespeare's play revolves around Shylock lending money to Antonio's friend, with the proviso that if he defaulted, Shylock would be paid a pound of Antonio's own flesh. This extraordinary arrangement reflected Antonio's confidence that he would be able to pay (he was expecting his ships to return with substantial profits), and Shylock's hatred at being constantly taunted by Antonio for being a Jew. In the event, the ships floundered and Shylock demanded his pound of flesh. There are many personal and social complexities in this play, but, as two legal scholars indicate, it also crucially illuminates the nature of the legal regime. Despite the palpable hatred between Christians and Jews, with the growth of international trade Venice needed to regulate commerce by embracing non-discriminatory legal principles. Only the need to commit to the letter of the law and to the ideology of the marketplace would have made the bizarre contract between Shylock and Antonio possible.[23] In effect, this early expression of capitalist principles combined impartiality at the state level with highly prejudiced forms of interaction at the social level. This is a familiar contemporary juxtaposition and one that makes Shylock's declaration of his common humanity all the more poignant:

> I am a Jew. Hath not a Jew eyes? Hath not a Jew hands, organs, dimensions, senses, affections, passions? Fed with the same food, hurt

with the same weapons, subject to the same diseases, healed by the same means, warmed and cooled by the same winter and summer as a Christian is? If you prick us, do we not bleed? If you tickle us, do we not laugh? If you poison us, do we not die? And if you wrong us, shall we not revenge? If we are like you in the rest, we will resemble you in that.[24]

Venice languished (though its glories are still on display in the magnificent palaces of its wealthy families). However, it demonstrated and anticipated some general characteristics of other port cities of the eastern Mediterranean. As Driessen notes, these cities exhibited 'multilingualism, religious plurality, openness, [an] enterprising ethos, intercultural exchange and at least a weak form of tolerance', which, he argues, was 'rooted in the Ottoman millet system of non-Muslim communities that were granted protection and relative autonomy'.[25] The key phrases here are 'weak tolerance' and 'relative autonomy'. While these port cities were certainly diverse in their population mix, the appellation 'cosmopolitan' (used in the sense of a disposition to celebrate difference)[26] was something of an exaggeration. Such cities combined residential segregation and ethnic/religious conflict with some limited forms of cultural interaction that fell far short of cosmopolitanism, let alone creolization. In like manner, despite the self-proclaimed cosmopolitanism of Periclean Athens, many residents were excluded from that ideal.

It took the massive expansion of capitalism and trade in the nineteenth century to change the character of the old port cities. To take one example of this growth, Britain's imports nearly tripled while exports multiplied nearly fivefold over a 40-year period, 1809–49, much of it routed through London.[27] The Mediterranean ports also expanded in the nineteenth century and notable wealthy traders ventured out of their ethnic enclaves to become municipal benefactors – sponsoring schools, hospitals and libraries and giving donations for other civic purposes. The trade with India opened up the ports of Bombay, Calcutta, Hong Kong and Shanghai. However, the bulk of trade, including the slave trade, had shifted from the Mediterranean to the Atlantic, which allowed the west European ports of Lisbon, Porto, Bordeaux,

Nantes, Bristol and Liverpool to thrive. Across the Atlantic in the Americas, the great port cities of Salvador de Bahia, New York and New Orleans became major landing points for goods and people, including slaves, settlers and seafarers. With this expansion came new possibilities for cultural interaction:

> Port cities have been gateways of migration and mobility control and locales for people from multi-confessional, multi-ethnic, and multi-lingual backgrounds, but they have also been locales for social and ethnoreligious inclusion and exclusion. They have produced self-governing spaces that mediated diverse worlds and functioned as geographical theaters and showcases for building technologies where individuals, societies, or states played various roles depending on their own interests.[28]

In a number of these newly energized port cites, creolized spaces – often red-light districts, zones of enticement, transition, criminality and menace – proliferated. District Six in Cape Town remained defiantly creolized, until the apartheid state finally ordered the area to be flattened with bulldozers. Tiger Bay in Cardiff fused, sexually and culturally, Somali, Yemeni, Italian, Spanish, Caribbean and Irish migrants with the Welsh. Toxteth in Liverpool housed some of Britain's oldest African, Caribbean and Chinese populations with admixtures of Irish and Welsh. Across the Atlantic, more dramatic and large-scale instances of creolization occurred. In Salvador de Bahia, *Candomblé* – a religion syncretized from African and Catholic traditions – spread to a number of other countries and is said now to have two million followers. Salvador is also the home of capoeira, a martial art developed by slaves, which combines dance, music and acrobatics. Samba, again creolized in Brazil, is enjoyed by countless dance enthusiasts throughout the world. And, as we shall see in chapter 4, creolized music emanating from New Orleans has formed the basis for much popular music globally.

Many of these traditions, particularly Brazilian and US dances, religions and music, remain vibrant and, in a healthy and creative way, are creolizing again and again as they find new audiences. However, in a number of port cities, multiethnic contact has eroded in the face of nationalism and civil war. Christian and Muslim Beirut are now zoned and separated by a 'green line'. Alexandria has become drearily monochromatic in comparison with its colourful past, which writers such as E. M. Forster, Lawrence Durrell and the much-admired cookery writer Claudia Roden celebrated. Roden waxes lyrical about the markets of Alexandria (and Cairo), which were used by resident Arabs, Greeks, Turks, Armenians, Copts and Jews (the last reduced to a population of 50 from a high of 50,000). Meals for the upper classes, she recalled, 'were a serious, almost erotically exhausting pleasure'.[29] Such intense nostalgia is also reported in the case of Anglo-Indians and Chinese from Calcutta living in Toronto and London, who pine for their 'diasporic city' (an inland port). Remembered neighbourhoods, streets, clubs and churches for the Anglo-Indians and wistful recollections of working as tanners, carpenters, shoemakers and dentists for the Chinese have generated a new kind of diasporic longing for city spaces, an important corrective to the common view that 'home' is a large, national space.[30]

Super-diverse cities

A score or so of large, well-known cities in the current era of global capital are, unsurprisingly, deemed 'global cities'.[31] They house the headquarters of major banks, insurance companies and stock exchanges. Some continue their functions as natural harbours (New York, London, Hong Kong, Tokyo), but what is more important is that they are hubs for airlines. They are centres of communication and information. TV channels are housed there, as are recording studios, major book publishers and newspapers. In geo-political terms, the notion of the 'global city' is widely used to categorize cities marked by new spatial hierarchies and a new international division of labour.

Many discussions of global cities derive from theories about globalization and depict the functions of such cities for global capital. We are much more interested in the sociology of such cities. They are major sites of cultural encounter because of their 'super-diverse' character. As Steve Vertovec explains, super-diversity is driven by the arrival of migrants from many countries of origin (with different ethnicities, languages, religions, local identities and cultural values). These migrants enter through different migration channels, manifest different legal statuses and arrive with different levels of human capital, thus making them either easily employable or highly exploitable.[32] We need also to remember that super-diversity is becoming increasingly apparent in cities that are not designated as 'global cities'. Many of the newest migrants to the USA, Canada and Europe are spreading out to cities not on the list of 'the usual suspects'. We concur broadly with the geographer Jennifer Robinson, who develops the notion of 'ordinary cities', which, she argues

> takes the world of cities as its starting point and attends to the diversity and complexity of all cities. And instead of seeing only some cities as the originators of urbanism, in a world of ordinary cities, ways of being urban and ways of making new kinds of urban futures are diverse and are the product of the inventiveness of people in cities everywhere.[33]

Stuart Hall also contends that cities in general, not just global cities, 'function as spatial magnets for different, converging streams of human activity'. This explains, he continues, 'why cities have a very long history as centres of trade, as markets, and thus as sites of cultural exchange and social complexity'.[34] Okwui Enwezor pertinently adds that cities are 'today's sites of creolization' where 'new diasporic formations have reconfigured the space'.[35] Like islands, plantations and port cities before them, super-diverse cities are contact zones characterized by varied ethnicities and religions, particular spatial configurations and a skewed division of capital, labour and power. In them we 'find echoes of the plantation in the modern world and the geopolitics of inequality'.[36] Many urban spaces become sites of encounter, which, like islands, promote processes of exclusion and the exacerbation of difference, while at the same time fostering new forms of intercultural exchange and the dilution of 'markers of difference' (see chapter 7).

Juxtaposing diaspora and creolization in urban spaces represents an attempt to bring a fresh perspective to recent debates around new 'geographies of encounter'.[37] Encounters between people from diverse origins and allegiances (ethnic, racial, class-based, gender-driven, religious or generational) have long been a subject of scholarly enquiry and public policy. Local and national policies aimed at addressing the challenge of living with such diversity have come full circle from a concern with assimilation and integration, to the promotion of multiculturalism, to a return to state-led programmes of assimilation in the guise of community cohesion. Setting their face against the far-reaching implications of creolization and diaspora, such programmes seek to impose hierarchical subordination to largely nebulous national myths like 'the American way', 'British values' or the French 'Republican ideal'.

In scholarly debates, the dethroning of multiculturalism has given way to what has been labelled a diversity turn, which reflects a shift from focusing on specific ethnic groups to looking at diversity itself, a move away from a 'focus on entities' to a 'concern with relations'.[38] Thus, rather than taking an ethnic group as the unit of analysis – and thereby reifying difference and creating an artificial sense of boundedness – research has moved to focus on new configurations of difference, manifested both across and within groups, which correspond to 'different conditions . . . different scales [and] particular places'. Within such research, there is an increasing acknowledgement that 'geography matters fundamentally'.[39] Thus, as we observed earlier in our discussion of islands and port cities, there is a dynamic and mutually constitutive relationship between social identity formation and the spaces within which such a process occurs.

Studies of diversity and difference in super-diverse cities have tended to take particular spaces *within* the city as their unit of analysis. To give a flavour of such studies, let us mention just four richly researched examples:

1 Using a notion of 'commonplace diversity', Susanne Wessendorf has described interactions of the assorted residents in the London borough of Hackney, where her meticulous ethnography has revealed subtle forms of allegiance and separation often cross-cutting ethnic, class and generational lines. Whereas an ethos of mixing is normal in public and associational life, social lives

remain separate while certain groups (namely ultra–Orthodox Jews and middle-class 'hipsters') remain aloof from the banal cross-cultural interactions of most of the residents.[40]

2 Ben Gidley has undertaken research in a housing estate in South London. Its three tower blocks (high-rises) contain people who, between them, speak 100 languages from nearly 100 countries. He deploys the expression 'everyday multiculture' to capture this extraordinary *mélange* of people gathered in a small space. 'The multiplication of axes of identification makes older notions of multiculturalism, based on the idea of several cultures, obsolete', he says. 'The term "multiculture" is better for conveying the sense of the irrevocably multiple nature of culture itself here.'[41]

3 Thomas Hylland Eriksen, a Norwegian scholar of creolization in Mauritius, finds himself in Furuset, an urban satellite district 20 minutes from Oslo with 70 per cent minority-born residents (often of Kurdish or Pakistani descent). Inverting the grammar of linguistic creolization, the second-generation migrants adopt a sub-stratal Norwegian mode of being, while continuing their sense of cultural difference from mainstream Norwegian society. Eriksen remarks, tellingly, that Vertovec might as well have developed his notion of super-diversity to describe Furuset rather than London.[42]

4 Alex Rhys-Taylor explores a small urban space within London through the prism of Ortiz's concept of 'transculturation'. His sensory ethnography of a market in East London focuses predominantly on the fusion of different smells and tastes that are experienced within this unique space. While not ignoring the history of racist violence and xenophobia in London and their new guises in the contemporary contexts, his study represents an attempt to move beyond the predominantly negative portrayals of intercultural exchanges and to point to instances where certain cultural elements meet and fuse, and in which 'the dangers of cultural difference fade'.[43]

We have taken a sample of just four of many studies, but they illustrate a pattern. Researchers find it difficult to agree on a common vocabulary – multiculture, commonplace diversity, creolization and transculturation are deployed in the titles and opening paragraphs of the studies just cited. In the narrative of their articles, even more near-synonyms (like hybridity, everyday cosmopolitanism, conviviality or transnationalism) appear. However, behind this unstable conceptual terminology, we notice highly congruent descriptions of emerging identities that draw selectively on the past and engage selectively in the present, what we have alluded to earlier as the delicate dance between diaspora and creolization. Difference is frozen or defrosted, transcended in everyday relations or sustained behind closed doors. Identities are 'islanded', intermittently connected to the metaphorical landmass that surrounds them, while being recurrently insulated and introspective. Moreover, the processes to which we allude do not necessarily (and indeed do not often) apply to the city as a whole. Rather, cultural contact occurs at particular spaces like neighbourhoods, streets, parks, markets, cafés, churches, sometimes in peoples' homes. What the concept of creolization adds to our analysis of these spaces is not merely a description of diversity or an ethnography of the possibilities for interaction, but rather an analytical framework for thinking about the irreversible shifts, the creative, combative (and still embryonic) emergence of new cultural forms and identities in these spaces which may not be easy to measure, to trace, but which are visibly in process. Creolization allows us to think beyond reductive or negative understandings of intercultural interactions, whereby they are considered as merely reproducing asymmetrical power relations, and to think about the productive possibilities that arise from everyday encounters with difference in particular spaces. Moreover, this framework is an emancipatory one, reversing the imposition of imperial terms on distant parts by importing an expression grown in the periphery to understand metropolitan realities.

Conclusion

In this chapter we have alluded to general theories advanced by social and cultural geographers validating the salience of space and showing how spatial and social relationships are mutually constitutive. We argue that this interactive process has particular bearing in three contact zones – islands/plantations, port cities and super-diverse cities. It is perhaps helpful to return to Mary Louise Pratt's use of the term 'contact zones'. Though her purpose is very different, namely to describe travel writing in imperial times, her observations uncannily parallel ours. She too points to the importance of understanding early forms of contact, particularly language contact (cf. chapter 2 above). Usefully, she distinguishes a 'colonial frontier' from a contact zone. The former is about trade and the expansion of the European powers, the latter 'invokes a space and time where subjects previously separated by geography and history are co-present, the point at which their trajectories now intersect'. Contact zones are those spaces where colonizer and colonized are involved in 'interlocking understandings and practices, and often within radically asymmetrical relations of power'.[44]

We have shown how islands and plantations were the *loci classici* of such interactions and how new social identities were born there. However, these islanded identities are to be understood both literally and metaphorically, the latter suggesting that traumatic historical experiences and new points of settlement isolate and connect, are both sequestered and open at the same time. Such a phenomenon is readily observable in port cities – open to the world of trade, seafarers and settlers, but prone to generate segregated spaces like ghettos, quarters and enclaves. Islanded identities also migrate from islands, one scholar pointing out that as Caribbean migrants moved, they 'creolized the metropole', thus 'mimic[ing] or represent[ing] the creolization(s) of the region itself'. In this sense, the Antillean diaspora in Paris and West Indians in the UK have transposed the encounter in the plantation to a metropolitan setting.[45]

As in islands and port cities, a key move forward in the study of cultural encounters in cities has been the acknowledgement of the crucial role of space, an emphasis captured by Michael Peter Smith's notion of 'transnational urbanism', which recognized the '*distanciated* yet *situated* possibilities for constituting and reconstituting social relations' in transnational cities.[46] Yet, despite his emphasis on the importance of historicizing these processes, it is somewhat surprising that many students of 'diversity' rarely discuss historical contexts and precedents. There are indeed striking parallels with contact zones of the past, for example, the islands of the New World, or the plantation spaces that, as the Réunionese scholar Vergès contends, 'were multicultural, multi-religious and multi-ethnic from the beginning. What Europe is discovering', Vergès continues, 'we experienced through loss, forced relocation, forced immigration, violence and resistance.'[47]

By bringing the concepts of diaspora and creolization to the study of ports and cities we can provide a new optic for thinking about how 'shared reciprocal forms of life' can emerge in contexts marked by 'glaring disparities of power, recognition, and material and symbolic resources'.[48] Our main contribution in this chapter is to insist on the importance of considering space (as well as history and power) in understanding how shared forms of life emerge. These three elements are fundamental to the processes of identity formation that emerge in particular spaces. These insights are also fundamental to other chapters in the book: in particular to the discussion of music, carnival, heritage construction and identity politics. In chapter 4, we examine how music develops from its diasporic origins in an island setting and a port city, how it creolizes, then sends out new diasporic outriders.

4

Expressing Merged Identities: Music

As we have established earlier, cultures are never intact, perfectly formed or historically immutable entitles. They are made and remade, selectively exchanged, repelled and absorbed. Social actors engage in forms of social conduct that recall or echo their diasporic pasts or develop ways of being, behaving and understanding that link them intimately to their neighbours, friends and surrounding communities – that is, they creolize. In this chapter, we consider how a crucial manifestation of popular culture, namely music, is developed and performed. Music seems unusually prone to cross-fertilization, perhaps because listening and participating happen at a number of levels, from the most simple forms of clapping, foot-stamping and repetition of chorus lines to the most complex blending of harmonies, scales and rhythms. Religious music usually crosses cultures easily, perhaps because we all know the emotions – sadness, grief, hope, love, devotion, joy, awe and fear – that religious music seeks to convey.

An acute French observer of popular music, Denis-Constant Martin, draws us closer to our interest in popular culture and to our two case studies, Cape Verde and Louisiana. He affirms that 'most forms of music described today as "popular" or "mass" music are derived, in one way or another, from practices that appeared within societies organized around slavery in territories conquered by Europeans ... within peculiar conditions of inequality and absolute violence all based on the denial of the humanity of people removed from their homelands.'[1] This capacity for creativity in the face of adversity is one of the key defining characteristics of creolization. After describing the major forms of social and cultural interaction in Cape Verde and Louisiana (which serves also as a background to the discussion of carnival in chapter 5), we detail the many ways in which popular music has developed at each site, before venturing a conclusion.

Encounters in Cape Verde

Cape Verde was arguably the 'first creole society in the Atlantic world' and, owing to its geo-strategic position between Africa, Europe and the Americas, it became the 'capital of the trans-Atlantic slave trade for the first century of that trade's existence'.[2] Given that this island nation came into being through conquest and settlement by European colonizers and through the import of slaves from several African countries, it is unsurprising that creolized cultural practices and identities emerged in a context in which a collective memory of 'roots' prior to colonization struggled to survive. The experience of creolization had become so naturalized that when asked what creolization and 'creole' meant in their opinion, several interviewees in Cape Verde responded that they had not realized that it referred to other places; they thought it referred only to Cape Verde, to the uniquely *crioulo* – mixed – culture of the archipelago. As one interviewee remarked, 'it's our way of being. It encompasses everything', while another added, 'creolization for us . . . is something that is neither African nor European but culturally in the middle'.

Yet, despite the indisputably creole nature of Cape Verde and its people, the search for a national identity – particularly since achieving its independence in 1975 – has been marked by contradictions between Africanness and Europeanness, somewhat paralleling the tension between tradition and modernity.[3] Its public manifestation took the form of an intense debate within the intelligentsia. The cultural and literary movement Claridade, which emerged in the late colonial period, sought to defend the unique creole cultural and linguistic identity of Cape Verde, while *mestiçagem* – the Portuguese near synonym for creolization – was put forward as an expression of the 'cultural Portugueseness' of the archipelago.[4] The policies of the post-independence governments of PAICG and PAICV,[5] by contrast, were aimed at a recovery of the nation's African heritage, in part through a revalorization of the culture of the *badius* – descendants of runaway slaves who lived in the remote regions in the interior of Santiago and who 'came to represent a romantic symbol of the twentieth century struggle for Cape Verdean legitimacy, authenticity and even independence'.[6] In a counter move, the subsequent government of the Movement for Democracy (MpD) emphasized the Europeanness of Cape Verdean identity, going as far as changing the country's flag and national anthem to create a sense of distance from Africa.

All three examples outlined above represent attempts – by cultural elites or government institutions – to define Cape Verdean 'authenticity' and to determine the strength of the different components of creolization and diaspora on the islands. Yet, missing from these 'top–down' efforts to define Cape Verde's cultural identity are the more hidden forms of creolization on the ground as well as its 'projective character . . . as a form of surpassing nationalism, ethnic exclusivism, and racism'.[7] There is also a tendency within elite definitions of authentic Cape Verdeanness to look to the past, to essentialize Cape Verdean identity through a quest for roots. As well as ignoring the dynamic history of Cape Verde and its 'deep creolization',[8] which in fact implies a high level of uprootedness, such discourses about authenticity also disregard the powerful influence of the Cape Verdean diaspora, which, if one includes second- and third-generation emigrants, greatly outnumbers those residing on the island. As Challinor argues, 'if the line between the past and the present were to be drawn differently, then what are perceived as "intrusions" upon Cape Verdean culture may equally be seen as contributions towards the ongoing processes of cultural production'.[9] Following this line of argument, we seek to redraw the line between past and present, to explore how different versions of Cape Verdean belonging and identity emerge from below in musical expression.

Diasporic and creolized identities in Louisiana

As Cape Verde represents a heartland and the original wellspring of insular creolization (despite Caribbean claims to the title), so Louisiana represents the most notable and important example of creolization on a mainland. To a degree, the original character of creole society had similar roots – French Louisiana was somewhat cut off from Hispanophone America to the southwest and Anglophone America to the northeast. Two of the component heritages were African and European and the language evolved into a superstratal French Creole, paralleling the dominant vocabulary of Portuguese in Cape Verdean Krioulu. As in Cape Verde, there was a strong predominance of Catholicism and a history of slavery, and again a phenotypically intermediate group emerged (known as *gens de couleur libres*, free people of colour or Creoles of colour), not only in New Orleans, but also in the Cane River area, as well as in Pensacola, Mobile and along the bayous and prairies of Louisiana.[10]

While the resemblances do not disappear, the evolution of diasporic and creolized identities in Louisiana was considerably more complicated. Unlike in many uninhabited or sparsely inhabited islands where creole societies took root, a significant set of Native American communities thrived in pre-European Louisiana. When French settlers penetrated the area in 1700 there were six Native American nations – the Atakapa, Caddo, Tunica, Natchez, Muskogean and Chitimacha – with Choctaw being a commonly spoken lingua franca. Within these nations were smaller bands or 'tribes' (the vocabulary to describe the social unit is contested), whose names survive in current place names. For example, the Opelousa band (part of the Atakapa) inhabited the area now known as Opelousas, while the Natchitoches (a sub-group of Caddo) lived near the present-day picture-postcard city of the same name.[11] While tuberculosis, smallpox, measles and influenza took their toll, Native Americans remained substantial elements in the creole mix. (A Creole with visible Native American origins is still referred to as *os rouge*, or red bone.)

Those of African origin were mainly West African slaves – Mandinkas,[12] Wolof or Bambara. But the key fissure among African migrants was between those who arrived directly from Africa and those who came via the French colonies of Saint-Domingue (modern-day Haiti) and, to a much lesser extent, Martinique and Guadeloupe. The Caribbean group were already Creoles, in the sense that they were born in the New World and had already evolved a creolized culture. Though all Creoles, they were divided roughly equally into white, mixed (*gens de couleur libres*) and black status groups. By 1804, when the revolution in Haiti resulted in independence, some 9,000 refugees from that country had arrived in New Orleans, a third of the total population of the city.[13]

We have alluded to the white Creoles from the French Caribbean, so it is perhaps useful to indicate that, in Louisiana, the word 'creole' initially followed the Iberian New World use – that is, it referred to whites who were born in the colonies, not in the metropole, and who, to varying degrees, had become culturally and socially localized. 'Localized' refers to wider forms of interaction, but it is also a euphemistic way of alluding to the informal marriages (*plaçage*) or more casual sexual relationships between white French Creoles and people of other phenotypes. Their reluctance openly to recognize exogamy was brilliantly portrayed in the controversial novel by George Washington Cable, *The Grandissimes: A Story of Creole Life*, first published in 1880,[14] which excoriated hypocrisy on the part of white Creoles and demanded justice for *gens de couleur*. Cable's honesty was too searing for some to bear and he was forced to leave his native Louisiana to spend the rest of his life in Massachusetts. It is important to add that the European population was by no means confined to the French. The Spanish (who ruled 'Luisiana' from 1762 to 1802 as part of New Spain) largely neglected the area, but Spanish traders and soldiers, and artisans from the Canary Islands, fashioned distinct Hispanic subcultures. One can add to the European mix German settlers from the Rhineland,

Italian plantation workers and English settlers, to nominate some obvious candidates.

Though all groups contributed to the creation of a regional creole cuisine, for the purposes of studying Louisiana's music, the most salient of the European sub-ethnicities are Cajuns, an Anglicization of 'Cadien', which, in turn, is a contraction of 'Acadien'.[15] Drawn from French Acadia (the Maritimes of modern-day Canada), between 1755 and 1763 the British military authorities expelled them and they settled mainly in the southwest of Louisiana. Although Cajuns frequently claim an authentic and unadulterated heritage from Acadia, a leading Cajun historian has made it clear that not only did Cajuns have other roots, but once they arrived in Louisiana they also formed intimate ties with black, Spanish, Métis (European–Native American descendants), Native Americans and other francophone groups.[16]

With apologies for the pun, creolization in Louisiana took on a whole new complexion when Napoleon sold the territory to the USA. As Susan Dollar recounts, at the acquisition ceremony at the Place d'Armes, New Orleans, in 1803, American officials witnessed Spanish and French troops, Creoles of colour, other Creoles, slaves and Native Americans. They confronted a 'gabble of tongues' and an array of complexions, 'ivory, café au lait, copper and ebony'.[17] The process of Americanizing this bewildering assortment of humanity into the standard American binary of white and black caused considerable confusion and social conflict, and much resentment and irritation, which persist to the present day.

Authenticity and longing: the music of Cape Verde

Having described the mix of identities in Cape Verde and the even more complex origins and components of the population of Louisiana, we turn now to showing how this *mélange* of cultures and peoples manifested itself in the popular music of both places. There is an intrinsic link between music and Cape Verdeanness, both on the islands and in the Cape Verdean diaspora. Indeed, music has formed an important part of nation-building projects in

Figure 4.1   Mural depicting different Cape Verdean musical styles in Praia, Santiago

Source: Jason Cohen, used with permission

the archipelago and in the struggle to determine the contributions of Africa and Europe to definitions of Cape Verdeanness.[18] While the origins of most Cape Verdean music genres remain contested, there is general agreement among scholars about their creolized nature in that they are 'rooted in a trans-Atlantic complex of hybridized Euro-African musical forms varying from island to island and from northern to southern island groups'.[19]

The musical style known as *Morna* is 'regarded as one of the most characteristic and quintessential expressions of national culture'.[20] Its origins are unclear, with some drawing attention to the traces of the Portuguese *Fado*, while others emphasize the African origins of the genre and, in particular, the style known as *Lundum*, which emerged in Brazil but has Angolan origins.[21] Indeed, the debates around *Morna* are reminiscent of the debates around Cape Verdean identity and the complex processes of creolization that have given rise to this identity, a unique identity that defies obvious references to particular roots. As a creolized musical form, the precise origins of *Morna* are untraceable, representing a singular 'reinterpretation' of musical styles in the new situation. The themes of the lyrics are rooted in the struggles of the archipelago, in particular that of departure, *saudade* (longing), or the sea as a key motif for representing an enabler for emigration, as well as a space marking separation.[22]

The internationally acclaimed singer Cesária Évora brought Cape Verdean *Morna*, as well as the faster paced *Coladeira*, to the global music market.[23] These musical exports drew international attention to Cape Verde and, arguably, contributed to the successful careers of several other Cape Verdean musicians. According to Arenas, this small archipelago is 'securing an identity and a niche within the world music industry'.[24] Yet, despite what we may describe as the 'commodification' of Cape Verdean music within the global music industry and the fact that many Cape Verdean musicians have made a career beyond the bounds of the archipelago, to focus solely on these aspects would be to ignore the ways in which popular music has formed, and continues to form, a powerful instrument of resistance to the seemingly hegemonic forces of cultural globalization.

The emergence of African-derived musical forms in the colonial era – and in their re-emergence in the postcolonial one – represents one way in which music became a means of resistance. Take the case of the *Batuque* (or *Batuku*), most probably the oldest musical style in Cape Verde, which emerged on the island of Santiago.[25] The music, song and dance are performed almost exclusively by women who are gathered in a circle known as a *terreiro*.[26] One cannot help but note the semantic link with the *terreiros de Candomblé*, the sacred spaces that practitioners of the Afro-Brazilian *Candomblé* religion use for services and ceremonies. One interviewee explained that the Portuguese word '*terreiro*' actually referred to the great open areas on the plantation where the coffee was dried and where slaves would meet, and it has taken on different meanings across the lusophone world. The *terreiro* – both for Brazilian *Candomblé* and Cape Verdean *Batuque* – signifies a space outside, a sacralized space that was the domain of slaves. Thus, historically, the *terreiro* represents a space separated from the space of the dominant power, which allows for the possibility of creativity and resistance.

During a *Batuque* 'session', the lead vocalist sings a verse, which is immediately repeated in unison by the rest of the group.[27] These verses, known as *Finaçon*, usually consist of improvised proverbs, which contain themes that range from quotidian scenes to social criticism.[28] Simultaneously, the lead player (*batukadera*) sets up the rhythm for the other members of the group – they respond by beating their knees or a piece of rolled up cloth between their legs – while one of the players goes to the centre to perform a dance. The *Batuque* performance is in two parts, the first as a kind of call-and-response,[29] the second involving all singers and players executing the same rhythm and singing the same refrain. The *Batuque* is usually accompanied by someone playing the *cimboa*, an instrument that, though uniquely Cape Verdean, bears a strong resemblance to instruments used on the west coast of Africa.[30]

Both *Batuque* and *Funana*, a style that emerged much later than the *Batuque* but also regarded as having strong African elements, were repressed during colonial times because their song lyrics and dances were regarded as too subversive and the style too 'African'. Indeed, this repression was particularly strong in the authoritarian years of Portuguese rule during the *Estado Novo* (1926–74). Yet, despite this history of marginalization, *Batuque* and *Funana* continued to be practised in the remote interior regions of Santiago and are closely associated with the culture of the *badius*. In an interview, local historian Moacyr Rodrigues said that women played on their knees or on wrapped up cloths because the Portuguese authorities prohibited the use of the African drum. Hence, rather than the prohibition leading to the suppression of the *Batuque*, practitioners adapted their practices to the circumstances, thus demonstrating both a resistance to these attempts at suppression and the gradual evolution of a musical style.

Since independence, Cape Verde's African-derived musical styles have re-emerged as important elements in the nation's musical culture, as well as valid subjects of ethno-musical research. Indeed, the promotion and celebration of these two genres were crucial elements in the 're-Africanizing' project of the post-independence government of the PAICV, regarded as an 'authentic Crioulo cultural tradition'.[31] Furthermore, having been practised after work in the fields or at special ceremonies such as weddings or baptisms, contemporary *Batuque* groups are often invited to 'perform' in more formal settings such as cultural centres or theatres, both in Cape Verde and internationally.[32] Although this emergence into the mainstream has arguably led to some loss in their original social meaning, some scholars argue that they continue to represent channels for political expression and, indeed, party politics. For example, Arenas writes that 'these musical styles underscore the distinctiveness of Santiago's *badiu* culture character-ized by its unabashedly independent and rebellious spirit rooted in the history of slavery on the island'.[33]

More recent musicians, such as Lura or Mayra Andrade,[34] have created inspired fusions of Cape Verdean styles with other musical genres. Thus, like their predecessors, contemporary musi-cians adopt and adapt the rhythms and styles available to them to create new Cape Verdean sounds, further creolizing these already hybrid musical forms. Rather than merely becoming products of monopolizing nation-building projects and acquiring 'folkloric status', the revival and evolution of these creolized musical styles in Cape Verde and in the diaspora can in fact provide spaces for social criticism and for the exposure of past and present injustices, as well as contribute to the ongoing evolution of a dynamic and unique Cape Verdean cultural identity.[35]

The second potentially subversive characteristic of Cape Verdean music derives from the fact that nearly all of it is performed in Krioulu as opposed to the official national language of Portuguese. As Arenas argues: 'Krioulu is the primary galvanizing force within Cape Verdean culture. Given its constitutively oral nature, it has a symbiotic relationship to music; thus together they are the quintes-sential medium to express a sense of "Cape Verdeaness", both on the islands and in the diaspora.'[36]

It would be a gross simplification to posit that Krioulu is in itself a means of subverting official Cape Verdean culture. Representing a convergence between the language and cultures of the coloniz-ers and slaves, as well as a form of differentiation and resistance to colonial rule, Krioulu was from the outset 'located, paradoxically, both within and outside the Portuguese language'.[37] Yet, the con-tinued widespread use of Krioulu in Cape Verdean music – it is regarded as a language better suited to express emotions – points to a desire to maintain a form of cultural distinctiveness and a rejection of the definition of their music as part of a wider 'lusophone' style. The relationship between music and Krioulu also lies in the fact that both belonged to more intimate and expressive spheres, in contrast to the public spaces of the church, the state and education dominated by Portuguese. This point is reminiscent of our earlier discussion of *terreiros*, suggesting that these musical, linguistic and religious practices emerged outside the sanctioned public sphere and were able to adapt, resist, or even destabilize, mainstream cultural practices.[38]

The 'symbiotic relationship' between music and Krioulu thus also lies in their relationship to official discourses and spaces, namely their practice both within the confines of official culture, where they can be appropriated for particular means, and their ability to maintain a certain distance from the dominant order. Despite attempts to officialize Krioulu, which of course receives wide support both in Cape Verde and in the diaspora, and attempts to categorize and fix certain forms of Cape Verdean music, the practice and constant evolution of both beyond the confines of these official spaces and discourses points to an ongoing, subtle resistance to such co-optation.

The third way in which popular music represents a form of resistance lies in the use of Krioulu in Cape Verdean music among the extensive Cape Verdean diaspora. Indeed, the fundamental role of the diaspora in the evolution of Cape Verdean culture and identity is apparent, despite co-optation into the world music market or attempts by the Cape Verdean state to support only what is regarded as 'authentic' Cape Verdean genres, namely the *Morna* or *Coladeira* or, more recently, *Batuque*, *Funana* and *Tabanca*.

Not only does Cape Verde embody a diasporic space from its very origin, as the uninhabited islands were populated by people displaced (either forcibly or voluntarily) from their original homeland, but massive waves of emigration since the beginning of the twentieth century have also given rise to 'today's deterritorialized transnation'.[39] The vast spread of the contemporary Cape Verdean diaspora, spanning multiple countries and involving waves of emigration due to diverse socio-political circumstances, means that there are many Cape Verdeans whose lives and cultural practices are, physically at least, outside the confines of the nation-state. Thus, given Cape Verde's long history of emigration – and indeed immigration and return – it is not surprising that music in the archipelago is, and has always been, strongly influenced by those who live outside the archipelago but who remain closely connected with people and events there. The sense of 'double loss' – of original roots and then of lives in Cape Verde – has long been a key motif in Cape Verdean popular music.[40]

Several interviewees remarked that one cannot talk about creolization in Cape Verde without referring to the diaspora. One argued that creolization in Cape Verde was more influenced by the practices of emigrants – who lived all over the world – than by Portugal. Yet, despite widespread acknowledgement of the fundamental role of the diaspora in cultural processes in Cape Verde, there were still many who lamented what was seen as the influx of external influences and felt that Cape Verdean culture needed to be protected from such pressures. There was a sense that the new musical styles emerging among the Cape Verdean diaspora posed a threat to what was 'authentically' Cape Verdean.[41] One example of a recent musical style that has emerged in the diaspora is *Cabo-Zouk*, a genre that derives from Antillean *Zouk* music and that emerged in the 1980s among Cape Verdeans living in France and Rotterdam.[42] While Rotterdam became the 'epicentre' of *Cabo-Zouk*, recordings are often mixed in Paris by sound engineers who have prior experience with Antillean *Zouk*. Consequently, critics have argued that *Cabo-Zouk* is 'simply not Cape Verdean' and that the musical freedom experienced by musicians in the diaspora has meant that they have been able to 'expand the boundaries of their music' and, in the process, disregard what is 'authentically' Cape Verdean.[43] Cape Verdean 'reality' is thus being constructed not merely by the top–down practices of states, cultural elites or the homogenizing processes of globalization, but, rather – or perhaps also – by the creative, counter-hegemonic practices of the nation's people both on the islands and beyond. The process of creolization thus continues – in this case through the transnational connections to the diaspora, but also through the powerful role of the media – which ensures that creole 'culture' is not frozen, but continues to creolize.

Louisiana: the wellspring of popular music

It is difficult to condense into a section of this chapter the massive array of creative musical genres associated with Louisiana. The roll–call includes country rock, work songs, hot music, gospel, rural blues, swamp blues, Dixieland, jazz (jass in earlier spellings), ragtime, rhythm & blues, second line, La La and zydeco. To get an intellectual grip on this diversity, it is worth distinguishing in the first instance between music that has no obvious element of protest or resistance, compared with genres in which some element of social criticism can be detected.

A useful initial contrast can be found between the sheet music written by Creoles of colour and popular folk songs. The former genre was produced by a number of composers, including Edmond Dédé, who worked as a theatre orchestra conductor in Bordeaux and wrote ballets, operettas, overtures, 250 dances and songs, six string quartets and a cantata, among other works.[44] Although there is evidence here of personal and small group mobility, such Creole composers were essentially augmenting a classical European tradition, with little evidence of social protest or critique. This is in decided contrast to popular folk songs. Remarkably, creolized slaves (already speaking creole) improvised satirical songs as soon as they arrived on the auction block in New Orleans. This song (below, with a translation following) took a spirited pot shot at a prominent lawyer, M. Etienne Mazureau, whose job it was to record slave sales in his ledger:

Mitchie Mazureau
Ki dan so bireau
Li semble crapo
Ki dan baille dodo.

Mr Mazureau
Who [is in] in his office
He looks like a toad
In a bucket of water.[45]

This open expression of derision derives directly from the African custom of praising, or where necessary satirizing, the powerful. Mockery could be hidden by language or by being part of a critical mass. Such a mass was found on Sunday afternoons in Congo Square, the informal name for an area now enclosed by the Louis Armstrong Park in New Orleans. With food vendors, neat paths and organized concerts, the newly laid-out park can be seen as a long-delayed move at gentrification, though the dearth of adequate public funding has induced some sordidness and provided a temporary haven for street people. Between 1800 and 1862, slaves were allowed to assemble in the square after church on their day off. This was an attempt to contain earlier unregulated assemblies. In 1799, for example, a visitor to the city wrote of 'vast numbers of negro slaves, men, women, and children assembled together on the levee, drumming, fifing and dancing in large rings'. The 'rings' represented Africans of different ethnic origins. Thousands of slaves came to Congo Square each Sunday. A British engineer and amateur ethnographer tasked with building the city's water-works noticed

> a most extraordinary noise which . . . proceeded from a crowd of five or six hundred persons, assembled in an open space or public square. [Africans were] formed into circular groups in the midst of [which] was a ring . . . ten feet in diameter. [Two dancing women] each held a coarse handkerchief extended by the corners in their hands. . . . [The music] consisted of two drums and a stringed instrument. An old man played a large cylindrical drum, and beat it with incredible quickness with the edge of his hand and fingers. Together with a second, smaller, drum they made an incredible noise.[46]

These assemblies in Congo Square attracted many whites to gape at the spectacle, but warily. The police dispersed the assembly at night to appease public fears and the music gradually lost some of its authentic African flavour. This was a matter of regret for folk-lorists and Afrocentric scholars trying to recover an intact diasporic heritage in the New World, but creolization is about invention not retention. It is thus hardly surprising to find that elements of the shared (creolized) African culture developed in the Congo

Square assemblies are found in surviving Bamboula and Calinda dances, in local Voodoo practices, in Mardi Gras songs and in the development of jazz, including the use of cross-rhythms found in ragtime.[47] The banjo (an African instrument) survived; we surmise that the European piano was turned from a melodic to a melodic-cum-percussive instrument to supplement the restrictions on drumming, a prohibition that matched that in Cape Verde. Under the Jim Crow laws, whereby 'coloureds' were not allowed to perform with whites, many who could play the piano teamed up with Africans who played horns, strings and percussion. Both ragtime and jazz could be connected to this 'enforced creolization'. Drumming was the most recognizable African survival, but in many areas the authorities banned drums and loud horns, surmising these might be used as signals for an impending slave revolt.

The double-face of creole music, being both respectable and subversive, can also be seen in the evolution of jazz. On the one hand, parades, marches, funeral dirges, concerts and the sacralization of figures like Louis Armstrong and Mahalia Jackson show the co-opted side of the music. Although the political elite never permanently drew Armstrong's fangs (for example, he suddenly denounced President Eisenhower over his inaction on civil rights), he accepted US State Department sponsorship to tour Africa, Asia and Europe and revelled in his nickname 'Ambassador Satch'. Mahalia Jackson was more vocal and explicit about the discrimination she experienced (as in her famous song 'I been 'buked and I been scorned'), but her outsider status was officially erased by the opening of the Mahalia Jackson Theater of the Performing Arts in Louis Armstrong Park, relaunched in 2009 in an official ceremony featuring, *inter alia*, Placido Domingo. On the other hand, there are some major jazz musicians whose lifestyles were so deviant that they escaped the fate of reputable incorporation. To mention just three, we think of Jelly Roll Morton, Billie Holiday and Charlie Parker.[48]

Creole music is also a rural music, the most buoyant example of which is zydeco, particularly associated with the southwest of the state. The origins of the name are obscure, and include theories that it derived from Atakapa music, is a corruption of *les haricots* (beans), or has murky creolized African origins, perhaps in the

Indian Ocean.[49] There is common agreement that it is a blend of African, Caribbean and European music. More contested is the sense that a predominantly African-derived genre is slowly being folded into Cajun music (sometimes this is designated as Cajun zydeco). Zydeco started as music of consolation and household recreation. The idea that its name was derived from '*les haricots*' is suggested by the common expression '*les haricots sont pas salés*' meaning not literally that the beans are not salted, but that there is nothing in the house with which to flavour the beans or, more plainly, people are being reduced to beans alone. Those with musical talents would hold La La house dance sessions in neighbours' homes. The percussion was provided by a washboard and, later, a dedicated zydeco *frottoir* (a rubboard with neck or shoulder straps). The accordion (imported from Germany), the banjo and fiddle completed the ensemble of instruments.

Though other instruments and English lyrics have now been introduced mainly for commercial reasons, 'the real stuff' is 'marked by exclusively French vocals and a percussive frenzy that clearly reveal that the style originated in the cultural creolization of Afro-Caribbean and Franco-American traditions'.[50] 'French' is understood to be creolized and this link between language and authenticity directly parallels Krioulu vocals in Cape Verde. However, joint hostility to Anglophone influence failed to suppress mutual suspicions between Creoles and Cajuns. Mattern argues that from the 1960s, 'Cajun musicians led a Cajun cultural revival that succeeded in drawing attention to some of the problems of Cajuns, such as cultural assimilation, poverty, and ethnic stigma. It also succeeded in helping to partially overcome these problems.' Black Creoles felt that this recognition was at their expense, that cultural property had been appropriated and that Cajuns were engaged in a bid for cultural dominance. This sense of injustice was particularly unfortunate, as the music reflected their shared history of common misfortunes as poor tenants and common everyday experiences, which contrasted with American segregationist and biracial doctrines. Mattern comments:

> The musical sensibilities and lyrical themes of Cajun and zydeco music also have much in common, reflecting similar experiences and

lives. Both, for example, contain strong blues inflections such as blues scales and vocal breaks evoking crying or sadness. Their lyrical themes emphasize economic marginalization, lost love, and unrequited love. Both zydeco and Cajun music nearly disappeared under pressure from Anglo assimilationist influences, going 'backporch' during the lean years of the 1930s, 1940s, and 1950s although not disappearing entirely.[51]

The official attempt to manage these strands has been to amalgamate them all into an undifferentiated 'gumbo', a Louisianan stew of many ingredients derived from most of the state's component cultures. Here is one example. Announcing that St Landry parish in west Louisiana provided 'a gumbo for your soul', the tourist brochure welcomed all to a place 'where accordions are cool, boudin is hot and history is not just in textbooks. Our festivals', it alphabetically continued, 'celebrate art, blues, Cajun music, catfish, cracklins, étouffée, herbs, spices, yams and zydeco.'[52] We have argued that officialization does not always succeed in repressing new creative forms of resistance from below. This is true too of zydeco. Again, a small example must suffice. Two local radio presenters kick off their Swamp 'n' Roll Show warning that the zydeco music to be aired 'contains adult language, nudity, and subversive political commentary'.[53]

Conclusion

In this chapter we have considered how a crucial manifestation of popular culture, namely music, is developed and performed in Cape Verde and Louisiana. The poet Henry Wadsworth Longfellow suggested that 'music is the universal language of [hu]mankind.' Certainly, it seems to have the capacity to sooth and inspire, to bridge emotion and reason, to connect apparent opposites. Writing of the creative, creolizing capacity of African music, Frank A. Salamone suggests that 'African-derived music is in fact a subversive and anomalous art form. It combines opposites in every aspect – performance, content, heritage, objectives. It demands technical proficiency and yet scorns mere technique. What really matters is the ability of the performer to create something new each and every time he or she performs.'[54] George Lipsitz provides a similarly enthusiastic endorsement of the power of Hip Hop, which, he argues, 'blends music and life into an integrated totality, uniting performers, dancers, and listeners in a collaborative endeavor'.[55]

The development of popular music in Cape Verde and Louisiana provides perfect examples of this collective endeavour. The ingredients in the musical stew have clear diasporic roots and routes. Particular cadences, forms of call-and-response, songs and fragments, scales and notes, lyrics and rhythms are borne by people as they migrate. Sometimes instruments make the journey too – the drums and banjos in Congo Square, New Orleans, and the *cimboa* (a bowed cordaphone) in Cape Verde have clear African origins. But something else happens too. New musical forms emerge from the plantation, from encounters with other religions (often Catholicism) and other musical traditions, from emancipation, isolation and having to survive in difficult circumstances. The impress of history (the diasporic inheritance), the attempt to resist oppression from plantation owners and the state, and the influence of particular contexts (islands, swamps or a port city like New Orleans) all combined to generate an extraordinary cornucopia of popular music.

We do not need to press this point in the case of Louisiana. There are more than 3,000 jazz clubs in over 100 countries. European and North American popular music is totally embedded in, and largely derivative of, the creolized musical forms that evolved in Louisiana. Sometimes this legacy is acknowledged by white musicians, sometimes it is repudiated. The British group, the Rolling Stones, took its name from a blues song by the African American Muddy Waters and copiously acknowledges its debt to blues, soul music and rhythm & blues. Elvis Presley, by contrast, made appallingly racist comments (like 'the only thing black people can do for me is shine my shoes and buy my music'), but it is apparent that he learned his music, and his moves, from growing up with African American neighbours. More cynically, Elvis was a creation of the music industry, intent on expanding an existing thriving musical genre to a new white audience.

The influence of Cape Verdean music is rather less well known but, nonetheless, significant. The late Cesária Évora made it big in the clubs and concert halls of Europe, while lusophone music lovers from Brazil to Portugal are plugged into Cape Verdean music. Elsewhere, the CDs and online filestores often bury the music under the vague category of 'world music'. At one level, this is a demotion and at another an appropriate recognition that Cape Verdean music draws not only from its diasporic past, but also from its diasporic present, including Cape Verdean musicians abroad. Cape Verdean *Cabo-Zouk* is also strongly influenced by Caribbean music. In short, musical genres can now creolize locally, region-ally and globally. Music that was reborn and remade in Louisiana and Cape Verde has gloriously demonstrated the capacity both to condense the local and to express the global, delighting fans and aficionados in many parts of the world.

5

Celebrating and Resisting: Carnival

We have been concerned in this book to focus on manifestations of creolization and diaspora emanating from below. However, élites can appropriate popular cultural practices as forms of cultural capital, or commandeer them to promote nation-building, heritage projects or tourism. Carnivals, which are now state-sponsored or approved in more than 60 countries, are a case in point. It is precisely the tension between the attempts to control and co-opt carnivals and the attempts by participants and organizers to elude official recognition that we wish to explore in this chapter. There is little doubt that carnival (Mardi Gras in the case of Louisiana) has become an increasingly globalized phenomenon with official emphasis more on attracting tourists than on either marking a religious ritual or creating a liberating space for creativity to flourish. We argue that the capture of a popular cultural practice from above does not end resistance from below; rather, both processes can take place sequentially or synchronously.

In this chapter we consider the examples of carnivals in Louisiana, Cape Verde and London and draw out the contrasts and similarities between all three. Taking into account Abner Cohen's notion that 'every major carnival is precariously poised between the affirmation and validation of the established order and its rejection',[1] we consider the extent to which these three carnivals enact this tension in different ways. Most notably, we suggest that creolization and diaspora offer valuable tools with which to capture this interchange between dominance, resistance and subversion as it is played out in the specific moment of the carnival.

Situating carnival and the 'carnivalesque'

The dominant scholarly accounts suggest that carnival emerged originally in medieval Italy and the name 'carnival' stems from the Italian words 'carne' and 'levare', which would mean 'to remove meat'. In this narrative, for some two weeks before Lent (when Christians were enjoined to fast), there was a prolonged 'letting go' or 'farewell' to meat. In effect, you succumbed to bodily pleasures because you know you would soon have to give them up. Philosopher and literary theorist, Mikhail Bakhtin, has made a major contribution to the study of carnival with his theory of the 'carnivalesque'. Also, through his discussion of the literary works of François Rabelais, he described the 'carnivalization' of society in the Middle Ages and Renaissance, with a particular focus on language and literature. For Bakhtin, carnivals were subversive and liberating because of the dissolution – for that short period – of existing hierarchies:

> Rank was especially evident during official feasts; everyone was expected to appear in the full regalia of his calling, rank, and merits and to take the place corresponding to his position. It was a consecration of inequality. On the contrary, all were considered equal during carnival. Here, in the town square, a special form of free and familiar contact reigned among people who were usually divided by the barriers of caste, property, profession, and age. . . . People were, so to speak, reborn for new, purely human relations. These truly human relations were not only a fruit of imagination or abstract thought; they were experienced.[2]

In this view, carnival and the carnivalesque were used metaphorically to depict the everyday practices that were temporally and spatially separated from the official, strictly hierarchical and dogmatic order. The notion of rebirth and renewal is a central motif, capturing a ritualistic reversal and renewal of established order and a moment for living only by 'the laws of carnivalesque *freedom*'.[3] In some ways, this notion of subversion and renewal reflects a dramatic enactment of creolization whereby old roots are eroded and something new is created, often through creative practices of resistance among marginalized groups that subvert power structures and relations. Thus, while Bakhtin uses carnival to make a wider comment on medieval society and culture, here we use it – as practised in three distinct locations – as a means of deepening our analysis of creolization and diaspora as they are manifested in different settings and at different historical moments.

Indeed, although carnival has taken on distinct forms in different places, since its origins it has come to represent a moment of release, a space where everyday life is put on hold, a time for one 'to determine to do all things normally impossible or forbidden in everyday life and perhaps even to fulfil oneself by trying out one or more roles or lifestyles, to be for a short time what one could never be in everyday life'.[4] Carnival is not merely a visual spectacle to be viewed from a distance. Rather, it blurs the boundaries between performer and audience; it involves, by necessity, 'interactive play' between player and spectator, and has 'layered meaning and multiple reference'.[5] Yet, despite the possibilities that carnival provides for the suspension, or indeed subversion, of the status quo, it is important to consider how its cultural forms and rituals cannot be separated from the socio-political contexts within which they take place. As Peter Jackson writes, 'the cultural is not separable from the political; it is fundamentally political'.[6] Thus, any analysis of carnival must take into account both its universal characteristics as an artistic spectacle and its political significance that is inscribed in the local landscape. Here, through our prisms of creolization and diaspora, we explore the interplay between the cultural and the political, between 'top–down' and 'bottom–up' expressions of power in carnivals in Louisiana, Cape Verde and London. In all three cases, we observe how, in different ways, the emphasis on glitzy, formalized parades, the desire to package them to attract tourists or, in the case of Notting Hill in particular, the desire to control what is widely perceived as a threat to the status quo, sometimes overshadows the liberatory potential of these festivities. However, attempts to commercialize or control these events do not necessarily prevent ordinary people 'using' carnival – albeit in more subtle ways – as a space in which to adopt new identities and contest the existing political order.

Mardi Gras in Louisiana

As we noted in chapter 4, the component cultures of colonial Louisiana were African, European and Native American. However, this is too bald a statement. Africans comprised Madinkas, Wolof and Bambara and there was a crucial distinction between those who arrived with their white Creole slave owners from the Caribbean (principally from modern-day Haiti) already creolized, and those who arrived directly from West Africa. There were six Native American nations, some with moderately flourishing cultures. The whites were also strongly differentiated between white Creoles, Cajuns (French speakers from Canada), the Spanish (who ruled the area for 40 years), other Europeans and 'the Americans', essentially English speakers who penetrated the area after the Louisiana Purchase and the Civil War. All but the last group creolized easily and created the local version of carnival, Mardi Gras.

Strictly, 'Mardi Gras' (Fat Tuesday) refers to the practice of eating richer foods immediately before the partial fast days commencing on Ash Wednesday, the beginning of Lent. More broadly, it is the culmination of the carnival season and, as Mardi Gras parades now take place over a 10–12-day period, the expression is nearly synonymous with 'the carnival season'. Ranking below only the massive event in Rio, Brazil, the Mardi Gras carnivals in New Orleans and Mobile are the most well attended in the world. By 2012, they had attracted more than a million visitors to each of these cities. The net fiscal benefit to New Orleans of staging the Mardi Gras there was US$13,108,538 (including 'brand value') and US$7,771,095 (without brand value).[7] Brand value refers to the downstream, reputational effects positively influencing tourist arrivals and expenditure at other times of the year. In short, Mardi Gras is big business and plays into a phenomenon known as 'place marketing', which Kevin Gotham analysed. He shows that because place marketing has become a key means of urban renewal in New Orleans, public officials and corporations have transformed 'a relatively amateur and informal activity into an increasingly professionalized, highly organized and specialized industry'. For some, Mardi Gras demonstrates that consumption capitalism (based on leisure and spectacle) is replacing production capitalism. By corollary, 'sign value' (the value of images and other semiotic objects) replaces use value. Gotham insists that this turn to issues of signification should not obscure the hard-headed interventions of corporations and city planners:

> New Orleans represents a prime example of 'creative destruction' as urban leaders and economic élites have attempted to strategically deploy Mardi Gras imagery and advertising to refashion the city into a themed landscape of entertainment and tourism. . . . Moreover, major developers and real estate interests now regularly rely on Mardi Gras imagery and motifs to create commercial spaces including arts districts, historical areas, museums, casinos and gaming facilities, and shopping areas.[8]

To service these interests, Mardi Gras has to be tamed, commoditized and sanitized. This is not always easy. Take the transgressive act of disrobement (exposing breasts, buttocks and genitalia), which frequently takes place at Mardi Gras. These acts are relatively recent (dating from the 1970s); they express some degree of class, ethnic and gender order and are nearly always enacted for the exchange of beads. Just as hundreds of thousands, perhaps millions, of beads have become *symbolic* forms of currency during Mardi Gras, temporary nudity has become a *symbolic* act of rebellion against the established order. Of course, we need to make clear that to describe social behaviour as 'symbolic' does not render such an act meaningless or inert. Licentiousness, of which disrobement is an example, evokes pre-Christian Dionysian behaviour associated with intoxication, unruliness, frenzy and ecstasy, none of which sits comfortably

with the managed, corporatized world of contemporary Mardi
Gras festivities and parades.[9]

A more explicit challenge to the officialized, commercialized Mardi Gras comes in the survival of Mardi Gras 'Indians',
earlier known as black Indians. They are not Native Americans,
but working–class blacks using the narratives of Native American
resistance and mystical connections to the spirit world to oppose
the social elite of New Orleans. As Lipsitz argued, while the
members of New Orleans 'high society'

> mask themselves in expensive costumes and ride motorized floats along
> the city's main thoroughfares, throwing beaded necklaces and souvenir
> doubloons to crowds of spectators, the Indians subvert this spectacle by
> declaring a powerful lineage of their own, one which challenges the
> legitimacy of Anglo-European domination. Their costumes are made,
> not bought. They avoid the main thoroughfares and walk through
> black neighborhoods. They define the crowds along their route as
> participants, not just as spectators. Their fusion of music, costumes,
> speech, and dance undermines the atomized European view of each
> of those activities as distinct and autonomous endeavors, while it fore-
> grounds an African sensibility about the interconnectedness of art and
> the interconnectedness of human beings.[10]

Even in the wake of hurricanes Rita and Katrina, when flood
waters devastated poor working-class areas, Mardi Gras Indians
were active, even defiant. With names like 'Creole Wild West',
'Fi-Yi-Yi' and 'Wild Tchoupitoulas', the 'tribes' (not 'krewes',
the more respectable name for the voluntary associations that
organize floats and group parades) stalked the back streets of New
Orleans on non–approved routes. They engaged in competitive
song and dance, and call-and-response lyrics, with strong African
resonances. The late 'Tootie' Montana (figure 5.1), the legendary
chief of the Yellow Pocahontas tribe, claimed that he dreamed up
his remarkable costumes by evoking African rituals.[11] This appeal
to the spirit world is all grist to our creolizing mill and displays a
splendid recklessness in combining the plausible and the implau-
sible, or even weird. Pocahontas was not of course a tribe, but a
person, the daughter of a Native American chief in the Virginia

Figure 5.1 Chief 'Tootie' Montana, who paraded with the Mardi Gras Indians for 52 years, died in 2005 at a City Council meeting, following accusations that police had roughed up youths in the poorer parts of the city
Source: Zada Johnson, Music Rising at Tulane

area. She married an Englishman and travelled to London, there being paraded as evidence of a 'noble savage' who could enter European civilization. Although 'Tootie' Montana was phenotypically black (not *os rouge*), he vehemently insisted that his cousins 'looked like Indian'. It is more than likely that his costumes were many-times reworked versions of those paraded in Buffalo Bill's Wild West shows, which combined depictions of the tragedy with the degradation of vanquished Native American cultures. As Roach perceptively comments, the performances of the Mardi Gras Indians were evocations of that pathos and ways of reimagining 'a space, a continent, from which the white man and his culture have vanished. . . . In other words, I believe that carnival in New Orleans permits, through the disguise of "masking Indian", the imaginative recreation and repossession of Africa.'[12]

As we have shown, Mardi Gras in New Orleans has not been totally co-opted, but we must remember too that the practice has spread throughout the state (and beyond). Carnivals along the Gulf Coast are particularly well established, and generally they are manifested by more local participation and fewer spectators. In Mobile, the oldest krewe, dating from 1867, depicted Folly chasing Death around a broken Greek column armed with a golden pig bladder. This may simply signify a Dionysian triumph, but it could be a reference to the broken dreams of the confederacy – Doric columns often supported old plantation houses.[13]

In the rural southwest, a different tradition has evolved – the Cajun and creole *courir de Mardi Gras*, or Mardi Gras run. Drawn from strong Acadian influences, riders on horseback or on flatbed trucks, or walkers, go from house to house, playing beggar-clowns and demanding *charité* before they leave. Chicken, sausage links and vegetables are especially welcome. If the householder is compliant, they are invited to join the revellers to eat the resultant gumbo and dance later that evening. Spitzer, who closely studied the rural Mardi Gras, observed that, despite sharing a cuisine, music and some common ancestry, Creoles and Cajuns have 'ambivalent and sometimes hostile' relations. Participating in the *courir de Mardi Gras* is a way of highlighting and perhaps resolving differences, or, at the very least, using the clowning to examine, exaggerate, neutralize or invert the travails of daily life.[14] Although most of the revellers are male, *courirs de Mardi Gras* have also become popular with women. Participants are particularly noted for the inventiveness of their masks, and for engaging in bawdy play and gender role reversals. They sometimes dress as hags or dolls, with ambisexual costumes, openly mocking conventional ideas of decorum and beauty.[15]

Carnival in Cape Verde

The attempt to capture carnival to develop tourism is also evident in Cape Verde. Many local people lament the 'Brazilianization' of carnival in Cape Verde, as it increasingly becomes a 'tourist product' competing in what has been labelled the 'carnival industry'.[16] Yet, despite these signs of commercialization and external influences within the official parades, the unofficial festivities in the streets, in rural areas and in unsupervised public spaces show

how popular resistance evades total order and official approval. While politicians hope carnivals can become 'nation-builders for tourism', for those who have taken part in these festivities throughout their lives, they become 'counter-festivities in the most extreme formulations, ones that comment negatively on the official ways of celebrating'.[17]

Carnival represents one of the major events in the Cape Verdean cultural calendar and it takes place every year at the start of Lent. It dates back to the colonial period and its origins lie in the Portuguese *entrudo* (or 'entrance' to Lent), which was celebrated in the sixteenth and seventeenth centuries. Yet, despite its Catholic and European origins, there is little evidence to suggest that it is a mere reproduction of the Portuguese festivities, for carnival in Cape Verde reflects the country's history of creolization. Carnival can thus be seen as a staging of Cape Verde's complex identity and its position at a crossroads between Europe, Africa and the Americas. Although each island has some form of carnival, the carnival of São Vicente is the biggest on the archipelago and many residents from the other islands come to partake in the festivities, as well as large numbers of Cape Verdeans living in the diaspora. Here, in Cesária Évora's translated song, is one representation of carnival in São Vicente:

> São Vicente is a tiny Brazil
> filled with joy and colour
> during those three days of extravagance
> there is no conflict, just carnival
> and unparalleled bliss.[18]

As the lyrics suggest, the Brazilian equivalent heavily influences São Vicente's carnival, both through the widespread propaga-tion of Brazil's carnival on the TV and other media and because many Cape Verdeans either live or have lived in Brazil. Several interviewees in São Vicente commented on the Brazilianization of the carnival, referring to how, rather than using locally produced artefacts, people buy the costumes, materials and drums in Brazil. Floats have also become the most visible part of the parade. Yet, despite such influences, people made a point of reiterating that the São Vicente carnival remains a uniquely Cape Verdean event. One interviewee also pointed out that the São Vicente carnival in fact preceded the one in Brazil, since the Portuguese brought it to Cape Verde first. The Brazilianization of Cape Verde's carnival can thus be seen as part of a long history of entanglement and cultural exchange within and across these two creolized spaces.

The notion of cultural entanglement is also an important consideration with regard to the echoes of Africanness, the diasporic traces, in this creole event. Typical figures in the São Vicente carnival are the *mandingas* – people who paint their bodies black with a mixture of coal and cooking oil and who dance bare-footed in grass skirts, violently shaking a stick bearing a doll's head, which is also painted black. These people were traditionally from Ribeira Bote, one of the poorest local neighbourhoods of Mindelo (São Vicente's main town), though nowadays they come from all over the city. While the name 'Mandinga' – or Mandinka – refers to a West African ethnic group, the so-called *mandingas* of the carnival are in fact based on a different ethnic group from the Bissagos Islands just off Guinea-Bissau. According to one account:

> A group of people from these islands came to Cape Verde in the 1940s on their way to a Colonial Exhibition in Portugal. They performed a dance . . . which remained in the collective memories of the people of Mindelo. And so people began to imitate them during carnival. And, since the Mandinkas were at the time the most well-known ethnic groups in Portuguese Guinea, this was the name they were given and it stuck.[19]

Apparently, the figure of the *mandinga* has been adapted and recreated over the years and is now uniquely São Vicentean. While the *mandinga* was initially a figure that evoked fear and played tricks, its role is now primarily to dance and entertain, in many ways becoming part of the more formalized, securitized, nature of the Cape Verdean carnival (figure 5.2). Yet, despite this apparent co-optation of the *mandinga* figure, one could also argue that the way in which the figure has evolved – involving people from all over the city – is part of the ongoing process of identity construction in Cape Verde. Far from being merely

Figure 5.2   Mandinga figure at Carnaval de Mindelo, Cape Verde, 2013
Source: Emma Klinefelter, used with permission

'top–down', the evolving social identity is an expression of the changing demographic makeup of the archipelago – including increasing migration from mainland African countries – and the changing everyday practices of Cape Verdeans. As well as their visibility during the official days of carnival, *mandinga* 'parades', accompanied by groups of percussionists, take place every Sunday for two months prior to the carnival and the *mandingas* are often seen painted in colours other than the traditional black. The shifting *mandinga* figure – both within and outside the carnival – thus raises important questions about Cape Verdean identity, about the relationship with Africa and the people power that arises through the creative play on this already creolized figure.

Several interviewees mentioned the increased police presence during the official parades. While the police presence seems insignificant compared with the Notting Hill or Brazilian carnivals, there is little doubt that on the days of the official carnival parades, some of the streets in Mindelo become heavily controlled and set out in specific ways. Another recurrent theme in the narratives of interviewees was the increased cost of the carnival: costumes and floats become ever more extravagant and, for members of the diaspora who return, the prices of food or hotel accommodation are inflated. Yet, despite this increased expense and formalization, for many, the most important moments of the carnival take place outside the official parades – in the streets, which become spaces of spontaneity and resistance as normal life is put on hold and everyday norms are subverted. It is a time–space where 'anything goes': men are dressed as women; women are dressed as men; children masquerade as elderly people; others wear elaborate masks and disguises; people make up chants critiquing the Cape Verdean government or the global situation; or they create new games and tricks to awaken complacent observers. As we saw earlier, all these features appear at the Louisiana Mardi Gras, though the suspension of conventional gender roles is probably more noticeable in Louisiana; women, in particular, are given much more sexual licence. It also represents a creolizing space where new cultural forms and practices emerge; through a combination of dance, play, theatre and music, carnival becomes an example of 'cultural creativity in process'.[20]

In addition to the many participants in the parades and unofficial carnival play, vast numbers of other people, including locals, visitors from neighbouring islands and members of the diaspora, come to watch the carnival and to seek out a spot that will provide the best views. Again, the everyday uses of the city are subverted: buildings under construction, railings, walls and trees – however high – become ideal viewing points, as do the rooftops and balconies of hotels and restaurants where people arrive hours in advance to get themselves the best place. Like the walkers Michel de Certeau describes in his seminal book, *The Practice of Everyday Life*, who tactically move around the city in ways that challenge the strategic plans of governments or town planners, during carnival city spaces take on new roles as the practices of users destabilize their official purposes.[21] Yet, while these creative and subversive uses of the city are concentrated on these few carnival days, their effect lingers. Carnival thus represents a staging, a making visible, a creative though spontaneous performance of the ongoing processes of creolization in Cape Verde's dynamic culture 'in the making'.

Carnival in London

Let us now turn our attention to a rather different creolizing space, to the carnival that takes place every year in the 'global city' of London, a city we refer to as a contemporary contact zone (see chapter 3). Many of the tensions outlined above – between commercialization and authenticity, co-optation and resistance, or past and present – are evident in London's Notting Hill Carnival. Although there were historical precedents to carnival in the Bartholomew and Southwark Fairs of the eighteenth century, the modern British revival dated from 30 January 1959 when Claudia Jones, a Trinidadian writer and activist, staged an indoor event as a deliberate protest against the Notting Hill race riots directed against Caribbean immigrants in August 1958. These colonial migrants, invited to help rebuild post-war Britain, had begun to arrive in the 1950s and their migration continued into the 1960s. Yet, despite expectations of a better life in the motherland – 'they take you here and they take you there, and they make you feel like a millionaire. So London, that's the place for me'[22] – the reality was far from welcoming and these migrants faced widespread discrimination. In the face of such hostility, cultural forms such as carnival emerged among Caribbean people in Britain, not just 'for recreation', but, importantly, 'for self-expression and self-affirmation and as a statement of identity'.[23] Not only has today's carnival in London dramatically grown, attracting more than a million revellers, but also its form and content have evolved to reflect London's ever more diverse population.

The early trajectory of the Notting Hill Carnival in many ways parallels that of its precursor in Trinidad (and other parts of the Caribbean) and, as Jackson argues, in both cases the political context is of key significance.[24] Prior to the abolition of slavery in 1834, the Trinidadian carnival was the realm of the white – predominantly French-speaking Catholic – elite. Yet, following emancipation, black slaves, who had formerly been prohibited from congregating in public, took to the streets and gradually took over the event as a way of celebrating their freedom and, through creative disguise and mimicry, criticizing and caricaturing their former masters. Through bringing together groups whose everyday lives are normally separate, both physically and socially, carnival came to represent a space where 'all the social, political and "racial" tensions of Trinidadian society' are made manifest.[25] On the other hand, governments and cultural elites have frequently used carnival as a form of nation-building, an 'integrative institution' that celebrates unity in diversity.[26]

In London, following several years of being celebrated in large halls, in 1966 carnival took to the streets of Notting Hill when a small street festival held for local children became an extensive street party as residents were drawn to the sounds of Russell Henderson's steel band.[27] At the time, Notting Hill was an area where many Caribbean migrants lived, predominantly due to low rental prices. In its early years, carnival represented a means for the celebration of shared Caribbean cultural identity in urban areas of settlement, and incorporated traditional masquerades, music and costumes. As one of its founders Rhaune Laslett remarked, the event emerged through the motivation 'to prove that from our ghetto there was a wealth of culture waiting to express itself, that we weren't rubbish people'.[28]

Protest was directed at poor housing conditions and the construction of the Westway flyover, which cut right through the area. Yet, it was not until the late 1970s, particularly following violent police action and the 'race riots' that erupted during the 1976 carnival, that the event took on a more explicitly political dimension. Carnival in this period became an affirmation of black identity in the face of alienation and discrimination, and a (re)claiming of public space in response to the contempt of those in power. Carnival also was increasingly identified with Jamaicans (the largest group from the Caribbean in Britain), particularly second-generation young people who were feeling more and more disaffected by their lives in London. The predominance of Jamaicans during this period saw the increased presence of big sound systems playing dancehall music, which was emerging on the scene in inner-city Kingston in Jamaica. The 1976 riots marked a significant turning point in relations between the police and black people in Britain, a transition to a period where 'the brute fact of institutional racism could no longer be disguised'.[29]

In this context, the symbolic meaning of carnival entered, like its Trinidadian antecedent, a more explicitly political domain.

Contestations over the Notting Hill Carnival have not assuaged over the years, despite the event's remarkable growth and reputation as a key marker of London's super-diverse character. More recent tensions have arisen largely because of the significant socio-demographic changes in the area brought on by widespread gentrification and the exorbitant rise in house prices. It is no longer a zone where low-paid Caribbean migrants live and work, but a space populated predominantly by a wealthy, white elite. These changes have led to repeated calls to relocate the carnival, either to confine it to a park or to reroute the procession to avoid some of the area's residential streets. Yet, these suggestions have met strong opposition from the carnival's organizers, not least because such changes would challenge the historical and symbolic significance of the event's location, which underpins its spirit of resistance. As Tompsett noted:

> The processional route at Notting Hill resonates with a particular and pertinent history. It is a microcosm of that macrocosm that is a shared history between colonizer and colonized. From the industrial canal behind Kensal Road and the old factory buildings and working man's club in the north of the area, down to the fine streets of Arundel Gardens, Kensington Park and Westbourne Grove, in the south, with their handsome white stucco fronted houses built with the wealth of empire, the route reflects every level of empire activity from the making of wealth in plantation and factory to the displaying of it in the grand houses.[30]

The Notting Hill Carnival thus bears traces of the past – a post-emancipation Caribbean where carnival represented a creative form of resistance to colonialism, and a postcolonial past in post-war London that involved the claiming of urban space among Caribbean settlers. The diverse carnival 'Mas bands'[31] reflect this complex history, with some, such as 'J'ouvert' or 'dirty Mas', explicitly evoking the history of slavery and the origins of carnival in the satirical mimicry of slave masters, often depicted as the devil; others, such as 'Mahogany Mas', more overtly adapt their design to correspond to the contemporary context (in 2008 Mahogany designed their carnival band around the theme 'Bling').[32]

Apart from the Mas bands of Caribbean carnival artists, the parades include various other ethnic groups. Brazilian Mas bands, echoing the more recent burgeoning Brazilian presence in the city and also with a proud tradition of carnival and history of slavery, are particularly strong. Following the choice of Rio as a site for the 2016 Olympics, the Notting Hill Carnival of 2014 was seen as a landmark year for the Brazilian presence, although Brazilian groups have participated in the event for several years – with two samba groups, three 'samba-reggae' groups, and two *maracutu* groups. *Maracutu* is a performance style that has its origins in the northeastern state of Pernambuco, dates back to slavery and incorporates elements of the Afro-Brazilian religion, *Candomblé*. The group, Maracutudu Mafua, formed in 2009, is illustrative of the evolution – and constant creolization – of the Notting Hill Carnival (figure 5.3). The group comprises more than 70 performers from a diverse range of countries and, basing its style on traditional *maracutu* forms, adapts and creatively reworks these forms as part of its carnival performance. It is a form of performing

Figure 5.3   Maracutudo Mafua at the Notting Hill Carnival, 2014
Source: chiffe.wordpress.com

Brazilian styles to 'an audience who would probably never have experienced them', as the artistic director of Maracutudo Mafua remarks.[33] It is also an example of how carnival evolves and adapts in response to new contexts.

The Notting Hill Carnival is, arguably, a more contested event than its Cape Verdean and Louisiana equivalents because it enacts contemporary *as well as* historical social and racial tensions in British society. It occupies a 'domain of threatening culture'.[34] The swarming masses at the Notting Hill Carnival can seem overwhelming and uncomfortable, a crowd that is 'potentially limitless and exists so long as it grows, pulling people, barbeque smoke and sequins into its wake as it rolls its way through the neighbourhood, disintegrating as quickly as it began when it reaches sunset'.[35] The edginess of Notting Hill is an integral part of the experience, without which it ceases to be carnival. As a Guyanese artist involved in a carnival-themed exhibition at the Tate Modern gallery commented, '[carnival] should be enjoyable but then it will be a bit edgy as well because that's how carnival always has been. Wherever you go in the world, carnival always comes out of some sort of tension.'[36]

Like its counterparts, the Notting Hill Carnival is frequently exposed to the charge of commercialization and the consequent loss of 'authenticity'. The commercialization of the event dates back to 1975 with the participation of Capital Radio and several other sponsors. Yet, such recourse to private funds and sponsorship has proliferated as the event has grown to its current size. Now, involving over one million people, it is the largest street festival in Europe. However, to see this commercialization as leading to an erasure of the event's 'authentic' grassroots would be to misinterpret the very nature of carnival's capacity to adapt, by necessity, to the socio-political contexts within which it finds itself: the carnival in London now has to accept an ever more diverse population, an increasingly paranoid (and armed) police force, a growing and more demanding public and ever scarcer recourse to public funds. Despite the wider use of private money and inevitable broadening of the event's scope beyond its original base, the Notting Hill Carnival retains much of its grassroots support, with the majority of Mas band participants and artists working as volunteers from homes, church halls or community centres.[37]

London's carnival at Notting Hill is a complex and contradictory event practised and interpreted on many different levels. As historical accounts tell us, carnival by its very nature has always been 'poised' between dominant and resistant ideologies, between 'compliance and subversion': on the one hand, it is 'exploited by dominant power interests', while on the other it has a strong capacity to foster 'criticism, protest and resistance'.[38] The Notting Hill Carnival has diasporic traces; it is an affirmation of black culture in Britain; and it draws on a shared cultural heritage that proclaims 'we are here to stay'. Yet, the carnival also embraces diversity and change: it adapts, evolves and creates new forms as it resists co-optation or domination. This three-day event, which temporarily transforms London's urban landscape, thus enacts processes of creolization, here transposed from the plantation, from the New World, back to the metropole.

Conclusion

Using the prismatic concepts of creolization and diaspora, and co-optation and resistance, we have analysed carnivals at three sites, not hitherto compared. Comparison is not merely about identifying similarities, but about deepening understandings of the unique through suggestive contrast. Indeed, one cannot separate carnival from the socio-political context from which it emerges and in response to which it evolves. We have considered how, in all three cases, carnival dramatically stages processes of creolization, while also retaining some diasporic traces. The common themes staged during carnival in Louisiana and Cape Verde are African slaves, European slave holders, colonialism and Catholicism. The London carnival retains some diasporic elements, though at once removed, for the people of African descent reworked social practices in the Caribbean before arriving in the metropoles of their colonial or postcolonial power (Britain, the Netherlands, France, Denmark or the USA). They have thus been described as 'a diaspora of a

diaspora'.[39] Of course, there are resonances of the original homeland in the evocation of African kings and ancient empires and in
the creolized and syncretized Rastafarian references. (Before he
became Emperor of Ethiopia, Haile Selassie was known as Ras
Tefari Makonnen.) Colonialism has also adopted a new, displaced,
character as 'the empire struck back' in the form of immigrants
from the former colonies in the Caribbean and South Asia.[40]

When we examined carnival/Mardi Gras practices in our three
creolizing spaces, we undoubtedly biased the examples towards
those displaying mimicry, social criticism, defiance, challenges
to dominant elites, inversions of gender roles and other forms of
resistance. We need to mention that not all forms of creolized and
diasporic carnivals are intentionally about resistance. Many carnival
organizers may choose to be co-opted. They not only make the
most of the situation, but by participating they also seek to influence the shape of officially and commercially sanctioned popular
culture. There are more prosaic reasons for playing the official
game too; musicians can gain exposure, while prominent carnival
organizers can augment their cultural and social capital. As we have
indicated, some music is produced for the fun of it, for recreation
and profit, not for protest.

The thrust of our argument is not that all creativity is an act
of resistance.[41] Rather, it is that carnival *permits* the creation of
a counter culture, one that is conditioned by relationships of
domination and subordination, one that draws inspiration from
sharing cultural traditions and one that is renewed by iterations
and nostalgic recreation – real, imagined, exaggerated, embellished
– of the diasporic experience. These are echoes of diaspora, not
retentions. The Garveyite and Afro-centric movements of the
1960s reconstructed a continent ravaged by colonialism and the
slave trade. Native Americans can no longer hunt the American
bison over wide swathes of the American West. Acadiens (Cajuns)
can no longer live by fishing and trapping alone. Africans can
no longer remain undisturbed in idyllic communitarian villages.
Carnival in Trinidad cannot be perfectly re-enacted by the largely
Jamaican-origin Caribbean people in Britain. But all these experiences and their embroidered versions can be mined to galvanize
claims for distinct identities and to re-energize creative impulses.

This capacity seems a particular property of music (discussed in chapter 4) and performances like carnival, which provide a code, a language or a ritual that allows, but does not guarantee, the deployment of traces of the past into a critique of the present. And, as the discussion of the role of the diaspora in the Cape Verdean carnival demonstrates, the diasporic present also feeds into cultural expressions and the possibility of dissent. Performance, perhaps especially public performance on the streets, is capable of uniting mind, body and intellect. As Carole-Anne Upton argues:

> Performance is the means by which life is played out: rehearsed, repeated and enacted. It is an infinitely rich and crucial part of the real world: the here and now of people gathering together to imagine, to contemplate, to question, to redress, to celebrate and to reflect upon the way people live. It engages the imagination, the intellect, and the body in the materiality of existence, and as such is an essential aspect of human experience. It's a deeply pleasurable pursuit, and for me, it's about nothing less than how to live well.[42]

In creating carnival costumes and music, in rehearsal and spontaneous dancing, in taking elements from here and there (what Lévi-Strauss calls 'bricolage'), creolization and diaspora are amalgamated. Such performances stand in notable contrast to the attempts at regulation and the destructive tolerance promoted by officialdom, both of which elide distinctiveness and imagination, often in the name of public safety or in pursuit of commercial ends. Carnival has struck deep roots and has become a crucial public ritual that disrupts the normal order for several days each year. In our next chapter, we shall examine attempts to create, embed and augment long-term heritage cultures in culturally mixed societies.

6

Constructing Heritage

Probably the most influential account of how heritage may be created and refashioned is contained in a book called *The Invention of Tradition*.[1] The title says it all. We tend not to question tradition because it has always been there: it conveys a sense of continuity, certainty and truth. In theological rhetoric, it is sanctified by divine will. Therefore, it is jarring to suggest that somebody has made it all up. Of course, the manipulation of history has to be convincing. To take one example, many people took Mel Gibson's bravura portrayal of William Wallace in the film *Braveheart* (1995) to be an authentic and stirring rendition of Scottish nationalism. Rather cruelly, a reputable Scottish historian has declared that the film 'hasn't an iota of fact in it'.[2] Nationalists are particularly prone to evoking history to foster patriotism by supposing a common identity and, in so doing, eliding inconvenient evidence of multiple ethnic, linguistic, cultural and religious traditions. Heritage construction can, however, also happen at a sub-national level and here we consider two contrasting cases. The first, in Mauritius, involved reactivating largely obsolete diasporic identities and refashioning them into heritage cultures. The second, in Louisiana, consisted of re-energizing and gaining official recognition for a long suppressed (often derided) creole way of life as a heritage culture.

Mauritius: the era of creolization

Mauritius is a creolized island *par excellence*. It had previously been uninhabited by humans (ignoring very remote hominids). Even the harmless dodo was clubbed to extinction by passing sailors, a testament to humankind's folly and incapacity to work harmoniously with nature. Nonetheless, all who settled on this remote island had perforce to get on with each other. Successive maritime and colonial powers – Portugal, the Netherlands, France and Britain – governed a diverse population, principally from Africa, India, China, Madagascar and Europe. There is widespread agreement among scholars that Mauritius is a textbook case of creolization. For example, in her authoritative history of the island, Megan Vaughan avers that Mauritius is unambiguously a 'creole island' in that, 'without natives [it] has always been the product of multiple influences, multiple sources, which to different degrees merge, take root and "naturalize" on this new soil'.[3] All the additional elements we associated with creolization and identified in earlier chapters are there. The locale is congruent – a relatively remote, small, colonial island based on plantations worked by imported slaves and, later, indentured labourers. The African, Malagasy, Chinese, French, Indian and mixed segments of the population were deeply riven by ethnicity, snobbery and social class, but a new *lingua franca* developed (*Kreol morisien*, or simply Kreol), as did a distinctive cuisine and dance/music, *sega*. Over the nineteenth and early twentieth centuries, Franco-Mauritians participated avidly in the new culture and shared a common religion. Catholicism had been adopted or imposed on Africans and Malagasies early in the slave period, while many Sino-Mauritians converted later. All elements of the population engaged with and helped to make the new language, cuisine and folkways and, for extended periods, they would have little connection with their countries and regions of origin.

This disconnection with home promoted and consolidated creolization, though the reasons for it varied between the different ethnic groups that constituted the Mauritian population. When the French social critic, naturalist and engineer Bernardin de Saint-Pierre visited the island in 1768–70, he was far from impressed with the Franco-Mauritians he encountered. A disciple of Rousseau, he had perhaps hoped for a more idyllic environment, one he imagined in his popular pastoral novel *Paul et Virginie* (1787). Instead, he found people who 'speculate, slander and talk scandal'. The men blamed their lack of financial success on their not being married, but Saint Pierre attributed it to 'the ease with which they find black mistresses'. He accorded the French women little more respect. They 'remain pale with good figures and most are pretty', but each woman, he thought, clung to 'some secret pretension, which comes from their fortune, their jobs or the birth of their husbands'.[4] The foibles and affectations of the French colonists survived for as long as the connection with their homeland continued. However, the Revolution and the Napoleonic wars effectively cut that link and the French settlers' surrender to a British naval squadron on 3 December 1810 followed. Thereafter, the island became a British colony with the Franco-Mauritians becoming localized (usually adopting the sobriquet 'Creoles'). Despite British rule, they retained their status and economic power while the French language survived, and a French-based creole (Kreol) developed. Unusually, the few British who actually settled in Mauritius (not just temporarily) became French-speaking. One of the country's best poets, for example, was the Englishman Robert Edward Hart, who wrote French verse.[5]

The majority Indo-Mauritian population was only fitfully connected with India during the colonial period and Jawaharlal Nehru strongly reinforced this detachment after India's independence in 1947. Anxious to ally himself with the non-aligned anti-colonial movement, Nehru advised people of Indian ancestry living elsewhere to adopt local citizenships and to identify with local issues and struggles. Once they had made their choice of citizenship, 'we have no concern with them', he said, as 'politically they cease to be Indians'.[6] Most of the Indians had come as indentured labourers; 450,000 were brought to the island between 1836 and 1907. Conditions on the plantations were extremely harsh. The 'protector' appointed by the colonial government to look after their welfare was ineffectual and, unlike in other sugar colonies, the 'coolies' (as they were pejoratively called) were not allowed to return to India after the expiry of their indentures.[7] Shutting

off an escape route home increased their engagement with movements to improve conditions on the island. Indo-Mauritians were
at the forefront of the 1937 riots over their exploitation on the
plantations. In addition, they started and signed up to trade unions
and, in significant numbers, to the Labour Party, which a Creole
medical practitioner, Dr Maurice Curé, founded in 1936. In 1940,
Curé wrote that 'the workers, Creole or Indians, are all basically
the same colour, with the same interests united under the same
banner. Today the leader of the Labour Party is a Creole; tomor-
row it will be an Indian.'[8]

The bulk of Indo-Mauritians were Hindu, but until recently
rarely observant or even knowledgeable about Hindu customs and
beliefs, though small local shrines can be observed at the side of
many roads. There was also a significant minority of Muslims, who
often came as traders rather than indentured workers. The Muslims
tended to form an 'islanded identity', meeting other Mauritians at
their shops but retaining a degree of residential segregation and religious piety. However, even Muslims participated in the common
social practices. Like everyone else, they spoke Kreol and, according to several sources, commonly found their way to the rum shop
or race track. Tempted by the superior education of the Catholic
schools, thousands of Indians from the emerging middle class
adopted Christianity. The story of the tiny Sino-Mauritian community is similar. Like the bulk of Indians, they came as indentured
labourers, then later as craftspeople and traders. A number moved
into retail trade or set up restaurants all over the island. Most are
Catholic and speak Kreol as their first language. Chinese food has
largely been absorbed into the general cuisine of the island.

At independence, people of African and Malagasy origin
formed the majority of the 27 per cent of islanders described as
'mixed'. The history of their settlement is complex, with people
landing from different parts of the continent in large groups, then
in dribs and drabs. Generally, Africans worked as slaves on the
sugar plantations. They did the gruelling work of clearing the
land (not easy when large chunks of volcanic rock needed to be
excavated, hoisted and broken up), planting, fetching water and
cutting cane. With Indians at their side, they were also the port
workers. Conditions were so brutal for some that they ran away

to seek refuge in the southwestern part of the country in what was virtually the only mountainous area. There, with Malagasy runaways from earlier unsuccessful Dutch settlements, they established precarious Maroon communities. They too were designated 'Creoles'. Lest this nomenclature is becoming too confusing, let us indicate that, at independence in 1968, Creoles comprised:

- From the top of the social ladder to the bottom, the following class categories: French Creoles (Franco-Mauritians), wealthy black Creoles (*klas bourzwa*, the local rendering of bourgeois), Creoles of colour (*gens de couleur*), working-class Creoles (*klas travailleur*), and marginalized or unemployed Creoles (*ti-Créole*, the contraction of *petit Créole* or little Creole).
- While there is some overlap between ethnicity and class in the above categories, there were also separate ethnically defined Creoles, for example *Créole Madras* (Indian Creoles), *Créole Sinwa* (Chinese Creoles) and *Créole l'Ascar* (Lascars were seamen, often from India or Yemen, so an occupational as well as an ethnic category).[9]

As these categories indicate, the island was thoroughly creolized; moreover, the many crossovers between them were embodied in the so-called 'general population', loosely *Créole Morisyen*. There was a strong interdependence between the different population groups who shared a creolized language, cuisine, music, dance, customs and habits. However, it is important to understand that we are not talking about an Edenic state of nature. Class, power and status separated people and, as independence dawned (1968), the diverse ethnic segments of the population reinvigorated their diasporic identities, turning distant echoes of the past into more insistent drumbeats of difference.

The revival of diasporic heritages in Mauritius

The reconstruction of local diasporic identities has been a product of both local electoral politics and an external process of identity validation. Internally, the political arithmetic and constitutional arrangements that led to decolonization encouraged the emergence of much more distinct communal blocs. The largest bloc, newly defined as 'Hindu', voted overwhelmingly for the Labour Party, which prominent Indo-Mauritians led. The remaining elements of the population loosely stitched together an electoral alliance, but this soon fell apart and disintegrated into riots in the months leading up to independence in March 1968. The son of an Indian indentured worker, Seewoosagur Ramgoolam, was appointed prime minister and he dominated Mauritian politics for the next 14 years. Although he sought an island-wide mandate and after his death was proclaimed 'the father of the nation', it was clear that the constancy of the Hindu communal vote underpinned his long pre-eminence.

Externally, the Indian government's policy to distance itself from people of Indian origin abroad changed from the 1970s, at first slowly and then in a rush. In Mauritius, it was marked by the construction of lavishly funded institutes designed to promote cultural, educational and literary links with 'mother India'. Luckily, a number of sensitive curators at the Mahatma Gandhi and Rabindranath Tagore Institutes attenuated the Indian government's plans by promoting cultural events and performing arts that were accessible to all Mauritians. However, the aggressive fly-posting and noisy megaphones mounted on the roving vehicles of newly imported militant versions of Indian-based religions, such as the Vishwa Hindu Parishad, alienated many Mauritians. Again, more militant varieties of Islam are serving to reshape and solidify ethnic and religious boundaries that had been being eroded for many years. Investment in the export-processing zone, Indian tourism to the island, the establishment of Indian banks (the Bank of Baroda alone had nine branches by 2014) and penetration by right-wing Indian political parties have followed the cultural and religious linkages. This enhanced connectivity with the 'homeland' has decreolized Indo-Mauritians and given them a greatly enhanced sense of their diasporic origins and links. This phenomenon is particularly marked in the case of language, with Hindi promoted in clear preference to Mauritian Bhojpuri and Kreol, thus generating a form of 'ethnolinguistic belonging' based on the recovery of a more prestigious ancestral language, which Indo-Mauritians do not actually speak, and 'the construction of [a] diasporic ancestral culture'.[10]

Another important way of reaffirming diasporic roots has been to persuade UNESCO to adopt particular places as World Heritage sites. Indian Prime Minister Indira Gandhi's visit to the Immigration Depot in Port Louis in 1970, where many Indian indentured labourers bound for the sugar estates had landed, triggered a long campaign for UNESCO recognition that finally succeeded. However, rebadging the site as Aapravasi Ghat (which means 'Immigration Landing' in Hindi) emphasized Indian arrivals to the detriment of other population groups also processed at the Immigration Depot. Attempts to restore and expand the site have been fitful and ineffective. One interviewee with close connections to the government said that 'the steam has now gone out of restoring Aapravasi'. When pressed, he explained that the 'Indian government wants to praise "India shining" not talk about [the] past',[11] the implication being that money from India to renovate the site had dried up.

Similar changes were afoot among the smaller population groups in Mauritius. Franco-Mauritians had long abandoned the self-description 'Creole', but deepened their ties with France. As sugar prices fluctuated or declined, they moved into the tourist and leisure industries. They reconstructed old plantations as restaurants, hotels, spas and golf clubs, developed beach sites, often in alliance with international hotel chains, and moved into the property (real-estate) business. One hotel owner cashed in on Saint-Pierre's romantic novel by calling his place the 'Veranda Paul and Virginie Hotel and Spa'. Another is badged 'Le Plantation Hotel', while 'Le Paradis Hotel and Golf Club' offers rest and recreation, so field observation disclosed, to spoiled members of French football teams and a discarded but infuriated mistress of a certain French president. For reasons that are unclear, successive British governments have abandoned any strategic interest in, or historical ties with, the Indian Ocean. By contrast, independence in 1968 coincided with a reassertion of French cultural power in the region. TV channels beamed from Réunion are popular in Mauritius, French language schools abound and French higher education has acquired renewed prestige.

Similar rumblings are happening among Sino-Mauritians. The community at large has rediscovered its roots and now boasts its own Chinese Heritage Centre, funded by local entrepreneurs. The centre, opened in 2013, is on the top floor of a Chinese-owned mall in Grand Bay, one of the upmarket parts of the island. Inside are depicted, *inter alia*, an early Chinese shopkeeper (in wax), many identity documents, pictures of rickshaws in Port Louis and lead type used to print the first Chinese newspaper on the island. The broad depiction is a 'rags to riches' story typical of, say, the received narrative of immigrant groups in the USA. There is little representation of encounters, intimate and hostile, with other parts of the Mauritian population. With the active assistance of Sino-Mauritians, China recently invested around US$1 billion to set up a special economic zone on the island, encouraged also by generous incentives by the Mauritian government.

Partly in reaction to the Indo-Mauritian, Franco-Mauritian and Sino-Mauritian reconstructions of their diasporic pasts, Creoles (defined now as a significantly reduced social category) have petitioned for Le Morne ('the sorrow') to become a UNESCO recognized 'cultural area'. This proposal, like that for the Aapravasi Ghat, has been successful. Le Morne is the name of a mountain in the southwest of the island where escaped African and Malagasy slaves established precarious self-provisioning communities. Rosebelle Boswell has documented this movement. One of her interviewees said, *'nu aussi nu bizin zwé nu filme'* ('we must also play our film'), which, Boswell suggests, means that Creoles must also play the political game of claiming a heritage identity 'if they are to obtain resources and a stronger position in Mauritian society'.[12] Such resources did appear, although not perhaps in the cornucopian quality imagined. The Le Morne Heritage Trust Fund (figure 6.1) manages government and international funds and runs educational tours of the Le Morne Cultural Landscape, covering the mountain, a sculpture park and archaeological digs of settlements, cemeteries and lime pits. A fieldwork visit coincided with the enactment and performance of heritage crafts on the seafront. Bystanders were shown how to make coconut brooms, grind maize, fashion fish-traps and lay traps. One ti-Créole enjoyed pretending to be a wild boar trapped in a sturdy wooden cage. Less

Figure 6.1   Le Morne: the heritage fund and educational centre
Source: Robin Cohen

enjoyable is the somewhat embellished story of a tragic misunderstanding on Le Morne, one version of which goes like this:

> It is said that when the first people to escape slavery made their way
> to the high rock at the extreme southwest of the island, it was in the
> hope that from there they might be able to see their homeland or even
> that one day a ship would come to take them home. When it was
> instead a detachment of armed British soldiers that they saw coming
> after them, even though, in fact, the orders these soldiers had were to
> tell them that slavery no longer existed . . . [they] flung themselves, all
> of them, from the high tops of the rock . . . toward the waiting ocean
> below. Men and women, children and the old, all died in the same
> way. It is a simply unbearable story.[13]

In the light of this story, the adjective 'unbearable' and the
appellation Le Morne ('the sorrow') seem appropriate, so it is

perhaps not surprising that a more affirming form of Creole heritage politics was constructed around the Nelson Mandela Centre
for African Culture, opened in 1986 in the centre of Port Louis.
The centre was tasked to project a positive image of African and
Creole culture in Mauritius and started soundly with some well-
attended public events and the production of an intellectually
challenging journal, *Revi Kiltir Kreol*. However, interviewees made
clear that official sponsorship by the Ministry of Arts and Culture
was 'the embrace of death'. There were internal disputes among
staff and our informants said that the '*klas bourzwa*', who ran the
centre, found it difficult to connect with working-class Creoles.
Indeed, many ti-Créoles find it difficult to accept African-origin
identities and simply affirm their localness.

Creolization in northwestern Louisiana

Creolization in New Orleans has been extensively described
(see chapters 4 and 5), but there are some significant examples
of creolization in other parts of the state, particularly in the
northwest (about four to five hours from New Orleans), where
our research is concentrated. In that area, creolization preceded
'Americanization' and is closely associated with the French and
Spanish presence. Despite strong opinions to the contrary, creolization is not a racially specific term. Africans, Europeans and
people of mixed heritage, including those of Native American
descent, declare themselves to be Creoles, exhibiting the sharing
and mingling of cultural practices and expressing themselves in
ways that are characteristic of creole societies. In a path-breaking
article, the folklorist Nick Spitzer notes that the expression *monde
Créole* is used locally 'to inclusively mean the Creole people, Black
Creoles or African French Creoles and more broadly their social
and cultural aesthetics and networks'.[14] As mentioned, 'Creole'
also included many Native Americans. For example, the Adai
Caddo, near Natchitoches, were hunters and traders who enjoyed
largely peaceful relations with the Spanish, who were determined
to Christianize them, and the French, who wanted to trade in val-

uable pelts and deerskins. Fur was used in the French and (after the Huguenots came to London) the British hat industries, and fetched substantial prices. This helped to sustain the Adai way of life, but they also, like other Native Americans, formed a significant component of the Creole population in the area.

Many other people of all phenotypes call themselves 'Creole'. One is the curator of the Campti Historic Museum. Her grandparents and parents all spoke fluent creole and French, but, by the time she went to school, French was discouraged and the Catholic nuns who taught her were 'from the north' and, thus monolingual in English. The town is named after the Native American chief Compte, who governed the area. It was a considerable transhipment point on the Red River. It is now a sleepy small town, but with a lively group of volunteers running the self-made museum. One of the volunteers mentioned that many prominent Creole families started in Campti, including the Lasyones (who run a famous meat pie restaurant in Natchitoches to this day) and the Prudhommes, who started the Oakland Plantation, and we will meet below. She averred that there are 'many Indian–Spanish' people in the area and even more 'Indian–French, who are Creoles'.

Creole cultures and subcultures made a particular mark in two areas, Opelousas and the Cane River area, south of Natchitoches. Most Opelousan Creoles were 'free persons of colour' (*gens de couleur libres*): across the state, those so legally classified numbered 18,647 in 1860. A local museum (figure 6.2) provides a testament to their distinctive culture and folkways. Opelousan Creoles held tenaciously onto their land grants, given mainly during the Spanish administration of the area. This provided the basis of wealth, respectability and access to superior education, often provided by Catholic nuns.

Immediately south of Natchitoches, a picturesque town that the French laid out in 1714, is the heartland of a notable creole culture, literally and figuratively an 'islanded identity'. The area is a large sausage-shaped island, bounded by the Little Red River on the right and the Cane River on the left. In the middle is the Isle Brevelle, where 'Creoles of colour' established themselves. Their history has been brilliantly and extensively recorded by the historian, Gary B. Mills, and his partner, the historical novelist Elizabeth Shown Mills.[15] The National Park Service, which has constructed a heritage trail, now owns some of the key properties in the area and the Cane River Creole National Heritage Park also contains several meticulously restored plantation houses. One such example is Oakland Plantation on the Cane River, which a (white) French Creole, Jean Pierre Emanuel Prudhomme, established under a Spanish land grant in 1789. His family, which retained ownership of the property for eight generations, had used slave labour to farm mainly indigo, tobacco and cotton. The main house and a number of subsidiary buildings survive, giving a tangible insight into how the slaves, other farmhands and the owners and their families lived.

The story of the Creoles of colour commences with an extraordinary woman, Marie Thérèse dite Coincoin (*c*.1740–1820), a slave sold along with five of her children to a French merchant from La Rochelle called Thomas Pierre Metoyer, who had settled in the area. She had a further ten children with Metoyer and became the founding matriarch of a powerful Creole family, which, through marriage or manumission, became *gens de couleur libres* (free persons of colour). When her relationship with M. Metoyer ended in 1786, Marie Thérèse owned 68 arpents of land along the Cane River on and around the Melrose Plantation. She and her energetic children adroitly switched crops between cotton, sugar cane, indigo, tobacco and pecan nuts as prices dictated. By 1850, she had expanded her holdings to 5,667 arpents (4,796 acres) and owned 436 slaves, making hers the most prosperous creole family in the USA. It is a further tribute to her character that Marie Thérèse treated her slaves with gentleness, never administered corporal punishment and ensured that they were baptized and buried with Catholic rites.[16]

The centre of the family empire was at Melrose and its main house, called Yucca, was built from hand-cut cypress beams, uprights and sleepers (the wood is very dense and resistant to rot). The walls were made with mud (adobe) from the river bed mixed with deer hair and Spanish moss. The architecture is distinctly creole, with wooden floors, balconies and through breezes; in fact, it is quite different from the Anglo-American plantation

Figure 6.2   The entrance to the Creole Heritage Folklife Center in Opelousas
Source: Robin Cohen

houses with their overblown resonances of ancient Greece. There
are two further architectural survivals of the glory days of Marie
Thérèse dite Coincoin and her descendants. The first, on Melrose
Plantation, is an 'African house', built around 1800, which has
been restored. The builders consciously imitated designs found in
the Congo and West Africa. With a prominent overhanging roof
and bricked inner section, the building was used both as a store-
room and a lock-up for recalcitrant slaves. The shingles are now
wooden, though the original roof in Africa would have been straw.

The second, and much grander, is the nearby substantial church
of St Augustine on the Isle Brevelle, which Nicholas Augustin
Metoyer built in 1829. Nicholas, the most successful and formida-
ble of Marie Thérèse dite Coincoin's children, both consolidated
the family's landholdings (adding 2,124 acres on his death) and

endowed the church. His life-size portrait is startling. With frock coat and top hat in one hand, he gestures towards the church with his other hand and stands with an easy sense of superiority on the marble steps of his stylized plantation house. The portrait continues to dominate the interior of the church, while, outside, the tombstones of Metoyers and other prominent Creole families litter the churchyard.

Decreolization and the recovery of a Creole heritage culture

Gary Mills and Elizabeth Shown Mills tell the epic story of the Cane River Creoles' collapse into relative poverty and obscurity with a deep sense of pathos. As in Mauritius, external events, in this case with calamitous economic and social consequences, interrupted the creolization process. The first blow was the Louisiana Purchase of 1803, when, in pursuit of funding his European wars, Napoleon sold two million square kilometres of French America to the United States: despite the name of the treaty, the sale extended to part (or all) of 13 states other than Louisiana, thereby doubling the US land area. For the Creoles, the sale was disastrous – bit by bit their hard-won social status, legal recognition and property rights were eroded. Their identity was intertwined with their Frenchness, but now Napoleon and their *patrie-mère* (motherland) had sold them down the river. When the American flag was hoisted at Natchitoches on 1 May 1804, the American commandant wryly remarked: 'I have understood some are not altogether pleased.'[17]

The second blow was the northern victory in the civil war. The Cane River Creoles had stayed neutral or allied themselves to the Confederacy. Flushed with victory, the Union troops rampaged through the plantations, destroying crops and buildings, excoriating the owners for being slave owners and reserving special insults for those who were not white. As Mills explains, Anglo-American attitudes and prejudices were superimposed onto French and Spanish laws:

The French–Spanish, Roman Catholic heritage of Louisiana produced an entirely different set of racial concepts from that which developed in the predominantly Anglo-Saxon Protestant societies of the other American colonies. Consequently, when Creole Louisiana was inducted into the American states the immediate result was a clash of racial concepts and ideals. . . . Those who lost most in the conflict were the members of the third caste. The people of Isle Brevelle and their counterparts in New Orleans, Opelousas, East Baton Rouge and thousands more scattered throughout the rural areas of the state lost their political and social 'escape hatch'.[18]

After the Civil War many Creoles of mixed heritage were slowly forced into the biracial categories of 'black' or 'white'. The locals did not see themselves as 'Americans' and often sought to resist any categorization. One interviewee, a creole-speaker interviewed in 2014 in Natchitoches, vehemently claimed that 'it was all alright until the Americans came'. As he explained, there was simply no way of bridging the gap between American biracial and creole non-racial outlooks. Another, born to a creole heritage in Opelousas and married to an African American, elucidated her views. For her, 'Creole is not a race. It's a culture and it has different meanings to different people.' She was close to her grandparents 'who spoke French'. Her parents spoke 'a mix of French and English'. But, in her generation, speaking French was discouraged and it was not taught at her school. As a child she 'didn't see race', but gradually became aware of differences in appearance. Her father was darker than her mother, but he had green eyes and red hair, probably from an Irish ancestor. Her siblings and wider family had 'different complexions', but they felt united by common traditions – they were Catholics, they were educated (both her parents went to college and were teachers), they had a French background, and some had land. They were sometimes under pressure 'to *say* . . . whether you are black or white. Now it's more acceptable to be biracial or multi-racial.' Although she is proud of her creole heritage, traditions and food, she connects strongly to her husband's heritage. 'It's easier to be accepted in the African American community. I embrace the community. Yes, I'm African American.'

Some Creoles of colour left the area to find work in California, Washington State and Chicago. One interviewee who had returned to the area around Natchitoches on his retirement had worked at Boeing assembling aircraft. At the factory he adamantly refused '*to say*' (again that expression), leaving his fellow workers to decide whether he was 'white, Mexican or whatever . . . they would *never* understand "Creole"'. Creoles from Louisiana also found their way to Hollywood and to the musical world. Of the many 'notable Creoles' who appear on the Wiki list covering categories like business, politics, law, journalism and the military, most fit the category Arts Culture and Entertainment, somewhat validating the idea that creolization and creativity have an elective affinity.[19]

Reaffirming creolization: Louisiana and Mauritius

The Wiki list of 'notable' Louisiana Creoles is emblematic of a discursive attempt to create and validate a separate creole identity. A brutal logic enforced the biracial prism of American social convention. If you were light enough, you could pass, but it was the Anglo-Americans who policed social acceptance and the outcome was never certain. By contrast, militant African Americans demanded that Creoles of mixed origin declare themselves African American or face being accused of self-denial and betrayal. Progress towards validating an intermediate identity finally came in a number of ways. US Census data show a quadrupling of children in self-identified 'interracial' families over the period 1970–90 (from fewer than 500,000 to about two million). It is also significant that when given the chance to respond to a question about multiple origins in the 2000 Census (for the first time), 6.8 million Americans availed themselves of this opportunity.[20] Although the Census takers insisted on using 'race', while Creoles think in cultural categories, at least mixed heritage was acknowledged. There were other shifts in the American zeitgeist. It did not take long before Obama was claimed as the first African American president, but during his candidacy and in the early years of his office, his mixed origins were recognized, sometimes in a slighting way, for example in the taunt that he was 'Halfrican not African'. In fact, another prominent politician had got there before him. Condoleezza Rice, the former secretary of state under George W. Bush, made fulsome acknowledgement of her 'half-Creole' grandmother from Baton Rouge, Louisiana.

Since the mid-1990s, the Creoles of the northwest have some-what recovered their social status and economic fortunes. Creole names pepper the ranks of local city councillors, fire chiefs and sheriffs, while doctors, dentists, accountants, attorneys, teach-ers and other professionals are commonplace in the younger generation. On the Isle Brevelle, descendants of prominent Creole families tenaciously cling onto properties, though their houses are now more suburban eclectic than creole plantation and their landholdings are seriously reduced. Nicholas Augustin Metoyer's St Augustine church is packed for Sunday services, and its adjoining community centre remains an important focus for community activities, including weddings and other celebra-tions. Each October, members of the Creole community with roots in the area, but who may be dispersed elsewhere (there are significant pockets in California, Chicago and St Louis), gather to cement their family ties. Another significant date in the calendar is 22 January (Augustin Metoyer's birthday), which, since 1994, has been celebrated as Creole Heritage Day; in 2001, it attracted a crowd of more than 3,000 Creoles from around the country.[21] For many Creoles, the church, community and Isle Brevelle have come to represent a kind of mini-diasporic home.

From being marginalized and somewhat invisible, heritage tourism, restaurant menus and much else besides have been 'recreolized'. It is difficult now not to find a creole gumbo on offer in a restaurant, with gumbo representing the quintessential creole cuisine. It comprises stewed meat or fish, vegetables (celery, sweet peppers and onions are always there) and various spices and thick-eners. The dish probably derived its name from either the Bantu word for okra (*ki ngombo*) or the Choctaw word for sassafras, locally called filé (*kombo*). In this imaginative reconstruction below, the food and the people are linked in a recipe:

1 part French, 1 part Spanish, 1 part German, 1 part Native American, 1 part Chinese, 1 part African (substitute more or less, or add others, to create your own personal flavor). Add above ingredients to bayous, rivers, lakes, swamps, country roads and city streets. Make a roux out of Louisiana, California, Chicago, Texas, and other parts of the US, as needed, for the base. Incorporate jazz and zydeco, Fais Do Do and La La, big families and solid communities, pride and loyalty, strong faith and an abundance of love. Sprinkle liberally with filé and red pepper. Mix well. Simmer for 200 years or more. Serve over rice. *C'est bon, chère.*[22]

As in Louisiana, recreolization is evident in Mauritius. The renewed appeal of diaspora has dealt a massive blow to historic forms of creolization on this island in the Indian Ocean, but many things still link the islanders. Christianity, generally Catholicism, links wealthy Franco-Mauritians with *gens de couleur* and ti-Créoles. A shared language, cuisine and everyday customs are taken for granted. Many people on the island are of mixed heritage and do not easily fit neat ethnographic labels. After generations of inter-marriage, a significant minority of the population have no clear ethnic background and remain, or describe themselves as, 'Creole'. Finally, although there is some spatial segregation between those who can be ethnically segmented, the island is small, and many villages – and the capital Port Louis – have ethnically hybrid zones in which separate islanded identities are visible but markedly attenuated by habits of interethnic cooperation. These crossovers and shared heritages also gained political expression in the election of Prime Minister Paul Raymond Bérenger (2003–5), a Franco-Mauritian who draws on the creolized section of the population. Political coalitions are complex, but essentially 40 per cent or more of the population vote for a non-communal party, a strong index of the continuity and revival of creolization.

Though failing to secure much by way of electoral support, a determined group of activists has mobilized strong cross-ethnic sentiments in the working class (*klas travailleur*). Its party, *Lalit de Klas* (class struggle), uses Kreol to get across its message in pamphlets, posters, magazines, books, a website and a well-attended Workers' Educational College.[23] Naturally, this is a collective

effort, but it is appropriate to single out the extraordinary dedication and contributions of Ram Seegobin and Lindsey Collen. The
former, a UK-trained medical doctor, ran a 'barefoot doctor' clinic
in a rather deprived village for four decades, while Lindsey Collen,
turning her back on her South African background, has fully
identified with the island and is a Commonwealth prize-winning
novelist, publishing at least two of her novels in English and Kreol.
Both are regulars at the Workers' Educational College.

Intellectuals at the University of Mauritius have also done a
good deal to promote Kreol and sustain a creole sensibility. Arnaud
Carpooran, a sociolinguist there and head of the Creole-Speaking
Union, has compiled an innovative and comprehensive Mauritian
Kreol dictionary, which contains translations into English and
French and provides contextual phrases and sentences.[24] In her
major historical contributions, Vijaya Teelock has been at the
forefront of trying to work across the Indo/Creole division.[25]
Although Indo-Mauritian by origin, she has been the guiding light
in compiling slave registers to allow those of African and Malagasy
descent to trace their ancestors. She has also played a significant
role in representing and understanding the Le Morne experience,
not only as a narrow expression of Afro/Malagasy Creole identity,
but also as part of a wider cross-communal struggle for human
dignity in the face of a history of slavery and indentured labour.
As she said, '*Le Morne symbolise la lutte pour l'indépendance, la lutte
contre la colonisation, la lutte pour la liberté*' ('Le Morne symbolizes the
fight for independence, the fight against colonization, the fight for
liberty').[26]

Conclusion

We can see a number of commonalities in the Mauritian and
Louisiana experiences. Both underwent a process of deep creolization, followed by 'decreolization'. As Thomas Hylland Eriksen
remarks, decreolization is a notoriously tricky and contradictory
term. In one sense, it occurs because in Mauritius creolization
has been *insufficiently* strong (despite considerable momentum

and political investment) to become a self-affirming nation with a shared past and common boundaries. In another sense, decreolization arises because the creolizing forces were *sufficiently* strong to trigger a counter-reaction, a yearning for rootedness and purity.[27] When, particularly in electoral contests, these reversions to invented prior identities resulted in violence and threats to the social order, some level of recreolization was advocated or actually occurred. Such experiences are a stark refutation of any simple notion of an uninterrupted unilineal movement towards an increasingly more creolized world.[28] There is no certainty here, no telos. The temporal, political and spatial dimensions matter. In earlier chapters, we argued that creolized societies cannot easily confront the vagaries of exogenous factors. The Creoles of Louisiana knew nothing and could do nothing about Napoleon's decision to sell French America to the USA. Likewise, the Indo-Mauritians had no influence over Nehru's decision to abandon Indians abroad or Indira Gandhi's policy to reach out to them. At certain moments, largely outside their own determination, Creole societies were connected, disconnected or reconnected to the circuits of capital, the caprices of big-power politics or the embrace of their homelands.

The vacillation between abandonment and reinsertion has different outcomes and rhythms. In Louisiana, creole cultures were islanded within a much larger ecumene. Even though there were moments of prosperity, Creoles survived precariously, and once France made that fateful decision to withdraw from America, there was no going back to an original diasporic home. In the face of this abandonment, this betrayal, diasporic roots could not be sustained. Imperfect adjustments to the USA could only be resisted by inventing a heritage that approximated the hyphenated ethnicities of other US citizens. The diasporic home became much more circumscribed – not France, not Acadia, not Haiti, but spaces like the Isle Brevelle or the French Quarter (*Vieux Carré*) in New Orleans. In Mauritius, creolization was once so encompassing that it almost transmogrified into indigeneity, but even there diasporic currents were switched on by heritage countries that wished to re-establish diasporic filiations and sometimes manipulate them in atavistic directions. It is a tribute to the islanders that they have fought back to re-energize political connections across communal lines, to revivify shared customs and to use heritage sites and events not merely to mobilize for narrow claims and loyalties, but also to reach out to their fellow citizens.

What our research yielded was a much greater appreciation of the way recreolization has emerged and developed. In both Louisiana and Mauritius, cultural and epistemic alliances developed between scholars and activists, public officials and museum curators, tour operators and public intellectuals, restaurateurs and guidebook publishers, teachers and heritage trusts. In Natchitoches and the Cane River area, Creole Heritage days, picnics and school visits are routine. Academics at the Creole Heritage Center, Northwestern State University of Louisiana, have undertaken genealogical, anthropological and historical research that has been fed back to community organizers, park officials and museum curators. Similarly, at the Aapravasi Ghat, but particularly at Le Morne, activists, educators, UNESCO funders, international scholars and students have found common cause. In her research on museums in Asia, Europe and the USA, Peggy Levitt has shown that this movement to connect is energizing many museums, turning them into 'community center[s], mounting exhibitions that directly address social problems and using art to jump-start social engagement'. She adds that new practices and initiatives include 'partnering with community members to create exhibitions, sharing the ownership and management of objects, and collaborating with the descendants of the people who made them to figure out what stories they should tell'.[29]

We started this chapter by evoking the phrase 'the invention of tradition'. Is that what we found and is that what Levitt is describing? We recognize something of this sort in the case of the constructed and reconstructed heritages we observed in Louisiana and Mauritius. However, it is vitally important to emphasize that the construction of heritage is not just a state project. Traditions are not merely invented or celebrated to consolidate the power of the ruling class and to intimidate the masses. Rather, construction of heritage is happening in two directions – as a state project (including the local state, nation-state and foreign state) *and* as a popular project, designed to contest and redefine the state project.

In the case of the USA, where a racialized form of discourse has allowed little room for mixed identities – be these complex ones such as those of President Obama or the Creoles of northwestern Louisiana – the recovery of a creole heritage has primarily been a recovery of dignity. It need hardly be said that contemporary Creole activists do not want to recover their history of slave ownership; rather, they want the right not to be steamrolled into identities with which they feel uncomfortable. They are neither inferior Anglo-Americans nor self-denying African Americans.

Dignity is also as the heart of the Le Morne project. With the dominance of Indo-Mauritians and the reduction of the category 'creole' to 'ti-Créole', the expression *'le malaise Créole'* became a sort of journalistic cliché, one widely diffused by the Indo-Mauritian middle class and by scores of university students.[30] The expression *le malaise Créole* is akin to the idea of a 'culture of poverty', or a 'culture of dependency', the implication being that some people in Mauritius were incapable of getting on with the modernist project or catching onto the logic of possessive individualism.[31] This is too large a debate to enter here, but our main point is that Creoles in Mauritius, like Creoles in Louisiana, were constrained to play the heritage game to gain recognition and acceptance.

Creolization, decreolization and recreolization are threaded between the activation and deactivation of diasporic pasts. As in music and carnival (chapters 4 and 5), the delicate dance between creolization and diaspora is found too in the construction of heritage. In our next chapter we turn to the intricacies of identity politics and how alternative tugs of loyalty are manifested in the French Antilles.

7

Marking Identities: The Cultural Politics of Multiple Loyalties

We have already shown how social identity formation 'from below' involves a complex articulation and disarticulation between the rival claims of diaspora and creolization, usually in a context of power asymmetries relative to a dominant society. However, these bottom–up voices are often set within a policy of nation-building or assimilation. Many newly formed nations engage in rather frantic attempts to unify disparate populations. Here is a sample of a few national mottos, from the blandly optimistic 'TOGETHER WE ASPIRE, TOGETHER WE ACHIEVE' (Trinidad and Tobago), 'UNITY IS STRENGTH' (Malaysia) and 'E PLURIBUS UNUM/FROM MANY, ONE' (USA), to the more cautious 'UNITY IN DIVERSITY' (South Africa and Indonesia). In nearly every country, there are multiple tugs of loyalty to places of origin and newer places of citizenship. We have taken the French overseas territories, the *départements d'outre mer*, as our chosen research site, where the contrasting, contradictory and complementary pressures of identity formation are played out in an intense way as a form of cultural politics. All the *départements d'outre mer* are formally integrated into the French nation, but maintain a strong sense of cultural difference. Martinique, which we consider here, is an exemplary case not only because all three elements of the identity mix (diaspora, creolization and assimilation) are transparent, but also because a remarkable group of local writers and intellectuals whose ideas have resonated across the world (including Frantz Fanon, Aimé Césaire, Suzanne Roussi, Édouard Glissant and Patrick Chamoiseau) has led the normative and analytical debates about Martinican identity.

In this chapter, we not only explore some of the complexities and nuances of their ideas, but also show how they relate to, or depart from, the lives of the Martinican people who have expressed their own views at key conjunctures through joining the French Resistance during the Second World War, voting in various referenda and elections, coming out on demonstrations and strikes, and developing ways of speaking, behaving and performing that show the conflicting tugs of Frenchness, diaspora and creolization. We suggest that the contradictions and tensions manifested in Martinican cultural politics – between the local and the universal, between closure and openness, between assimilation and assertions of difference – in fact closely parallel the complex and often contradictory processes of identity formation in everyday life in many other settings. Drawing on examples of different 'markers' of identity, we argue that rather than focus purely on contradictions and cleavages between different spheres of influence on Martinican identity, it is perhaps more useful to map the discursive markers (or theories of difference) on Martinique's physical, social and cultural landscape. We draw on examples of what we have labelled:

- *environmental markers* – how external influences make their mark on the Martinican landscape;
- *social markers* – how the social practices, values and hierarchies of people migrating between France and Martinique mark identity; and
- *cultural markers* – how linguistic and cultural practices mark Martinican (creole) identity.

We use these as analytical tools with which to explore the complexities of Martinican identity formation. Yet by using such labels, we are by no means seeking to create new categories of identity or gloss over the fuzzy boundaries and multi-layered histories of identity formation in Martinique (as well as the other *départements d'outre mer)*. We suggest that as long as we take into account *who* is 'marking', and the *context* in which identity is being 'marked', we can move beyond the notion of contradictory or clashing identities and consider how different markers of identity can coexist or relate to one another.

French *and* Martinican: in harmony or at odds?

The small Caribbean island of Martinique (with a population of approximately 390,000) is an 'overseas department' and 'overseas region' of France, so thus an integral part of the French Republic. Martinique's official language is French, the island's currency is the Euro and the predominant religion is Catholicism. Its people vote in elections in France, benefit from the French social security system and, indeed, almost every Martinican family has or has had a member living in metropolitan France, *la métropole*, colloquially known as *l'Hexagone* (after the shape of the country). One only need arrive in Martinique's glitzy airport, drive on clean and highly functional *autoroutes* past the Carrefour supermarket and Peugeot showroom to the capital city of Fort-de-France, with its tantalizing patisseries and stylish boutiques, to gauge the extent to which France is deeply embedded in the island's socioeconomic infrastructure and way of life.

These contemporary markers of Frenchness reflect the long and multifaceted history of France's relationship with its overseas 'possessions', which were assimilated into the *mère-patrie* in the wake of the Jacobin revolution at the end of the eighteenth century.[1] Following the abolition of slavery in 1848, emancipated ex-slaves (or at least adult males) in the French Antilles became simultaneously free men *and* French citizens, and, although these rights were revoked during the regime of Napoleon III (1851–70), French Antilleans have been incorporated into the values and institutions of French republicanism since its inception. As William Miles asserts in his discussion of the conundrum of 'national' identity formation in Martinique, 'one cannot overemphasize the extent to which *la nation* became the secular equivalent of dogma. Jacobin ideology and Napoleonic imperialism conjoined to elevate the idea of nation as the linchpin of Frenchness.'[2]

Yet, this assimilationist drive has not been unidirectional. Ever since the abolition of slavery, Martinicans have sought to integrate into metropolitan France, forsaking the possibility of a separate identity to acquire equal rights with French citizens in the metropole.[3] Indeed, proof of this dedication to the motherland came in the willing enlistment of thousands of French West Indians in both world wars.[4] The transition of the island's status from colony to *département d'outre mer* in 1946 formalized Martinique's integration into France. In contrast to the wave of decolonization and quest for independence sweeping neighbouring Caribbean islands, Martinicans – as well as other French Caribbean colonies, Guadeloupe and Guyane – voted overwhelmingly in favour of full integration into the French nation and the values of *liberté*, *egalité* and *fraternité* that such membership promised. The poet, intellectual and left-wing politician Aimé Césaire, who was elected mayor of Fort-de-France in 1945, played a pivotal role in drafting the policy of departmentalization, arguing that membership of France as fully fledged citizens would dramatically improve the social and political situation on the island. To be Martinican is thus, to all intents and purposes, to be French, to be integral to the French nation and its extensive *francophonie*,[5] and to be part of Europe. From the results of recent referenda on the future status of the island, it is clear that Martinique will remain French for the foreseeable future.[6]

However, to be Martinican is also to be distinctly 'not French'. The visual markers of Frenchness and seemingly willing political assimilation into the metropole mask a deeply rooted and complex struggle among islanders to establish an identity apart from the 'motherland'. Many Martinicans believe that, irrespective of the promise of equal rights as French citizens living in any other French department, their political status has not only cemented centuries of economic exploitation, but also initiated new forms of cultural, economic and financial domination and dependence. Even Césaire became disillusioned with what had become a neo-colonial relationship with France and lamented the ecological and cultural destruction of the island that had resulted from the assimilation project.

Although there is no politically viable independence movement in Martinique, the islanders' resentment of *l'Hexagone* and what they depict as a neo-colonial relationship of inequality and dependence has long created social pressures, with unrest and a series of labour strikes testifying to their antipathy and resistance to 'the mother country'. Disillusionment with departmentalization mounted when it became apparent that their French citizenship did not give them perfect equality with mainland *metropolitains*. Tensions surfaced dramatically during the general strikes of 2009, when thousands of Martinicans – following the example of neighbouring Guadeloupe – took to the streets for more than a month to protest against the high cost of living and to proclaim that 'Martinique is ours', or in Kréyol, *'Martinik ce ta nou'*. In addition to challenging the complex economic order of over-consumption, reliance on assistance and lack of local control of the island's economy,[7] the strikes also brought to the surface the deeply entrenched racial inequality that still haunts the island, as well as the continued economic power of the island's white (*béké*) minority.[8]

Three years after the strikes, it was apparent (from interviews) that very little had changed in Martinique: dependence on France, growing unemployment and inequality continued apace.[9] Our findings suggested that the strikes reflected a deep dissatisfaction with Martinique's relationship with France; they also pointed to the superficiality of assimilation and to the often hidden voices of Martinicans in asserting this dissatisfaction.[10] They were, we would argue, testament to how 'just below the surface of modernization and assimilation there lurks the spirit of resistance'.[11] In other words, behind the overarching veil of Frenchness, other counter-narratives of identity and resistance are emerging 'from below'. Before going on to explore in more depth different markers of identity as they are manifested across Martinique's physical, social and cultural landscape, we shall examine some of the ways in which some writers and intellectuals on the island have analysed questions of identity.

Marking difference from the metropole

France's assimilationist policies and the rapid inculcation of French values, products and indeed people created the threat of what Glissant termed 'cultural genocide': the erosion beyond recognition of Martinique's identity and culture and the subsequent detachment of Martinicans from their own environment.[12] This sense of alienation and loss has been a major preoccupation of French Caribbean thinkers and writers, whose ideas have greatly influenced debates on cultural difference in both the francophone and anglophone worlds. In this section we discuss how the key 'theories of difference'[13] that developed in Martinique since the 1930s continue to have resonance in the social and cultural life of the island.

For the *négritude* movement, which emerged in the 1930s, difference from and resistance to the dominant white power was expressed through the powerful acclamation of black people's identity and culture as originating in precolonial Africa and thus 'outside the realm of the colonial project'.[14] This hostility towards French political and cultural domination and assimilation emerged among students from France's colonies who were studying in Paris at the prestigious École normale supérieure. Contrary to the expectation that these colonial students would assimilate into the French education system, for many the experience merely exposed the hypocrisy of France's assimilationist policies *vis-à-vis* its colonial citizens.[15] The movement's principal founders were Léopold Senghor from Senegal, Léon Damas from French Guyana and Aimé Césaire from Martinique. All three were talented poets and writers who expressed the ideas behind *négritude* most powerfully in their literary works. Yet, all three also went on to have important political careers – Senghor as president of Senegal, Damas as a member of the French National Assembly and Césaire as National Assembly member and mayor of Fort-de-France. This fact is important because it illustrates the close relationship between intellectual, cultural, political and everyday life in Martinique. These individuals were not only writing literature and political commentaries, they were also deeply embedded in both these worlds.

In response to the centuries of subjugation, repression and alienation of black people's identity and culture, *négritude* formed a doctrine for the expression of difference and the discovery and rediscovery of a particular black or African 'essence' that the 'reductive universalism' of the French colonialist project had concealed.[16] It was reformulated and refashioned in Africa and the African diaspora, but was clearly an important movement in asserting black pride. The French writer and intellectual Jean-Paul Sartre described *négritude* as 'anti-racist racism', which he saw as a necessary step towards 'the abolition of racial differences'.[17]

Despite its widespread resonance as a key precursor of movements in the USA like 'black power', the reassertion of a diasporic identity rooted in Africa was later criticized by those who felt that it merely replaced one essentialist and purifying racial definition, that of European definitions of blackness, with another essentializing ideology, also grounded in the language of race. On the one hand, it inverted the stereotypical image of blackness; on the other, it reaffirmed such stereotypes through its 'apparent lack of critical distance from the European definitions of knowledge, culture and literary values'.[18] Moreover, critiques of this affirmation of 'black' or African particularity in the face of French universalism were particularly strong in the context of the French Caribbean, whose societies are marked by centuries of physical and cultural mixing, known as '*métissage*'.[19]

A vigorous alternative to *négritude* and its insistence on a diasporic identity came in the form of the *créolité* movement, which the linguist Jean Bernabé and writers Patrick Chamoiseau and Raphaël Confiant founded. In their manifesto (*Éloge de la créolité*) for the movement, published in 1989, they declared: 'neither European, nor African, nor Asian, we proclaim ourselves Creoles' and went on to stress that we 'are simultaneously Europe, Africa, enriched by Asian, Levantine and Indian elements, and we also draw from survivals of pre-Colombian America'.[20] So, while *négritude* responded to a wider imperative to affirm the dignity and unity of the African diaspora, *créolité* had a more local focus in that it attempted to articulate a national identity in response to French assimilationism. Again, it was predominantly a literary movement, but one based on the socio-cultural concept of *créolité* – it was an

assertion of the ethnically mixed character of Martinique consequent upon the island's history of colonization, slavery, indentured
labour and migration.[21]

For more than two decades, *créolité* exemplified the successful affirmation of a unique Martinican identity to counter the
French assimilation project and an implied critique of *négritude*.
Increasingly, however, intellectuals both on the island and beyond
began to criticize the movement, mainly on the grounds that it
contained a contradiction between the very open and dynamic
identity that the proponents of *créolité* celebrated and the sense that
créolité was itself becoming an essentializing identity.[22] Moreover,
the very notion of a manifesto to promote an open-ended creole
culture seems contradictory in that it suggests the imposition, or
at least delineation, of an identity 'from above'. Another charge
made against the *créolistes*, with reference to their works other
than the *Éloge*, was the tendency towards folklorization, whereby
Martinican identity is located in a picturesque past that is evoked
nostalgically. As Price and Price remark:

> In our view, there is a tendency for the literary works of the *créolistes*
> to be complicitous with the celebration of a museumified Martinique,
> a diorama'd Martinique, a picturesque and 'pastified' Martinique that
> promotes a 'feel-good' nostalgia for people who are otherwise busy
> adjusting to the complexities of a rapidly modernizing lifestyle.[23]

The idea of the *créolité* project as an attempt to impose an identity
through definition and closure surfaced in several interviews. To
examine the wider impact of the movement, we asked respond-
ents how they felt about the term *créolité* and if they thought it
was relevant to the social realities of Martinique. One woman, a
practising artist, commented: 'I'm not really happy with this idea
of *créolité* because there is something like – still, you know the idea
of domination . . . you know, the idea of a lower level of black
people, or people who claim to be descendants of African people.'
Another woman, an academic at the university, went so far as to
describe it as 'dangerous' or 'terrifying'. Thus, both *négritude* and
créolité, as responses to the colonial and postcolonial condition, as
well as to the identarian awakening in Martinique, were regarded

as falling into the trap of essentializing or reifying difference and, arguably, failed to respond to the complexity of identity formation on the island and beyond.

It is apposite to note that Édouard Glissant had influenced the authors of the *Éloge* when, in an earlier declaration of '*antillanité*' or 'Caribbeanness', he stressed the heterogeneous nature of West Indian identity and the multiplicity of relations and interconnections of Martinique with elsewhere. Yet, Glissant distanced himself from the *créolité* movement and made a distinction between the 'process' of *créolization* and the 'state' of creoleness (or *créolité*).[24] We can add here that our own use of the term creolization closely mirrors that of Glissant. In this sense, rather than referring to something fixed, stable and predictable, creolization represents a dynamic opening to the world, what Glisssant describes as a *mise en relation* (loosely, in English, 'establishing a connection'). Glissant's conception of identity replaces the singular root with the image of the rhizome – a chaotic mass of roots in which it is impossible to trace a specific source. From this rhizomatic reading, Caribbean identity is (and always has been) 'relational', in a process of continual creation and transformation through ceaseless creolization and intermixing. Glissant developed this notion of relation in his later work, when he linked his Caribbean-oriented visions of identity and diversity to a more universal notion of identity as necessarily 'relational'. As mentioned in chapter 3, Glissant understood the Caribbean as a creolized space, one that emerged from its terrible history by galvanizing new ways of thinking about the world. Patrick Chamoiseau, himself a key expositor of *créolité*, declared himself a convert in an interview for this book:

> Whereas the traditional definition of identity was what is 'mine': this is our essence, our blood, our identity, in the face of the 'other', today relationships in the world are more characterized by fluidity of relationships, a relational fluidity to others and to the diversity of the world, which means that we exist in a flow that is constantly changing. So the master term for today is no longer *créolité* but 'relation'.

These intellectual discourses, or markers, of identity clearly diverge in their attempts to define Martinique's position in the world. Yet, if we consider them diachronically as opposed to syn-chronically, the ways in which they correspond to particular social realities become more apparent. Thus, while *négritude* was clearly a powerful movement, which responded to a need to affirm and give pride to the African diaspora, *créolité* formed part of a nation-building project for a unified but distinct Martinican identity in response to French assimilation. Yet, as social realities shift, it seems that cre-olization and 'relation' become more salient concepts, responding to a context of growing interdependence and high levels of mobil-ity. However, as creolization and relation move beyond charges of essentialism and parochialism in their more universal application, we argue that it is important not to lose sight of the importance of place, the local specificity, in the shaping of identities (see chapter 3). As one interviewee remarked, 'the Martinican territory exists socially, we have created it'. It is to some more tangible 'markers of identity' in Martinique that we now turn.

Environmental markers: what lies beneath?

Once again we turn to Glissant, who made clear that identity formation needs to be located in a specific landscape.

> The relationship with the land, one that is even more threatened because the community is alienated from that land . . . [is necessary, but] describing the landscape is not enough. The individual, the com-munity, the land are inextricable in the process of creating history. Landscape is a character in this process. Its deepest meanings need to be understood.[25]

Martinique's physical landscape exposes visible markers of the island's complex colonial and postcolonial condition and its relationship with metropolitan France. The years following depart-mentalization, particularly the 1960s and 1970s, saw a dramatic transformation of Martinique's landscape and agriculture-based economy, with the widespread appearance of supermarkets, shop-ping malls, new roads, hotels and airports, what was locally labelled *bétonisation* (concretization).[26] This reflected France's 'aggressive programme of development and integration that transformed this island neo-colony into a modern consumer society'.[27]

Martinique's socio-political shift from colony to French department was thus visibly inscribed on the island's countryside and these markers of Frenchness, or Europeanness, become particularly salient in contrast with many neighbouring Caribbean islands. As the above quotation from Glissant suggests, the social and urban development of Martinique not only affects the land itself, but also contributes to the steady alienation of Martinicans from taking part in their own history. In her discussion of the ecological impact of departmentalization, and the varying responses to it, Renée Gosson uses the metaphor of 'covering over':

> Covering over the landscape with symbols of development and progress (buildings, roads, marinas, airports, etc.); covering over history as so much of Caribbean history has been silenced, obliterated, and forgotten; and covering over the culture, identity, and imagination of a people who have been taught that the only valuable part of their identity and history is that part which is French.[28]

However, just as intellectuals and cultural elites put forward 'counter-discourses'[29] to the inculcation of metropolitan values, so the Martinican landscape itself reflects some resistance to complete Frenchification. Of course, there is the obvious fact that Martinique is an island with a distinct climate and ecology, which makes it impossible for it to be a mere replica of official and quotidian life in mainland France. As we argued in chapter 3, it is important to consider the symbiotic relationship between a contact zone and the social forms and relationships that emerge within that space.

Full assimilation is countermanded through the sheer physicality of the island. Our fieldwork in Martinique revealed organized attempts to resist total transformation, the resilience of local environmental markers and, significantly, actual efforts to *preserve* and *rearticulate* Martinique's local specificity and its links to multiple places beyond the metropole. The ambitious regeneration projects proposed for the tourist area of Martinique called Trois-Îlets and for the island's former capital St Pierre are examples of just such an attempt. The regional council is funding these projects headed by Patrick Chamoiseau who, in addition to being an important literary figure, continues to play a central role in Martinican cultural politics. Research for this book coincided with the inauguration of *L'Embellie Trois Îlets*,[30] which aims to resist 'industrial tourism' and the 'exploitation of Martinique as an exotic paradise', and to encourage a new form of tourism (or rather 'travel') in which people experience the 'real Martinique', with its multiplicity of histories and interconnections.

Representatives from the regional council and local tourist board gave presentations at the inauguration, as did Chamoiseau, who explained that a key feature of the project was its participatory nature, for it aimed to empower people to reconnect with their local surroundings and to play a role in the island's future. This local participation is achieved through so-called '*ateliers d'imaginaire*' ('workshops for the imagination'), which are held regularly to ensure that local people have a 'voice in defining their future'. In interview, Chamoiseau said: 'My role is to try to find ways to make the spaces express totally all the complexity that we've just talked about. We are at the same time Amerindian, African, colonizers – we're all that. And all of that should be filtered into our urban development. That's what we're trying to do.'

In some ways, one could argue that this represents yet another attempt to mark the Martinican landscape with a particular vision, a kind of applied *créolité*, or model for a new identity.[31] Moreover, it is possible to criticize the project for its somewhat nostalgic celebration of a picturesque Martinique buried beneath the damaging mask of modernization. By contrast, 'giving voice' to local people, and to some extent challenging the existing model of development, arguably provides the scope to promote a collective responsibility to redefine Martinique's future and its place in the world, to 'speak back' to centuries of exploitation. Seen in this light, the project reflects not so much an applied *créolité* as an identity in the making; it recognizes the relational nature of Martinique's identity. It has the potential to capture the interplay between local specificity and relationship to the landscape, as well as past, present and future connections between Martinique and multiple elsewheres. The

Martinican landscape thus represents a canvas upon which the struggle for identity is marked. We turn next to the role of those who 'people' that landscape in this quest for defining Martinican identity.

Social markers: Martinican or *metropolitain*?

Substantial demographic shifts accompanied the physical transformation of Martinique's landscape. There was widespread migration when an official programme designed to fill particular economic niches in *l'Hexagone* and to resolve the growing problem of unemployment in Martinique lured thousands of Martinicans to France: meanwhile, enticed by a 40 per cent premium in public sector salaries, increasing numbers of French citizens (locally referred to as *metropolitains*) were arriving in Martinique to work or retire, a phenomenon that Césaire rather luridly described as 'genocide by substitution'.[32]

These migratory movements expose several significant markers of identity in Martinique. First, they reveal the salience of race, which remains a powerful marker of difference despite discourses of equality and harmony. Martinicans living in Paris are continually reminded that they are not French; they face widespread racial discrimination in their everyday lives and are often mistaken for undocumented Malian migrants during sweeps on the metro, or denied access to housing and private sector jobs.[33] Yet, the difference between Martinicans and metropolitans is also played out 'at home', where, as Price and Price observe, 'white immigrants from metropolitan France now constitute more than 10 per cent of the island's residents' and 'the battle for who "owns" Martinique is played out through hundreds of minor confrontations each day'. They go on to suggest that such incidents, which become highly charged, 'leave unresolved the personal tension inherent in being simultaneously Martiniquan [*sic*] and French'.[34]

These clear differences emerged from fieldwork interviews. When asked about her identity, one woman who had lived and worked in Martinique for almost 30 years replied: 'I would never

call myself Martinican, because I know I would never be regarded
as such, never. I am white.' Contrastingly, a man who described
himself as black, went on to say: 'I am not French, I am not
French', and then repeated the phrase eight times to make clear
that his citizenship status had no bearing on his personal sense of
identity. A movement founded in 2007 called Tous Créoles represents an attempt to transcend racial markers of difference and to
embrace a common creole identity. One of its founders, a 'white'
béké, understands a creole identity as something visceral, embodied
and beyond explanation. He explained during our interview:

> I'm naturally Creole and many of my friends – everyone in Tous
> Créoles – are naturally Creole. We feel Creole. Today we have some
> *metropolitains*, French people, who are members of the association
> because they feel Creole. . . . When I'm in Paris I can distinguish a
> Creole from an African. I can't explain it. You can recognize a Creole.
> I don't know how but you can.

The Tous Créoles example is clearly problematic because many
people feel that its celebration of creoleness ignores the violent
history of the term, as well as the class and racial hierarchies that
still exist in Martinique. Yet, our research revealed that other
factors played a part in distinguishing a Martinican from a *metropolitain*, often expressed with examples of how returning or visiting
migrants from the metropole (*Négropolitaines/Négropolitains*) bring
back 'Parisian attitudes, aspirations, values and lifestyles'.[35] One
woman spoke of how the decision about what to do with her
late mother's body caused serious tension between herself and her
older brother who had been living in France for several years. She
contrasted the 'European detachment from death' with the fact
that her mother – living in Martinique before she passed away –
had asked her to 'bury her and have the wake in the traditional
way'. She continued, 'and when my older brother came and he
arrived just like a tourist – you know – and he asked for the body
to be taken to the morgue . . . we came to fight physically. So that
was really a drama for me.'

Just as Martinicans are categorized as 'outsiders' in Paris, despite
being French citizens, so returning Martinicans become outsiders

as they return home, thus '(re)marking these departmental subjects and the metropolitan experience as doubled avatars of both "otherness" and "the same"'.[36] Martinican identity is thus consistently marked and remarked in relation to the distant yet ever-present, envied yet scorned, welcomed yet kept apart, metropolitan and 'other'. We turn next to the ways in which this unique Martinican identity is apparent through what we designate 'creole markers', linguistic and cultural manifestations of Martinican particularity.

Cultural or creole markers

Martinique's landscape and demographic makeup reflect the multiple tugs on Martinican identity and, in particular, the impact of the colonial/postcolonial relationship with metropolitan France on processes of identity formation. In what follows, we consider how beneath these visible markers of Frenchness are several examples of the resilience and adaptability of Martinique's creole culture.

Language is a significant area of resilience and revival in that, since the 1970s, the Kréyol language has undergone an important process of revalorization. Language as an important marker of creole identity emerged in several interviews. Some people mentioned that Kréyol had been considered shameful in the past and that their parents were forbidden to speak it at home, whereas others pointed out how it has now entered spheres from which it had been formerly absent, including 'love songs' and 'courting'. One interviewee, a teenager working as a petrol attendant in the town of St Anne, said that he definitely thought the language would survive because he spoke it with his friends every day. During our interview, his mobile phone rang and he immediately switched to speaking Kréyol (albeit mixed with some French words), only to return effortlessly to textbook French when we resumed our exchange. While Kréyol is being revalorized, it is also clear that both Kréyol and French are being recreated every day through inventive combinations of both languages. Indeed, if, as Michael Dash asserts, language 'not only reflects but enacts the power relations in Martinican society',[37] our research certainly revealed the complex intertwining of language, power and identity. As one interviewee remarked:

> I think identity has to do with language . . . I don't know what language I speak and, more than that, I don't know what language I live in . . . I would say that what comes to my mind, I switch between languages. My mother didn't speak French – she couldn't speak French. But I was not allowed to speak Kréyol to her, even if she would reply in Kréyol . . . of course I speak French, and of course I speak Kréyol, and I happen to speak a bit of English. But the point is I have no language of my own so . . . I have no identity of my own . . . it's a weakness, but at the same time it's a form of strength . . . it helps you to be flexible.

In addition to language as a marker of the complex identity many Martinicans experience, we observed examples of cultural markers, or 'traces', that expose a Martinican specificity. As the surrealist writer and philosopher, René Ménil, wrote:

> [These traces are the] beliefs widely held in our rural areas and our cities . . . these celebrations and dances, these objects crafted by our artisans, the books the literature produced by our writers, these gestures and body movements when walking or dancing, the facial expressions while talking, the way of telling a story and the turns of phrase, the particular elements . . . which as a whole have given rise to the creation of a community of one mind with a common way of thinking.[38]

One example of cultural revalorization is the growing popularity of *bélé*, a dance and musical style that emerged during slavery. Indeed, what were seen as 'African-inspired' dances and drums were prohibited under the rigid stipulations of the *Code noir*, yet Martinicans responded by finding new ways of disguising their dancing – mimicking European square dancing formations – and finding different ways to beat the rhythm. *Bélé* music and dance were increasingly marginalized following departmentalization, but it has re-emerged in recent years and is widely practised among people from all age groups and from different socioeconomic backgrounds, thus coinciding with renewed efforts to promote and assert the Kréyol language and culture on the island.

During fieldwork interviews with cultural practitioners, it emerged that the French government provides funds to promote creole cultural forms as part of its concerted effort to celebrate Martinique's patrimony, a development that may be exposed to Richard and Sally Price's charge (see above) that cultural movements tend to recreate a Martinican past rather than respond to a modernizing present. Yet, there was also a sense that, beyond this folklorization, these 'traditional' cultural forms were themselves evolving, changing and adapting to current realities, albeit those that processes of cultural globalization are influencing. As a Martinican choreographer commented: 'I think that as traditional dance moves forward, it adapts to new socioeconomic situations. The *bélé* that was danced 30 years ago is not the same as the *bélé* that is danced today – and I accept that because dance evolves.' Another challenge for cultural practitioners in Martinique, she explained, is that Martinican contemporary dance is an oxymoron in the eyes of the French government: 'When I need to export our work to France . . . we have to get rid of our identity – they couldn't care less about Martinican contemporary dance – I have to fit into the framework of French contemporary dance.' This is illustrative of a significant tension that many cultural performers on the island experience: the reality of Frenchness denies the possibility of Martinican 'difference' on its own terms, so entry to the elite European world of contemporary dance necessarily involves a renunciation of one's particularity.

Surprisingly, this metropolitan denial of Martinican culture as a dynamic and modern phenomenon can result in greater creativity: several people commented on the vast number of artists, musicians and dancers on the island. Rather than being co-opted into France's image of Martinican culture, the cultural practices in Martinique – albeit less widely recognized on the global scale – demonstrate resistance through creativity, a phenomenon we documented in our chapters on music and carnival. Despite the notion that cultural promotion became a 'top–down' prescription of Martinican identity, for choreographers such as the one interviewed here, dancing and creativity became a political act, an expression through the body of the complexities of Martinican history and identity. As she commented with reference to one of her most recent works:

I am still concerned with Martinican identity, this backbone that works differently – as a result of its many inheritances – compared to other populations. . . . So the point of departure is Martinique, a singular regard towards the universal. What is this Martinican being? [It is] an inheritance of African culture, of European culture, of Caribbean culture and a distant inheritance of Chinese. So it's very much a melting-pot, a real cocktail of blood.

As this interviewee suggests, Martinican identity is marked through cultural practices not merely as a folkloristic revival of past practices but, rather, through revisiting and refashioning the past, as a way of responding to the mystifying present and an unpredictable future.

Another cultural practice to have re-emerged in recent years is *Damnye*, a martial art type dance closely related to the Brazilian capoeira and, like capoeira, it originated among slaves as a creative form of self-defence. During our fieldwork in Martinique, the cultural centre in the town of Le Lamentin (figure 7.1) hosted a large *Damnye* event. Each year the organizers invite a group from

Figure 7.1   Car park mural at Le Lamentin 2012, featuring a stylized portrait of Aimé Césaire

Source: CarteMartinique.com

another country to participate in the performance and, in 2012, it chose China to take part in an encounter between *Damnye* and the Chinese martial art *Shou-bo*. On the one hand, one could see such an event as a co-opted, rather commercialized use of a historic cultural form, reminiscent of the commercialization of carnival discussed in chapter 5. On the other, however, it is also possible to look upon it as part of the ongoing process of identity formation. Echoing the example of carnival, the identity process at work here incorporates traces of the past – or diasporic traces – yet also speaks to the future, integrating the new migrants who reside on the island and who are part of an ongoing process of creolization.

Conclusion

Our aim in this chapter has been to interrogate the question of difference in Martinique and the multiple, seemingly contradictory, 'tugs' on identity in the island, which are theorized and prescribed 'from above', but lived, practised and contested 'from below'. While, in many cases, these efforts illustrate a top–down projection that bears little relation to what is happening on the ground, we suggest that it is important to give more agency to those whose identity is supposedly 'imposed' and to consider how these discursive markers actually parallel and intersect with the complex processes of identity formation from below. Thus, while Martinican identity is undoubtedly marked and pulled in multiple directions from above, we argue that such markers are not necessarily contradictory and do not prevent Martinicans resisting or creatively combining such 'pulls'.

French colonial and assimilationist policies have undoubtedly made their mark on identity formation in Martinique, evidenced through the transformation of the Martinican countryside in the image of the mainland, as well as through the inculcation of products, ideas and, indeed, people onto the island. Yet, as one interviewee remarked, Martinicans are 'extremely vocal in asserting their difference', always ready to assert their identity through what it is not – in this case, French. The concepts of *négritude* and later *créolité* encompassed a spirit of resistance and embodied important counter discourses with which to carve out Martinique's dissimilarity with France. As movements, they reflected the wider politics of identity emerging globally and in delineating and defining identity among marginal groups represented an important form of empowerment. The concepts of creolization and, more recently, *relation* emerged in analyses of identity in Martinique and again reflected both new ways of thinking about identity and shifting socio-political realities in Martinique and beyond. Indeed, the way the 2009 strikes spread so rapidly from Guadeloupe to Martinique and Réunion arguably testified to the possibility of solidarity and resistance transcending geographical boundaries and perhaps 'circumvent[ing] Western metropolises altogether'.[39] Thus, while Martinicans may continue to vote in favour of remaining part of France, their cultural practices and the formation of local identity reveal how the pull of the metropole will not prevent the ongoing process of creolization. As Miles writes: '[Martinique] behoves students of nationalism to consider the possibility that local expressions of cultural nationalism (here, as expressed in Antillean music and dance and in the Kréyol language) may indefinitely trump those of political nationalism (with the conventionally anticipated outcome of sovereignty).'[40]

A discussion of different identity markers in Martinique can provide insights into social identity trajectories elsewhere. The prism of 'markers' allows us to consider that living with diversity need not necessarily imply transcending difference or going *beyond* identity, but that it is possible for individual and collective expressions of coexisting identities to complement rather than contradict one another. It validates the right of people to carve out spaces of belonging and to refuse to be 'marked' by dominant 'others'; it also accommodates an inclusive acceptance of diverse markers of difference. The Martinican case not only reveals a multiplicity of often conflicting yet sometimes converging identity markers, but also demonstrates how these markers are neither indelible nor fixed. Thinking about identity in this way enables one to express and expose difference, yet simultaneously retain space in the ongoing construction of identities to connect and create. This chapter demarcates identarian tensions and possibilities in the context of

Martinique. The next and final chapter will consider the relevance of these examples, as well as those explored in our previous chapters, to wider debates about identity and encountering difference in the contemporary world.

8

Encountering Difference: A Conclusion

Our aim in this book has been to address the question of how people can learn to live with difference, but, in so doing, we do not mean to elide difference. Why do we not go further to assert a normative preference that people should set aside all differences and embrace their common humanity? There are, of course, many practical difficulties in realizing this cosmopolitan dream. However, as Stuart Hall noted, there are also some more fundamental objections to simply disregarding difference:

> I am, from the moment of birth, from the moment of entry into language and culture, dependent on that which is different from me. Otherwise love is self-love, love is narcissism, love is locked in solipsism, never gets out of the confines of the reflection in the mirror. It's not enough. We are dependent on the other – to feed us, to recognize who we are, to speak a language. Our common humanity, which is what you are speaking about, is the process of reciprocity with that which is not us, which is other than us, which is different.[1]

How then do we imagine and construct that which is 'us' and that which is 'not us'? This process happens at a personal and social level. As Mark Wallace argues, everyone needs a story to make sense of his or her life:

Without a narrative, a person's life is merely a random sequence of unrelated events: birth and death are inscrutable, temporality is a terror and a burden, and suffering and loss remain mute and unintelligible. In other words, narratives allow narrators to give meaning to their lives by locating themselves in their time and place.[2]

At a social level, these stories are diffused, mediated, enacted, memorialized, negotiated, shared, inscribed, performed, told and retold.

Concepts

Stories and narratives become the building blocks of social identity formation, and language is at the heart of this process. We are not the first scholars to spot that what happened in the sphere of language contact, notably creolization, could be widened to understand many other forms of social interaction; indeed, as we have acknowledged throughout the book, there is a wide body of scholarship that engages with a broader application of creolization. To eschew false modesty, perhaps we are among the first to address the concept of creolization comprehensively – conceptually, comparatively, historically and empirically. As in the study of language formation, we maintain that creolization is a significantly more powerful concept than bland variations on the theme of mixity, multiculturalism or hybridity, which assume a rough equivalence of the different cultures in play. On the contrary, creolization is structured in dominance and imbalances. The concept helps to 'de-centre' Euro-American theories of identity formation and encounter: although coined in the New World, the concept now has increasing traction in many other settings.[3] The notion of creolization forces one to recognize inequalities (socioeconomic, gendered, imperial and racial) and the manoeuvres for advantage that underlie many intercultural encounters. Creolization involves not just a question of dominance on the part of the powerful; it also necessarily encompasses creative forms of resistance on the part of the less dominant. As Michel-Rolph Trouillot affirms, this feature of endurance and invention in the face of dominant actors was unlikely and unexpected. 'Creolization', he writes, 'is a miracle begging for analysis. Because it first occurred against all odds, between the jaws of brute and absolute power, no explanation seems to do justice to the very wonder that it happened at all.'[4]

We have provided at least a partial explanation of why creolization occurs in our second major conceptual intervention, which explicitly recognizes that what the players bring to the field of cultural encounter are not only differential resources (or power), but different pasts. These pasts are assemblages of known forms of social behaviour, habits, distinct languages and religious practices and, in general, ways of being that have been socially accepted and legitimated. Above all, they bring with them collective memories, some more or less accurate renditions of the group's traditions, some invented or reconstructed to serve new needs. These pasts we have described as diasporic. Where traditions are strongly upheld and the ethnic group remains insular, creolization is interrupted. However, memories fade; they are rarely totally encompassing and gradually connections and crossovers with neighbours and outsiders lead to fresh imaginings and shared forms of social behaviour. Where these pooled interactions totally envelop the participating groups, creolization has morphed into a new social formation (a nation, society or culture) that is distinct unto itself. If this occurs, creolization has ended. However, total elision of the past rarely happens. To recollect the past is a search for meaning, a response to the question 'where are we from?'. It is a powerful source of resistance in adverse conditions, which can then be used to ameliorate hardship through cross-cultural exchanges. In these circumstances, the diaspora survives as a resource, even if, as we have put it, the collective memory and recounted oralities are reduced to diasporic traces. Moreover, a diasporic present soon complements a diasporic past as additional emigration and displacements affect the newly, or shall we say nearly, creolized society.

Our third conceptual intervention is to hold diaspora and creolization simultaneously in play. At first, they appear to work in opposite directions, the one to a recovery of a past identity, the other to a severance of that identity in the interests of establishing an integrated, alternative, identity of the present. However, as we have seen, this apparent contradiction plays out in more unexpected ways in different settings. In situations of conflict or exogenous intervention, diasporic attachments may be amplified and a degree of decreolization commences. An opposite logic might apply if the emerging society is suddenly or decisively cut off from its metropolitan connections or trade links. For example, until independence the dominant elite of Sierra Leone comprised a composite of African diasporic groups – returnees from the Americas and England and 'recaptives' (freed slaves) – who created a composite language, Krio, and who creolized with each other and with the British colonial forces.[5] Undermined by democracy, which activated the voices of the interior population for the first time, the elite effectively decreolized or went into exile. Despite their uncertain fate, the diminished number of Creoles of Sierra Leone, organized particularly in Masonic lodges, remain socially and culturally influential, in marked contrast to the marginalized '*ti-Créoles*' (little Creoles) of Mauritius who, without such grand narratives of their origins and glorious achievements, were sidelined by dominant Franco-Mauritian and Indo-Mauritian elites. We have represented such unexpected outcomes as 'a delicate dance'. As new social identities congeal or fracture, become solid, ductile or liquid, the delicate dance between creolization and diaspora has revealed unexpected moves, clumsy steps and not a few sore toes.

Encounters

There are, literally, hundreds of accounts of the meetings of groups hitherto unknown to each other – observations and interpretations provided by literate missionaries, explorers, adventurers, traders and travellers, on the one hand, and oral histories by illiterate people, which were later recovered for general use, on the other. We have reviewed only a small sample of them, but enough to show that instances of suspicion and hostility were more than matched by mimicry, curiosity and genuine attempts to create an intercultural dialogue. It is perhaps not surprising that some returning travellers

wildly embroidered their experiences. Tales of legendary king-
doms (like Prestor John's), of unimaginable riches (like El Dorado)
and unusual sexual practices (recounted, for example, in Richard
Burton's *Arabian Nights*) sold well and led to further sponsorship
for would-be voyagers. Perhaps the most enduring embellishment
was the persistent talk of cannibalism in Africa and the Pacific.
However, accounts of this practice were mainly invention, not
reality.[6] So we can venture a first and obvious generalization; in
describing cultural practices and cross-cultural encounters, it is
crucial to penetrate beyond the self-interested and sensational to
the commonplace and quotidian.

Using this yardstick, contact led overwhelmingly to connection and cooperation, sometimes to conflict and almost never to
cannibalism. Where, literally, there was no language in common,
people danced together, clapped hands and made music. They
engaged in a silent trade for the goods they needed or wanted.
Later, pidgins and creoles developed a basis for intercultural communication. It is from the linguistic study of creoles that we were
to excavate our first master concept, creolization. Eminent linguists had concluded that creole languages were crucially different
from pidgins; the plantation was different from a trading post.
Creoles were wholly new creations that gradually became mother
tongues with enriched vocabularies, the capacity for abstract reasoning and conceptual depth. Pidgins were, by contrast, limited
shared vocabularies designed to facilitate simple transactions or to
enable powerful actors to issue commands while still retaining the
original languages.

Spaces

We have crafted the main steps in the dance between diaspora
and creolization, but said nothing of the dance floor. We think it
important to understand not only *how* new social identities emerge,
but also to situate *where* they emerge. We have highlighted three
major contact zones – islands/plantations, port cities and 'super-
diverse' cities. These creolizing spaces conform closely to Mary

Louise Pratt's notion of contact zones as 'social spaces where disparate cultures meet, clash, and grapple with each other, often in highly asymmetrical relations of domination and subordination – such as colonialism and slavery, or their aftermaths as they are lived out across the globe today'.[7]

We found islands and plantations to be particularly instructive sites; they are micro laboratories where intersections, links, connections and disconnections can be observed in bite-sized spatial nodes and at certain historical moments. Many plantation societies demonstrated how creolization and diaspora interlaced in complex ways, sometime reinforcing, sometimes contradictory. Moreover, the political economy that suffused such spaces – mercantile capital, a monoculture, slavery and other forms of unfree labour – served both to condense and dissipate the matrix of identity formation. Identities often creolized, but they rarely did so in an inward and exclusionary way. Instead, the domination of colonial metropoles and similar experiences in adjacent islands and territories meant that identities became archipelagic, a scattering of islands providing a chain of partly insulated and partly connected social structures and experiences.[8]

Just as islands and plantations were the sites for new forms of social identity formation in the mercantile period, so many port cities, together with generating more and more commodities for export and import, later acquired an enhanced role as cultural entrepôts. In port cities, global cities and so-called ordinary cities, where trade, industrial capital and new financial interests intersected with multifaceted patterns of immigration, 'super-diversity' has resulted. Within them, 'islanded identities' have developed. As Ralph Crane has suggested of Anglo-Indians in India, the 'enclosing borders of the "island" serve to emphasize the cultural differences between those within and those beyond the island. The metaphorical island is enormously useful in defining identity.'[9] As we explain in more detail below, islanded identities lead to peaceful, if superficial, cohabitation between people in super-diverse cities, though deeper forms of creolization have also begun to embed themselves in many social practices in a variety of shared spaces.

Music and carnival

Two popular practices that epitomize the entrenching of creolization into the warp and weave of contemporary life are music and carnival. Margaret Kartomi argues that syncretism or transculturation (what we call creolization) in music arises from the 'halo' surrounding a dominant culture, the need for artistic communication between diverse groups and the lure of success if a new music looks like becoming commercial. The elements that foster transculturation, she maintains, are mainly 'extra-musical', deriving from wider social group relations. In a quasi-Hegelian analysis, Kartomi suggests that, as the tensions between two or more musical traditions are resolved into a new music that is accepted by the group concerned as 'representative of their own musical identity', this genre is exogenously challenged and the process of transculturation begins again.[10] Most popular music in Europe and the USA can be traced to crossovers between African and European music and, as Frank Salamone contends, the imprint of its creole origins is still palpable:

> African-derived music is in fact a subversive and anomalous art form. It combines opposites in every aspect – performance, content, heritage, objectives. It demands technical proficiency and yet scorns mere technique. What really matters is the ability of the performer to create something new each and every time he or she performs; what really counts is the ability to think on one's feet, to bring to bear on the situation all one's being and experience.[11]

Similar 'combinations of opposites' are at work in carnival, where diasporic groups play out old myths, sometimes drawn from their own folk histories, but often derived from the stock of youthful recollections of history lessons or stylized Hollywood renditions of great historical figures. It would not be at all surprising to see Zeus, Fu Manchu, Shaka Zulu, Buddha, Napoleon, a Pharaoh or two, Montezuma, Haile Selassie, Lincoln, Neptune, Caesar or Cleopatra on a passing float. But, in each case, the masquerades reinterpret such figures in a socially playful or politically charged way. Carnivals are now accepted parts of the public space in 60 countries and in many more cities. However hard officials and politicians seek to appropriate carnival for commercial or national purposes, it remains a fascinating illustration of the interplay between imagination and reaction, between creativity and resistance, between creolization and diaspora. Carnival enacts the creative and resistant elements of creolization: it is a moment when cultural identities merge and transform as official culture is challenged and often explicitly critiqued, while still retaining strong resonances of their diasporic origins.

Other cultural practices

We have provided chapter-length accounts of how music and carnival illuminate and crystallize the formation of shared cultural practices, but, of course, there are many other ways in which the processes of creolization and diaspora interconnect. Whenever it was appropriate, we interpolated examples or illustrations from language, dance, religion and food. Each of these could easily have merited a separate chapter but, alas, we can only make summary comments here:

1 As we have discussed language at some length, all we need to recall is that language is at the heart of cross-cultural interaction and communication. What has vividly been styled 'the miracle of creolization' is both analogous to and derivative of the evolution of creole languages.

2 Strictly, the expressive quality of dance allowed communication before a shared language developed. Body preceded mind. Nowadays, the blending of dance styles, the development of transnational ballet companies and the consumption, refashioning and what we have metaphorically described as a delicate dance between creolization and diaspora have all become a lived reality among dance professionals, tourists and migrants.[12]

3 Although the expression 'syncretized religion' is more common than 'creolized religion', the processes of interpenetration are

similar. Sometimes in unexpected ways, elements from prior religious traditions are absorbed and reprocessed. The cases of Shango (also called Orisha) in Trinidad, Santeria in Cuba, Vodou in Haiti and *Candomblé* in Brazil all combine West African and Catholic foundations and all derive from slave societies with highly asymmetrical power relations. There are many other creolized religions. For example, Malbars in Réunion combine Hinduism and Christianity, while Konkokyo in Japan combines Shintoism and pantheism. Certainly, the 'revealed religions' resist seeing themselves as syncretic but, to take just one example, open-minded adherents of the Abrahamic faiths might concede that the Ten Commandments bear more than a passing resemblance to the Code of Hammurabi.

4 In the mid-nineteenth century, Ludwig Feuerbach coined the memorable phrase '*Der Mensch ist was er isst*' (loosely, 'humans are what they eat'). He explained this further by adding, 'eating is the subjective, active form of being'.[13] Blending herbs and spices, meats and fish, fruits and roots, nuts and berries, flavours and aromas, then stewing, boiling, frying or grilling the ingredients in a myriad of ways have drawn millions of people worldwide into acts of sharing, exchanging and mingling food. Human existence depends on food, though this self-evident materialist proposition is not all that Feuerbach is saying. He correctly intuited that food was to become much more than a means of survival; its preparation and consumption embody and express cultural choices and treasured rituals, truly an 'active form of being'.

To language, dance, religion and food need to be added other cultural and social practices like crafts, art, theatre, markets, poetry, literature, parades, festivals, schoolyard games, storytelling, clothing, jewellery-making and body-marking. No doubt, many of these activities are about not much more than leisure and fun, so there is a danger of over-interpretation. Yet, one cannot help noticing, for example, that in the apparently innocent act of a Jamaican grandmother telling her grandchildren the story of Anancy, the spider man, she is also recounting the history of how the powerless can use cunning and trickery to outmanoeuvre the powerful. Granny's hidden message intuitively evokes a Hegelian logic; the master can be enslaved by the shrewdness of his slave.[14] In short, ordinary forms of social behaviour can manifest deeper elements of creativity and resistance, sometimes generating the vocabulary, consciousness, set of convictions or modes of performance necessary to oppose established authority.

Heritage

Henry Ford once said: 'I don't know much about history, and I wouldn't give a nickel for all the history in the world. It means nothing to me. History is more or less bunk. It's tradition.' Conversely, history means a great deal to those who wish to claim ownership of a particular heritage. When ownership is uncertain or hybrid, a battle royal ensues between curators and heritage seekers who are happy to accept impurity and those who seek to purge any impure elements in defence of a singular ideological position, nationalist project or religious conviction.

As de Jong points out, the stakes are often high.[15] If ancient Egypt is 'captured' by the West as the fount of its civilization, this can be seen as a racist appropriation designed to deny the African origins of European civilization (the Diop thesis). Likewise, if ancient Greece is nominated as the beginning of European civilization, this negates those who point to the Asiatic and African roots of Greek civilization (the Bernal thesis).[16] The rival claims of Jews and Muslims to the Temple Mount/Haram al-Sharif in Jerusalem may appear to have a certain farcical quality as particular ramps, fences and walls are guarded by heavily armed soldiers, but when the micro territories of either side have been transgressed, conflict erupts, sometimes with murderous consequences. There are many similar examples of the anger and mayhem caused by those who want to turn a creolized heritage into an exclusive prerogative of one party. To bring this lugubrious story to more recent times, we can refer to the operations of the so-called Islamic State in Syria and Iraq in 2015. Determined to eliminate from their self-declared caliphate any traces of its diverse religious and ethnic origins, they have turned their fury (*inter alia*) on the Assyrian Christians and destroyed priceless pre-Muslim art and artefacts in Nimrud, Mosul, Nineveh and Palmyra.

The curatorial challenge for hybrid or creolized sites presents particular difficulties for those managing cultural heritages. As we explained in chapter 6, UNESCO, the international body charged with the recognition of world heritage sites, found it difficult to mediate between rival sub-national claims in Mauritius and took the path of least resistance, recognizing two sub-national projects and, in so doing, inadvertently helping to decreolize the island. Perhaps there is an understandable tendency to yield to the loudest noise made by the group with the most effective lobby. This has resulted in UNESCO having recognized more than 1,000 world heritage sites by 2014. In Louisiana, state and municipal authorities have sought to appropriate the history of creolization in the area and cement it into a series of Creole heritage trails, museums, streets and districts, reconstructed plantations, homes, books, pamphlets and exhibitions. Inside these museums, people are asked to dress and perform 'creole', thereby displaying forms of imitation and appropriation that seriously negate the idea of creative resistance at the heart of creolization and the fact that the distinctiveness of creolization lies in its resistance to completion, closure or boundary-making.

Markers of identity

In the French Antilles three tugs of identity – creolization, diaspora (expressed as *négritude*) and assimilation – are in competition, a sort of identity market with parallel 'markers'. Can we capture these markers in a literal and self-evident way? Can we, to be blunt, take the approximate skin colour 'brown' to signify Creole (creolization), 'black' to signify African descent (*négritude*) or 'white' to indicate French *metropolitain* (assimilation)? In fact, this clumsy and literal understanding does not translate well into the islands' identarian politics. Assimilation has great salience precisely because it was not totally imposed by France but partly chosen by Antillean people. Indeed, the embrace of the French republican project was even tighter in the colonies than in the metropole, for if 'Liberty, Equality, Fraternity' could be made to work, that offered an escape from the plantation, from colonialism and from racial discrimination. When France and French values buckled during the period of Nazi occupation, it was the colonies (several later to become overseas departments of France) that started the fight back. In Martinique, that great protagonist of *négritude*, Aimé Césaire, used his immense political influence, as mayor of Fort-de-France and deputy to the French National Assembly for Martinique, to draft the law on departmentalization, often represented as an assimilationist project. His extraordinary prose-poem *Cahier d'un retour au pays natal*, published in 1939, is a searing account of the joys and pains of living in a creole society. A fragment from this poem displays Césaire's astute understanding of how space, emotion and identity connect:

> What is mine these few thousands death-bearers who turn in circles in this calabash of an island and what is mine too, the archipelago arched with the anxious desire to deny itself, as though eager to protect with maternal anxiety the more delicate tenuity separating the two Americas; and its flanks secreting for Europe the sweet liquor of a Gulf Stream; and one of the two slopes of incandescence between which the Equator funambulates to Africa. And my non-enclosure island, its clear boldness standing at the back of this Polynesia, before it, Guadeloupe split in two along its backbone and sharing our misery, Haiti where *négritude* stood up for the first time and said it believed in its humanity and the comic little tail of Florida where the strangulation of a nigger is about to be completed and Africa gigantically caterpillaring as far as the Hispanic foot of Europe, its nakedness where Death swings its scythe widely.[17]

Césaire's own life mirrors the complexity of cultural politics in Martinique at large. The tug of the metropole, expressed in several referenda to remain part of France, does not inhibit an interrogation of diasporic pasts or the ongoing process of creolization. To capture this complexity, this deviation from the crude marker of phenotype (or 'race'), we have discussed the convergences and discrepancies between environmental markers (emanating from outside, but affecting a society), social markers (embodying social practices and values) and cultural markers (expressing linguistic and cultural practices). The prism of 'markers' allows us to generalize the experience of the Caribbean, to show why living with diversity does not necessarily imply transcending difference or going beyond identity, but rather points to the ways in which coexisting identities can be complementary rather than contradictory.

Conflict, cohabitation or creolization

We ranged far and wide in our enquiry and in several places (particularly in chapters 3 and 5) indicated how our arguments could be universalized. Here we want to focus on contemporary cities, the contact zones of the globalizing, urbanizing, super-diverse world. We want to distinguish between three alternative forms of interaction in urban settings – conflict, cohabitation and creolization. These are not the only forms of interaction (and we accept that cohabitation provides a generic category for many sub-variations), but they provide a useful trichotomy in which to organize a discussion.

Conflict

Super-diverse cities rarely display continuous expressions of conflict – cohabitation is the default trajectory – but there are important exceptions to this generalization. Anger, hostility, xenophobia and racism are evident where longstanding residents complain that they are being overwhelmed by the number of newcomers and competition for housing, welfare payments, employment and sexual partners. The authorities usually manage such conflict with little difficulty. However, such low-level conflict can escalate rapidly if populist politicians fan the flames and/or sections of the police force adopt nativist loyalties. (The links between some police and the Golden Dawn ultra-nationalist movement in contemporary

Athens provide a good contemporary example.) Conflict can become fossilized or frozen, earning the appellation 'divided city' – with longstanding territorial divisions, usually sustained by barriers and fences (Jerusalem, Nicosia and Belfast are cases in point). Long-supressed forms of oppression can erupt in violence after a particularly gross act of injustice. A case in point occurred on 9 August 2014 in Ferguson, Missouri, when a white police officer shot and killed an 18-year-old African American, Michael Brown. Vandalism, rioting and protest erupted across the USA, with numerous protesters asserting that routine acts of oppression of African Americans remained endemic in many US cities. Finally, exogenous conflicts can overwhelm cities with longstanding patterns of cohabitation. A sad example is Aleppo, historically one of the most diverse and tolerant of all cities, which now lies in ruins, a grotesque symbol of diversity blown to bits.

Cohabitation

In many cities, cohabitation is the norm, though it is difficult to capture the sheer range of possibilities loosely grouped under this category. Such an appellation might cover all interactions from the friendly smile and warm handshake to a reluctant acceptance of the presence of a disliked minority or even the barest acknowledgement of the other's existence. Even where legal segregation (as in apartheid South Africa) does not apply, self-segregation is common, with people living in parallel bubble worlds. This is mediated and diminished if there is enhanced contact in public spaces (parks, streets, leisure facilities, stadia, shopping centres, exhibitions). However, parallelism is unlikely to be totally overcome without integrated schooling or, in the increasingly rare cases where it applies, citizen community or military service. In many instances, the development of three spheres, or domains, marks cohabitation. These are the private sphere (where separation is sanctioned), the public sphere (where shared norms are enforced, for example in the courts) and the ambivalent sphere (where modes of coexistence are not finalized and thus have not entered the public habitus or become marked by intimate exchanges).[18]

It is perhaps unsurprising that scholars have struggled to find an agreed conceptual vocabulary to capture these ambivalent modes of cohabitation. For example, as we indicated in chapter 3, Susanne Wessendorf described the forms of allegiance and separation between different ethnicities and generations in Hackney (London) as 'commonplace diversity'. Interactions at her research site seem sufficiently frequent to allow peaceful cohabitation, but they also reveal a shallowness and lack of depth.[19] This combination of accepting diversity and banal forms of associational life underlies a number of cognate terms like 'multiculture', 'everyday cosmopolitanism' and 'conviviality'. For Ben Gidley, 'everyday multiculture' has now become normal because extraordinary mixes of people are forced to inhabit small spaces, for example public housing.[20] Similarly, Steven Vertovec and Robin Cohen note that, with enhanced travel and migration, strangers are required to develop cheek-by-jowl relationships 'at work, at street corners, in neighbourhoods, schools and recreational areas'. Such relationships, they argue, could be described as 'everyday cosmopolitanism'.[21] More innovatively, Paul Gilroy has used the term 'conviviality' to capture 'the processes of cohabitation and interaction that have made multiculture an ordinary feature of social life in Britain's urban areas and in postcolonial cities elsewhere'.[22] And finally, American sociologist Elijah Anderson evokes the concept of a 'cosmopolitan canopy', which, he argues, 'becomes ever more significant as a setting in which people of diverse backgrounds come together, mingle with strangers, and gain from their social experience a critical folk knowledge and social intelligence about others they define as different from themselves'.[23]

Creolization

Gilroy's notion of conviviality provides a good bridge to our preoccupation with deeper forms of interaction and 'thicker' encounters, namely creolization. At one level, his choice of the word conviviality is counterintuitive. Gilroy is not alluding to a *bon viveur* who greets all and sundry with a warm handshake, a drink and a pat on the back; rather, the etymological reference is to *convivir* (Spanish for cohabitation). He is seeking to transcend conventional ideas of communities and ethnicities in talking instead about 'the evasive, multicultural future prefigured everywhere in the ordinary experiences of contact, cooperation, and conflict across the supposedly impermeable boundaries of race, culture, identity and ethnicity'.[24]

This nearly captures, but does not quite convey, our understanding of creolization, which goes beyond conviviality and well beyond most understandings of cohabitation. Creolization indicates that long-established and imported cultures go through a fundamental process of transmutation as they interact. New social identities and practices arise that supersede the old ones in strength if not also esteem. Component 'creolized' cultural forms and identities often retain traces of their origins, which are revalorized for the purposes of cultural renewal – a revisiting of the remembered, dismembered and invented past that we alluded to as a 'diasporic echo' or 'diasporic trace'. In addition to being incomplete, intercultural exchanges are asymmetrical and hierarchical. Yet using creolization as a framework to explore such encounters allows us to consider how, while born out of unequal encounters, they do not merely reproduce such asymmetries. A creolization framework points to how these encounters may be creative, productive and often subversive. Understanding the contexts is also important to understanding the contents. Historically, we have seen creolization in island societies and port cities. We are seeing it again in contemporary cities manifesting the characteristics of super-diversity.

Imagining the future

There are three key senses in which creolization – mindful of its relationship with diaspora – is useful for analysing identity in the contemporary world, and for addressing some of the challenges of living in ever more super-diverse spaces. We allude to history, space and power. First, a focus on the intersections between diaspora and creolization compel us to think about the importance of history in the emergence of social and cultural forms and identities.

Second, we can use the same intersections to plot the dynamic relationship between culture and space – from the space of the plantation or the island, to port cities and contemporary contact zones in super-diverse cities. Finally, and most importantly, diaspora and creolization are crucial concepts for thinking about identity in our dynamic, ever more interconnected world: a world of movement, a world of migrants and a world of 'relation' (to use Glissant's term). Diaspora and creolization both represent alternative expressions of identity in the context of forceful assertions of nationalism or religious certainties, and challenge the solidity of closed ethnic and racial categories. It is in this challenge that power from below is found. Expanded uses of diaspora, and certainly creolization, 'demonstrate that people thrive not by getting stuck in fixed quasi-racial identities but at the nodes and connection points where original ideas and bold inventiveness are nurtured and fashioned'.[25]

The very premises of our book are, first, that the concept of creolization is applicable to other spaces in which similar processes of relative isolation, inequality, repression and diversity lead to the emergence of new cultural forms and, consequently, the term can usefully (though not unreflectively) be expanded to incorporate other phenomena related to processes of cultural globalization in the contemporary world. We need to record here a significant objection to such an exercise by Mimi Sheller, who asks if, 'as theories (and theorists) become mobile and ungrounded, are they at risk of being consumed within mainstream culture and stripped of their oppositional meanings?'.[26] As our concepts have travelled – and in writing this book we are contributing to the evolution of the ideas of diaspora and creolization – we need to ensure that we do not lose sight of connotations of loss and displacement in the first case, and of creativity and resistance in the second. Our responsibility in using, promoting or expanding these concepts is to acknowledge and maintain many of the original meanings behind the terms, even as we apply them to different contexts. We also need to remember the potential for the co-optation of popular counter-hegemonic practices and cultures by cultural elites (as we saw in the examples of music and carnival in chapters 4 and 5). And finally, in deploying these terms beyond their original contexts, we need to be attentive to how processes of creolization and diaspora – and the power dynamics inherent within them – play out in people's everyday lives and social realities. To what extent, we must ask, would your social position – job opportunities, social networks, housing situation – affect your decision or ability to adopt a bounded diasporic identity, rather than embrace creolization?

Two other issues need airing in the final paragraphs of this conclusion. We have mentioned that we do not want, or think it possible, to elide difference. In adopting the expression 'encountering difference', we have shown that many of the cultural and social practices we covered in the book demonstrate that people can connect and relate across the faultlines of ethnicity, religion, language, nationality, gender, class and generation (to mention the principal ways in which humankind is divided). To be sure, retaining diasporic longing does not preclude communication and indeed collaboration with neighbouring groups. However, in these cases mixing occurs while boundaries remain intact. Creolization challenges boundaries as such.[27]

Perhaps it would not be too much of a simplification to say that the divisions wrought by race/ethnicity and religion are those that currently cause most concern. However, as we suggested in chapter 1, to resolve our anxieties by embracing cosmopolitanism seems to be a step too far. Think for a moment of Zeno, the pioneer Greek Stoic and cosmopolitan philosopher who even designed unisex clothing to ensure that men and women should look alike. This is a trivial example, but one that illustrates the point – difference cannot be willed away by philosophy or ideology. As Stuart Hall argued, such an exercise is narcissistic and arrogant. It is not demonstrable that *our* way is the best way or that there is one alternative way on which we can agree. Indeed, the very essence and definition of the self depends on contrasting it with the other.[28] So difference has to be acknowledged and accepted. The conceit of a uniform and undifferentiated humanism, fashioned by an elite (who else?), has to be rejected. So too does the self-righteousness of those who proclaim that they will remain apart from the rest of humanity. The leading theorist of *créolité*, Patrick Chamoiseau, put it well:

No one can foresee what will happen in the *totalité-monde*. In all epochs there are going to be people who take refuge in singular identities. There will still be people saying 'I'm a Negro!', 'I'm African!' One person will proclaim 'I'm an!' Another will find safety in some obscure religious tradition. There will always be retractile tendencies, there will always be desires for ethnic purification, there will always be a desire to preserve some lost, phantasmatic [*sic*] source. But in the face of all this, there is the grand poetics of creolization: there will be imaginaries that express the totality of languages, the totality of cultures.[29]

The grand poetics of creolization cannot, however, neglect the rewind and playback of diaspora. As we have made clear at several places in this book, decreolization can occur and indeed has occurred. Creolization and diaspora need to dance together in a warm and intimate embrace, a 'creospora', if we can indulge in a final neologism. Even then, even with the smoothest of choreographies and the most accomplished of dance partners, there is no teleology, no inevitability that a creolized imagination teamed with a diasporic recall will triumph. Things do not inevitably roll out according to a divine design or a social evolutionist's plan.

Notes

Framing the Question: A Preamble

1 Stuart Hall, 'Living with difference: Stuart Hall in conversation with Bill Schwarz', *Soundings: A Journal of Politics and Culture*, 37, 2007, pp. 150–1.

Chapter 1   Shaping the Tools: Three Concepts

1 See, notably, William Safran, 'Diasporas in modern societies: myths of homeland and return', *Diaspora: A Journal of Transnational Studies*, 1(1), 1991, pp. 83–99; William Safran, 'The Jewish diaspora in a comparative and theoretical perspective', *Israel Studies*, 10(1), 2005, pp. 36–60; Khachig Tölölyan, 'Rethinking diaspora(s): stateless power in the transnational moment', *Diaspora: A Journal of Transnational Studies*, 5(1), 1996, pp. 3–36; and Robin Cohen *Global Diasporas: An Introduction*, 2nd edn, London: Routledge, 2008.

2 Haim Hazan, *Against Hybridity: Social Impasses in a Globalizing World*, Cambridge: Polity, 2015, p. 2. The most notable and heroic effort to rescue hybridity from its unfortunate origins was undertaken by Homi Bhabha. See Homi Bhabha, 'Signs taken for wonders: questions of ambivalence and authority under

a tree outside Delhi, May 1817', *Critical Inquiry*, 12(1) 1985, pp. 144–65.

3 Charles Stewart, 'Syncretism and its synonyms: reflections on cultural mixture', *Diacritics*, 29(3), 1999, p. 40. We commend Charles Stewart for his balanced account comparing hybridity, creolization and syncretism, though is worth noting that eight years later he edited a major collection favouring the term creolization. See Charles Stewart (ed.), *Creolization: History, Ethnography, Theory*, Walnut Creek, CA: Left Coast Press, 2007.

4 Interculturalism has had a major re-engineering in the context of community cohesion in the UK. See Ted Cantle, *Interculturalism: The New Era of Cohesion and Diversity*, Basingstoke: Palgrave Macmillan, 2012. For the sake of completeness we should also acknowledge our debt to the concept of transculturation developed by the Cuban sociologist Fernando Ortiz, which, regrettably, has not been widely diffused. See Fernando Ortiz, *Cuban Counterpoint: Tobacco and Sugar*, Durham, NC: Duke University Press, 1995 (originally published in Spanish in 1940).

5 Richard Jenkins, *Social Identity*, London: Routledge, 2004, pp. 8, 11.

6 Erik H. Erikson, *Childhood and Society*, New York: W. W. Norton, 1963 (originally published 1950).

7 Social constructivism implies that reality is determined by social interactionism (or intersubjectivity), rather than by objectivity (the recognition of a known natural or material world) or by subjectivity (a world determined by individual perceptions). Social constructivism tends to favour accounts based on human agency and voluntarism rather than those based on history, structure or habit.

8 Peter L. Berger and Thomas Luckmann, *The Social Construction of Reality: A Treatise in the Sociology of Knowledge*, New York: Anchor, 1967.

9 Benedict Anderson, *Imagined Communities. Reflections on the Origin and Spread of Nationalism*, London: Verso, 1983.

10 See Ulf Hannerz, 'Flows, Boundaries and Hybrids: Keywords in Transnational Anthropology', Working Paper, Transnational Communities Programme, University of Oxford, WPTC-2K-02, 2002; http://www.transcomm.ox.ac.uk/working%20papers/hannerz.pdf.

11 *E pluribus unum* ('from many, one') has appeared on the seal of the USA since 1776.

12 These ideas were first developed in Robin Cohen, 'Social identities, diaspora and creolization', in Kim Knott and Seán McLoughlin (eds), *Diasporas: Concepts, Identities, Intersections*, London: Zed Books, 2010, pp. 69–73; and Olivia Sheringham, 'A delicate dance: creolization, diaspora, and the metropolitan "pull" in the French Antilles', paper given at the Caribbean Studies Association annual conference, 28 May–1 June 2012, Guadeloupe.

13 Ralph Premdas, 'Public policy and ethnic conflict', Management of Social Transformations, Discussion Paper Series No. 12, Paris: UNESCO, 1996.

14 A number of philosophers have denounced the exclusive focus on humanity, deeming it 'speciesism' and arguing in favour of extending moral standing to animals or to the biosphere at large (the Gaia hypothesis). These positions, which we think are worthy of sympathetic consideration, go beyond the scope of this book and are not considered here.

15 Thucydides, *The Peloponnesian War*, London: J. M. Dent, 1910, 2.39.1; http://www.perseus.tufts.edu/hopper/text?doc=Perseus%3 Atext%3A1999.01.0200%3Abook%3D2%3Achapter%3D34.

16 Steven Vertovec and Robin Cohen, 'Introduction', in Steven Vertovec and Robin Cohen (eds), *Conceiving Cosmopolitanism: Theory, Context and Practice*, Oxford: Oxford University Press, 2002, p. 9.

17 We should add that the expression 'everyday cosmopolitanism' partly offsets the predominant use of the expression.

18 Stuart Hall, 'Living with difference: Stuart Hall in conversation with Bill Schwarz', *Soundings: A Journal of Politics and Culture*, 37, 2007, p. 155.

19 David Chariandy, 'Postcolonial diasporas', *Postcolonial Text*, 2(1), 2006; available at http://journals.sfu.ca/pocol/index.php/pct/article/view/440/159.

20 Rogers Brubaker, 'The "diaspora" diaspora', *Ethnic and Racial Studies*, 28(1), 2005, pp. 1–19.

21 Stephan Palmié. 'Creolization and its discontents', in Robin Cohen and Paola Toninato (eds), *The Creolization Reader: Studies in Mixed Identities and Cultures*, London: Routledge, pp. 55, 57.

22 Ulf Hannerz, 'The world in creolization', *Africa*, 57(4), 1987, pp. 546–59.

23 Édouard Glissant, 'Creolization in the making of the Americas', *Caribbean Quarterly*, 54(1/2), 2009, pp. 81–9.

Chapter 2   *Exploring Difference: Early Interactions*

1 Samuel P. Huntington, *The Clash of Civilizations and the Remaking of World Order*, New York: Simon & Schuster, 1996.

2 Brenna M. Henn et al., 'Hunter-gatherer genomic diversity suggests a southern African origin for modern humans', *Proceedings of the National Academy of Sciences*, 108(13), 29 March 2011, pp. 5154–62; Sarah A. Tishkoff et al., 'The genetic structure and history of Africans and African Americans', *Science*, 324(5930), 22 May 2009, pp. 1035–44. See also, for a popular account of the new science of 'genography', Paul Salopek 'Out of Eden', *National Geographic*, 224(6), 2013, pp. 21–60. The announcement of the discovery of *Homo naledi* in the Cradle of Humankind in South Africa on 10 September 2015 has caused considerable excitement, but it is worth remembering that the researchers only claim that Naledi *shares* characteristics that are otherwise encountered only in *Homo sapiens*.

3 Charles Darwin, *On the Origin of Species by Means of Natural Selection, or, the Preservation of Favoured Races in the Struggle for Life*, Harmondsworth: Penguin, 1968 (originally published 1859); Charles Darwin, *The Descent of Man, and Selection in Relation to Sex*, Princeton, NJ: Princeton University Press, 1981 (originally published 1871); http://www.christs.cam.ac.uk/darwin200/pages/index.php?page_id=c8.

4 Tabari's work is monumental. The first translation into English took 40 volumes. More accessible to the non-specialist is the selection and translation provided by Franz Rosenthal, *Tārīkh al-rusul wa-al-mulūk: General Introduction* and *From the Creation to the Flood*, Albany: State University of New York Press, 1989.

5 James George Frazer, *Folk-lore in the Old Testament: Studies in Comparative Religion, Legend and Law*, vol. 1, London: Macmillan, 1918, pp. 377–87.

6 http://www.elyricsworld.com/tower_of_babel_lyrics_elton_john.html.

7 http://www.saatchi-gallery.co.uk/artists/diana_hadid.htm?section_name=unveiled.

8 Leonard Schwartz, 'After Babel' (2002) http://towerofbabel.com/sections/bard/thenewbabel/.

9 Peter Bradshaw, 'London: The modern Babylon – review', *Guardian*, 2 August 2012. To cap this, an innovative team of architects and designers has invented the city of 'Babylondon', complete with a fake Wiki entry: http://www.theaoc.co.uk/docs/texts/babylondon.html.

10 Robert Fine and Robin Cohen, 'Four cosmopolitan moments', in Steven Vertovec and Robin Cohen (eds), *Conceiving Cosmopolitanism: Theory, Context and Practice*, Oxford: Oxford University Press, 2002, pp. 140, 144.

11 David Harvey, 'Cosmopolitanism and the banality of geographical evils', *Public Culture*, 12(2), 2000, pp. 524–64.

12 Emmanuel Chukwudu Eze, *Race and the Enlightenment: A Reader*, Oxford: Blackwell, 1967, pp. 48–9, 65.

13 Norbert Elias, *The History of Manners*, Oxford: Basil Blackwell, 1978, pp. 49–50.

14 Fred Inglis, *Culture*, Cambridge: Polity, 2004.

15 http://www.statemaster.com/encyclopedia/Johann-Gottfried-Herder.

16 We thank Thomas Hylland Eriksen for adding to our understanding here (private correspondence).

17 James Axtell, *Natives and Newcomers: The Cultural Origins of North America*, New York: Oxford University Press, p. 40.

18 Inga Cledinnen, *Dancing with Strangers: The True History of the Meeting of the British First Fleet and the Aboriginal Australians, 1788*, Edinburgh: Canongate, 2005, pp. 8–9.

19 Cledinnen, *Dancing with Strangers*, pp. 6–7.

20 Barbara Ehrenreich, *Dancing in the Streets: A History of Collective Joy*, London: Granta Books, p. 1.

21 Ehrenreich, *Dancing in the Streets*, p. 3.

22 William Arens, *The Man-eating Myth: Anthropology and Anthropophagy*, New York: Oxford University Press, 1979, p. 21.

23 Gananath Obeyesekere, *Cannibal Talk: The Man-Eating Myth and Human Sacrifice in the South Seas*, Berkeley: University of California Press, 2005, pp. 255–8.

24 Charles van Onselen, *Chibaro: African Mine Labour in Southern Rhodesia, 1900–1933*, London: Pluto Press, 1976, pp. 234–5.

25 Sometimes popular and scientific uses coincide. Thus Kweyòl

(in St Lucia, Dominica and Haiti), Creolese (in Guyana), Krio (in Sierra Leone) and Creole in Belize are used identically. See Donald Winford, *An Introduction to Contact Linguistics*, Malden, MA: Blackwell Publishing, 2003, p. 305. However, there are some misleading designations. Scholars regard Tok Pisin ('talk pidgin') in New Guinea as a creole language. Many of the 86 or so creole languages also do not indicate their scholarly classifications in their names.

26 Donald Winford, *An Introduction to Contact Linguistics*, Oxford: Wiley-Blackwell, 2002, p. 268. Winford is the editor of the authoritative *Journal of Pidgin and Creole Languages*.

27 Derek Bickerton, *Bastard Tongues: A Trailblazing Linguist Finds Clues to Our Common Humanity in the World's Lowliest Languages*, New York: Hill and Wang, 2008, pp. 3–16, 97–114.

28 Rajend Mesthrie, 'Language contact 2: pidgins, creoles and "new Englishes"', in Rajend Mesthrie, Joan Swann, Andrea Deumert and William L. Leap (eds), *Introducing Sociolinguistics*, Edinburgh: Edinburgh University Press, 2009, pp. 279–315, quote at p. 297.

29 Bambi B. Schieffelin and Elinor Ochs (eds), *Language Socialization across Cultures*, Cambridge: Cambridge University Press, 1987.

30 Bickerton, *Bastard Tongues*, p. 247. Bickerton somewhat distances himself from Noam Chomsky, but there are clear echoes of Chomskian ideas.

Chapter 3   Locating Identity Formation: Contact Zones

1 Doreen Massey, 'Politics and space/time', *New Left Review*, 196, 1993, pp. 70, 81.

2 Françoise Vergès, 'Is creolization a useful concept today?' Presentation at a conference, 'Identities: Creolization and Diaspora in Comparative Perspective', University of Oxford, 6–7 December 2012.

3 Françoise Vergès, 'Postcolonial challenges', in Nicholas Gane (ed.), *The Future of Social Theory*, New York: Continuum, 2004, p. 195.

4 Mary Louise Pratt, *Imperial Eyes: Travel Writing and Transculturation*, London: Routledge, 2008, p. 7. In some respects Pratt's views echo earlier discussions of 'plural societies', peoples brought together by colonialism, who 'mix but do not combine', each group holding firmly to its own religion, culture and folkways. In the classic account

by the British colonial administrator, J. S. Furnivall, imported groups would meet only in buying and selling, a prediction that proved far too pessimistic. See J. F. Furnivall, *Colonial Policy and Practice: A Comparative Study of Burma and Netherlands India*, Cambridge: Cambridge University Press, 1948.

5　Françoise Vergès, 'Kiltir kréol: processes and practices of créolité and creolization', in Okwui Enwezor et al. (eds), *Créolité and Creolization*, Kassel: Documenta, 11, 2003, p. 181.

6　ISISA (International Small Islands Study Association), 2010; http://tech.groups.yahoo.com/group/ISISA/message/468.

7　Maeve McCusker and Anthony Soares, 'Introduction', in Maeve McCusker and Anthony Soares (eds), *Islanded Identities: Constructions of Postcolonial Cultural Insularity*, Amsterdam: Rodopi, 2011, pp. xii–xiii.

8　David Pitt, 'Sociology, islands and boundaries', *World Development*, 8(12), 1980, pp. 1055, 1056.

9　Michaela Benson and Karen O'Reilly (eds), *Lifestyle Migration: Expectations, Aspirations and Experiences*, Farnham: Ashgate, 2009, pp. 1–13.

10　Phillip Vannini, 'Constellations of ferry (im)mobility: islandness as the performance and politics of insulation and isolation', *Cultural Geographies*, 18(2), 2011, p. 267.

11　Melville J. Herskovits, *The Myth of the Negro Past*, Boston, MA: Beacon Press, 1996; and Gilberto Freyre, *The Master and the Slave: a Study in the Development of Brazilian Civilization*, New York: Knopf, 1964.

12　Michel-Rolph Trouillot, 'Culture on the edges: creolization in the plantation context', *Plantation Society in the Americas*, 5(1), 1998, pp. 8–28.

13　Aisha Khan, 'Journey to the center of the earth: the Caribbean as master symbol', *Cultural Anthropology*, 16(3), 2001, p. 272.

14　Édouard Glissant, *Poétique de la relation*, Paris: Gallimard, 1990; Antonio Benítez-Rojo, *The Repeating Island: The Caribbean and the Postmodern Perspective*, Durham, NC: Duke University Press, 1996. See also Thomas Hylland Eriksen, 'In which sense do cultural islands exist?' *Social Anthropology* 1(18), 1993, pp. 133–47.

15　Stuart Hall, 'Créolité and the process of creolization', in Robin Cohen and Paola Toninato (eds), *The Creolization Reader: Studies in Mixed Identities and Cultures*, London: Routledge, 2010, p. 29.

16 Richard D. E. Burton, 'The French West Indies *à l'heure de l'Europe*: an overview', in Richard D. E. Burton and Fred Reno (eds), *French and West Indian: Martinique, Guadeloupe, and French Guiana Today*, London: Macmillan, 1995.

17 Maeve McCusker, 'Writing against the tide? Patrick Chamoiseau's (is)land imaginary', in Maeve McCusker and Anthony Soares (eds), *Islanded Identities: Constructions of Postcolonial Cultural Insularity*, Amsterdam: Rodopi, 2011, p. 42.

18 Glissant, *Poétique de la relation*, p. 71.

19 Édouard Glissant, 'Creolization in the making of the Americas', *Caribbean Quarterly*, 54 (1/2), 2008, p. 81.

20 It would indeed be reasonable to expect that creolization will assume different forms as it 'migrates' from island settings. This is argued, for example, by Benítez-Rojo (in *The Repeating Island*), who maintained that creolization on the mainland in Mesoamerica and South America was different because depopulation was incomplete, despite millions of deaths. As the indigenous populations gradually recovered demograph-ically, they allied with Spanish settlers to develop distinctive nationalist and creolized political movements. In the contemporary period, new forms of creolization, particularly at the level of popular culture, are emerging in globalized and 'super-diverse' metropolitan settings. See H. Adlai Murdoch, *Creolizing the Metropole: Migrant Caribbean Identities in Literature and Film*, Champaign, IL: University of Illinois Press, 2012.

21 Henk Driessen, 'Mediterranean port cities: cosmopolitanism recon-sidered', *History and Anthropology*, 16(1), 2005, p. 131.

22 Information from http://www.jewishvenice.org/.

23 Anita L. Allen and Michael R. Seidl, 'Cross-cultural commerce in Shakespeare's *The Merchant of Venice*', *American University International Law Review*, 10(2), 1995, p. 858.

24 William Shakespeare, *The Merchant of Venice*, Act 3, Scene 1.

25 Driessen, 'Mediterranean port cities', p. 138.

26 This, Vertovec and Cohen argue, is one of the six ways in which cos-mopolitanism may be defined. See 'Introduction' to Steven Vertovec and Robin Cohen (eds.) *Conceiving Cosmopolitanism: Theory, Context, and Practice*, Oxford: Oxford University Press, pp. 8–14.

27 Paul Atterbury, 'Steam and speed: industry, power & social change in nineteenth century Britain'; http://www.vam.ac.uk/content/articles/s/industry-power-and-social-change/.

28 Nurçin İleri, 'Rewriting the history of port cities in the light of contemporary global capitalism', *New Perspectives on Turkey*, 47, 2012, p. 206.

29 Anon, 'Spice routes: Cladia Roden's culinary diaspora', *New Yorker*, 5 September 2007; http://www.newyorker.com/magazine/2007/09/03/spice-routes.

30 Alison Blunt and Jayani Bonnerjee, 'Home, city and diaspora: Anglo–Indian and Chinese attachments to Calcutta', *Global Networks*, 13(2), 2013, pp. 220–40.

31 See, for example, John Friedman, 'The world city hypothesis', *Development and Change* 19(2), pp. 69–83; Saskia Sassen, *The Global City: London, New York, Tokyo*, Princeton, NJ: Princeton University Press, 1991; and Peter Marcuse and Ronald Van Kempen (eds), *Globalizing Cities: A New Spatial Order?* Oxford: Blackwell, 2000.

32 Steven Vertovec, 'Super-diversity and its implications', *Ethnic and Racial Studies*, 30(6), 2007, p. 1049.

33 Jennifer Robinson, *Ordinary Cities: Between Modernity and Development*, London: Routledge, 2005, p. 1. See also Shail Mayaram (ed.), *The Other Global City*, New York: Routledge, 2009, for a critique of the global cities paradigm.

34 Stuart Hall, 'Cosmopolitan promises, multicultural realities', in Richard Scholar (ed.), *Divided Cities: The Oxford Amnesty Lectures 2003*, Oxford: Oxford University Press, 2006, p. 25.

35 Okwui Enwezor, 'Introduction', in Okwui Enwezor et al. (eds), *Créolité and Creolization*, Kassel: Documenta, 11, 2003, p. 16.

36 Vergès, 'Is creolization a useful concept today?'

37 Gill Valentine, 'Living with difference: reflections on geographies of encounter', *Progress in Human Geography*, 32(3), 2008, pp. 323–37.

38 Karen Fog Olwig, 'Notions and practices of difference: an epilogue on the ethnography of diversity', *Identities: Global Studies in Culture and Power*, 20(4), 2013, p. 471. It is worth noting that the widespread attack on multiculturalism by European politicians and commentators represents more of a discursive shift than a substantive change of practice. See Steven Vertovec and Susanne Wessendorf (eds), *The Multiculturalism Backlash: European Discourses, Policies and Practices*, London: Routledge, 2009.

39 Mette Louise Berg and Nando Sigona, 'Ethnography, diversity and

urban space', *Identities: Global Studies in Culture and Power*, 20(4), 2013, p. 352.

40 Susanne Wessendorf, *Commonplace Diversity: Social Relations in a Super-diverse Context*, London: Palgrave Macmillan, 2014.

41 Ben Gidley, 'Landscapes of belonging, portraits of life: researching everyday multiculture in an inner city estate', *Identities: Global Studies in Culture and Power*, 20(4), 2013, p. 367.

42 Thomas Hylland Eriksen, 'Rebuilding the ship at sea: super-diversity, person and conduct in eastern Oslo', *Global Networks*, 15(1), 2015, pp. 1–20.

43 Alex Rhys-Taylor, 'The essences of multiculture: a sensory exploration of an inner-city street market', *Identities: Global Studies in Culture and Power*, 20(4), 2013, pp. 393–406. The author draws on Fernando Ortiz, *Cuban Counterpoint: Tobacco and Sugar*, Durham, NC: Duke University Press, 1995, for his concept of transculturation.

44 Pratt, *Imperial Eyes*, p. 8.

45 H. Adlai Murdoch, *Creolizing the Metropole: Migrant Caribbean Identities in Literature and Film*, Bloomington, IN: Indiana University Press, 2012, p. 207.

46 Michael Peter Smith 'Transnational urbanism revisited', *Journal of Ethnic and Migration Studies*, 2005, 31(2), p. 237.

47 Vergès, 'Postcolonial challenges', p. 193.

48 Hall, 'Cosmopolitan promises, multicultural realities', p. 23.

Chapter 4   Expressing Merged Identities: Music

1 Denis-Constant Martin, 'The musical heritage of slavery: from creolization to "world music"', in Bob W. White (ed.), *Music and Globalization*, Bloomington: Indiana University Press, 2012, p. 17.

2 Tobias Green, 'The evolution of creole identity in Cape Verde', in Robin Cohen and Paola Toninato (eds), *The Creolization Reader: Studies in Mixed Identities and Cultures*, London: Routledge, p. 157.

3 Márcia Rego, 'Cape Verdean tongues: speaking of a "nation" at home and abroad', in L. Batalha and J. Carling (eds), *Transnational Archipelago: Perspectives on Cape Verdean Migration and Diaspora*, Amsterdam: Amsterdam University Press, 2008, pp. 145–59. See also Elizabeth Challinor, 'A history of Cape Verde: centre/periphery relations and transnational cultural flows', paper given at the International

Conference on Cape Verdean Migration and Diaspora in the Centro de Estudos de Antropologia Social (ISCTE), Lisbon, 6–8 April 2005.

4 Miguel Vale de Almeida, 'From miscegenation to Creole identity: Portuguese Colonialism, Brazil, Cape Verde', in C. Stewart (ed.), *Creolization: History, Ethnography, Theory*, Walnut Creek, CA: Left Coast Press, 2007, pp. 108–32. See also Challinor, 'A history of Cape Verde'.

5 PAICG is the African Party for the Independence of Cape Verde and Guinea-Bissau. The struggle for independence in Cape Verde was fought in Guinea Bissau and involved a strong alliance between anti-colonial forces in the two Portuguese colonies. Following a coup in Guinea-Bissau in November 1980, five years after independence was declared in Cape Verde (it had been declared in Guinea-Bissau in 1973), relations between the two countries became strained, and the party was renamed the African Party for the Independence of Cape Verde (PAICV).

6 Richard Lobban, *Cape Verde: Crioulo Colony to Independent Nation*, Boulder, CO: Westview Press, 1995, p. 61.

7 Lobban, *Cape Verde*, p. 129.

8 Nick Spitzer, 'Monde Creole: the cultural world of French Louisiana Creoles and the creolization of world cultures', in R. Baron and A. C. Cara (eds), *Creolization as Cultural Creativity*, Jackson: University Press of Mississippi, 2011, p. 44.

9 Challinor, 'A history of Cape Verde', p. 32.

10 Bayou is a Choctaw word alluding to the marshy stretches of water frequently found in the Mississippi delta, often difficult to penetrate. The bayous provided a rich marine life (crawfish, turtles and catfish) and were conducive to remote community formation on a very small scale, thus resembling the intermittent patterns of isolation and connectedness found in many creole island communities. See Robin Cohen and Olivia Sheringham, 'The salience of islands in the articulation of creolization and diaspora', *Diaspora: A Journal of Transnational Studies*, 17(1), 2008, pp. 6–17 (published in 2013).

11 John D. Folse, *The Encyclopedia of Cajun and Creole Cuisine*, Gonzales, LA: Chef John Folse & Company, 2005, p. 6.

12 See the discussion of 'mandingas' in Cape Verde below, where they assume a more wraithlike and less literal form.

13 Gwendolyn Midlo Hall, *Africans in Colonial Louisiana: The Development of Afro-Creole Culture in the Eighteenth Century*, Baton Rouge: Louisiana State University Press, 1992.

14 George Washington Cable, *The Grandissimes: A Story of Creole Life*, New York: Charles Scribner's Sons, 1880. The legal uses of the term 'Creole' and its changing definitions over time are well portrayed in Virginia Dominguez, *White by Definition: Social Classification in Creole Louisiana*, New Brunswick, NJ: Rutgers University Press, 1986.

15 Mark Mattern, 'Let the good times unroll: music and race relations in Southwest Louisiana', *Black Music Research Journal*, 17(2), 1997, p. 159.

16 Carl A. Brasseaux, *The Founding of New Acadia: The Beginnings of Acadian Life in Louisiana, 1765–1803*, Baton Rouge: Louisiana State University Press, 1987.

17 Susan E. Dollar, 'Ethnicity and Jim Crow: the Americanization of Louisiana's Creoles', in Michael S. Martin (ed.), *Louisiana beyond Black and White: New Interpretation of Twentieth-Century Race and Race Relations*, Lafayette: University of Louisiana at Lafayette Press, 2011, pp. 1–2.

18 Timothy Sieber, 'Popular music and cultural identity in the Cape Verdean post-colonial diaspora', *Etnográfica*, 9(1), 2005, pp. 123–48.

19 Fernando Arenas, *Lusophone Africa Beyond Independence*, Minneapolis: University of Minnesota Press, 2011, p. 45. See also Lobban, *Cape Verde*, and Sieber, 'Popular music'.

20 Lobban, *Cape Verde*, p. 78.

21 Sieber, 'Popular music', pp. 142–3; see also Arenas, *Lusophone Africa*, p. 65.

22 Fieldwork notes, February 2013; see also Arenas, *Lusophone Africa*, p. 69.

23 The *Coladeira* is often described as a faster paced *Morna*, with influences from Latin American rhythms such as the Colombian *cumbia* (Interview with Margarida Brito Martins, 5 February 2013; see also Arenas, *Lusophone Africa*, p. 67.) During fieldwork in Cape Verde, several interviewees spoke quite bitterly about Cesária Évora. While conceding that her success had brought international attention to Cape Verde and its music, it was argued that she had abandoned her compatriots and that her success had monopolized the Cape Verdean music scene and marginalized other, equally talented, musicians.

171

24 Arenas, *Lusophone Africa*, p. 102. See also C. F. Gonçalves, *Kab Verd Band*, Praia, Cape Verde: Instituto do Arquivo Histórico Nacional, 2006.
25 Gonçalves, *Kab Verd Band*, p. 17.
26 Gonçalves, *Kab Verd Band*, p. 17.
27 Interview with Margarida Brito Martins, 5 February 2013.
28 Margarida Brito, *Os Instrumentos Musicais em Cabo Verde*, Praia–Mindelo, Cape Verde: Centro Cultural Português, 1999.
29 This call-and-response pattern is common in African music and also forms an important component of music developed in the USA, field hollers, work gang chants, boat songs and spirituals being the most obvious examples.
30 Interview with Margarida Brito Martins, 5 February 2013. See also Gonçalves, *Kab Verd Band*, pp. 16–27, for an in-depth discussion of *Batuque*.
31 Lobban, *Cape Verde*, p. 78.
32 Lobban, *Cape Verde*, p. 82.
33 Arenas, *Lusophone Africa*, p. 80.
34 Short profiles can be found on the web at the following links: http://www.luracriola.com/ and http://www.bbc.co.uk/radio3/world-music/a4wm2008/2008_mayra_andrade.shtml.
35 Sieber, 'Popular music', p. 144.
36 Arenas, *Lusophone Africa*, p. 49.
37 Márcia Rego, 'Cape Verdean tongues: speaking of a "nation" at home and abroad', in L. Batalha and J. Carling (eds), *Transnational Archipelago: Perspectives on Cape Verdean Migration and Diaspora*, Amsterdam: Amsterdam University Press, 2008, p. 147.
38 Sieber, 'Popular music', p. 138.
39 Sieber, 'Popular music', p. 123.
40 This is the theme of Cesária Évora's famous song *Sodade* (Longing), which is virtually ubiquitously known in the diaspora. Its haunting character is hardly captured in this translation: Who will show you / this distant way? / Who will show you / this distant way? / This way / to São Tomé? // The longing, the longing / The longing / For this land of mine, São Nicolau // If you write me letter / I will write you back / If you forget me / I will forget you. // Until the day / You come back. (This translation found at: http://lyricstranslate.com).
41 Fieldwork notes; see also JoAnne Hoffman, 'Diasporic networks,

political change, and the growth of cabo-zouk music', in L. Batalha and J. Carling (eds), *Transnational Archipelago: Perspectives on Cape Verdean Migration and Diaspora*, Amsterdam: Amsterdam University Press, 2008,pp. 205–20.

42 It is interesting to note the similar historical and cultural 'roots' of both Antillean *Zouk* and Cape Verdean *Cabo-Zouk*. As Hoffman, 'Diasporic networks', pp. 209–10, observes, Cape Verdeans related very strongly to this Antillean style, 'not simply because of the similar rhythms, but similar colonial pasts, including slavery'.

43 JoAnne Hoffman, 'Diasporic networks', p. 207 and p. 211. See also Timothy Sieber, 'Popular music'.

44 Lester Sullivan, 'Composers of color of nineteenth-century New Orleans.' In Sybil Kein (ed.) *Creole: The History and Legacy of Louisiana's Free People of Color*, Baton Rouge: Louisiana State University Press, 2005, p. 77.

45 Sybil Kein (ed.), *Creole: The History and Legacy of Louisiana's Free People of Color*, Baton Rouge: Louisiana State University Press, 2000, pp. 12–13. She translates 'crapo' as frog, but we surmise the reference is to a cane toad, a large, ugly toad used in the sugar cane fields to control pests.

46 Gary A. Donaldson, 'A window on slave culture: dances at Congo square in New Orleans, 1800–1862', *Journal of Negro History*, 69(2), 1984, pp. 64, 65.

47 James Lincoln Collier, *The Making of Jazz: A Comprehensive History*, London: Macmillan, 1984, p. 43.

48 'Jelly Roll' is black slang for a woman's labia. Morton's exploits were described as a 'litany of misadventure'. He was a 'pimp', 'hustler', 'poolshark', 'gambler', 'sensitive', 'ebullient', 'a braggart', among many other descriptions (see Lincoln Collier, *The Making of Jazz*, p. 95, 96). Billie Holiday was an alcoholic, insatiable drug-taker and masochist. Charlie Parker was addicted to heroin and died aged 34.

49 Barry Jean Ancelet, 'Zydeco/zarico: the term and the tradition', in James H. Dorman (ed.), *Creoles of Color of the Gulf South*, Knoxville: University of Tennessee Press, 1996, pp. 126–143; and Hubert Daniel Singleton, *The Indians who Gave Us Zydeco: The Atakapas–Ishaks (a-TAK-a-paws EE-shaks) of Southwest Louisiana and Southeast Texas*, Place of publication unstated: Author, 1998.

50 Ancelet, 'Zydeco/zarico', p. 139.

51 Mark Mattern, 'Let the good times unroll: music and race relations in Southwest Louisiana', *Black Music Research Journal*, 17(2), 1997, pp. 159, 151–2.

52 St Landry Parish Tourist Commission, *We Live Our Culture* (Tourist Brochure), Opelousas: SLPTC, 2013. In Louisiana, boudin is usually a white sausage, without blood. Cracklins comprise pork skin, refried in pork lard. Both are Cajun dishes. Étouffée is a thick shellfish sauce 'smothering' a base of rice, and claimed by both Cajuns and Creoles. Yams are associated with West Africa, but are sometimes confused with sweet potatoes in Louisiana.

53 R. Reese Fuller, *Angola to Zydeco: Louisiana Lives*, Jackson: University Press of Mississippi, 2001, p. 60.

54 Frank A. Salamone, 'Nigerian and Ghanaian popular music: two varieties of creolization', *The Journal of Popular Culture*, 32(2), 1998, p. 22.

55 George Lipsitz, *Dangerous Crossroads: Popular Music, Postmodernism and the Poetics of Place*, London: Verso, 1994, p. 36.

Chapter 5   Celebrating and Resisting: Carnival

1 Abner Cohen, 'A polyethnic London carnival as a contested cultural performance', *Ethnic and Racial Studies*, 5(1), 1982, p. 34.

2 Mikhail Bakhtin, *Rabelais and his World*, Bloomington: Indiana University Press, 1984, p. 10.

3 Bakhtin, *Rabelais and his World*, p. 10.

4 Daniel J. Crowley, 'The sacred and the profane in African and African-derived carnivals', *Western Folklore*, 58(3/4), 1999, p. 224.

5 Adela Ruth Tompsett, '"London is the place for me": performance and identity in Notting Hill Carnival', *Theatre History Studies*, 25, 2005, p. 43.

6 Peter Jackson, 'Street life: the politics of carnival', *Environment and Planning D: Society and Space*, 8, 1988, p. 213.

7 Toni Weiss, 'The economic impact of the Mardi Gras season on the New Orleans economy and the net fiscal benefit of staging Mardi Gras for the city of New Orleans', unpublished paper prepared for the Carnival Krewe Civic Foundation, Inc., New Orleans, 2001, p. 20.

8 Kevin Fox Gotham, 'Marketing Mardi Gras: commodification,

spectacle and the political economy of tourism in New Orleans', *Urban Studies*, 39(10), 2002, pp. 1735, 1752–3.

9 Wesley Shrum and John Kilburn, 'Ritual disrobement at Mardi Gras: ceremonial exchange and moral order', *Social Forces*, 75(2), 1996, pp. 423–58.

10 George Lipsitz, 'Mardi Gras Indians: carnival and counter-narrative in black New Orleans', *Cultural Critique*, 10, 1988, p. 115.

11 Roger D. Abrahams, with Nick Spitzer, John F. Szwed and Robert Farris Thompson, *Blues for New Orleans: Mardi Gras and America's Creole Soul*, Philadelphia: University of Pennsylvania Press, 2006, pp. 71–2.

12 Joseph Roach, 'Mardi Gras Indians and others: genealogies of American performance', *Theatre Journal*, 44(4), 1992, pp. 469, 478.

13 Abrahams et al., *Blues for New Orleans*, p. 75.

14 Nicholas R. Spitzer, 'Mardi Gras in l'Anse de 'Prien Noir: a Creole community performance in rural French Louisiana', in James H. Dorman (ed.), *Creoles of Colour of the Gulf South*, Knoxville: University of Tennessee Press, 1996, pp. 88, 95 et seq.

15 Carolyn E. Ware, 'Anything to act crazy: Cajun women and Mardi Gras disguise', *Journal of American Folklore*, 114(452), 2001, pp. 225–47.

16 João Manuel Chantre, 'Opinião: a industria do carnaval', Expresso das Ilhas, 11 March 2011; http://www.expressodasilhas.sapo.cv/opiniao/item/23578-opiniao--a-industria-do-carnaval.

17 Roger D. Abrahams, 'Questions of criolian contagion', *Journal of American Folklore*, 116(459), 2003, pp. 73–87.

18 Lyrics on the Café Atlántico album. Quoted in Fernando Arenas, *Lusophone Africa beyond Independence*, Minneapolis: University of Minnesota Press, 2011, p. 76.

19 Moacyr Rodrigues, cited in *A Nação*, 'Carnaval: "Mandingas" na verdade são Bijagós' (online edition 27 January 2013); http://www.alfa.cv/anacao_online/index.php/destaque/4119-carnaval-mandingas-na-verdade-sao-bijagos.

20 Robert Baron and Ana C. Cara, 'Introduction: creolization and folklore: cultural creativity in process', *Journal of American Folklore*, 116(459), 2003, pp. 4–8.

21 Michel de Certeau, *The Practice of Everyday Life*, trans. S. Rendall, Berkeley: University of California Press, 1984, pp. 91–110.

22 Lord Kitchener (Alwyn Robert), 'London is the place for me', London: Honest Jon's Records Ltd, 2002.

23 Tompsett, '"London is the place for me"', p. 43.

24 Jackson, 'Street life: the politics of carnival', p. 214.

25 Richard D. E. Burton, 'Cricket, carnival and street culture in the Caribbean', *The International Journal of the History of Sport*, 2(2), 1985, pp. 179–97.

26 Cohen, 'A polyethnic London carnival', p. 35; see also Jackson, 'Street life: the politics of carnival', p. 215.

27 See http://thelondonnottinghillcarnival.com/about.html for a brief history of the Notting Hill Carnival.

28 Rhaune Laslett, quoted in Esther Peeren, 'Carnival politics and the territory of the street', *Thamyris/Intersecting*, 14, 2007, p. 70.

29 Jackson, 'Street life: the politics of carnival', p. 221.

30 Tompsett, '"London is the place for me"', p. 49.

31 'Mas bands' is the term used to denote the different groups of artists and performers that participate in carnival. 'Mas' is an abbreviation of masquerade.

32 See http://www.carnaval.com/london/2008/bands/.

33 Mariana Pinho, 'Escolas brasileiras brilham no carnaval londrino de Notting Hill'; http://www.portugues.rfi.fr/geral/20140825-car naval-de-notting-hill-tem-apresentacoes-de-escolas-brasileiras.

34 Kwesi Owusu, *Struggle for Black Arts in Britain: What Can We Consider Better Than Freedom?* London: Cengage Learning, 1986, p. 8.

35 Melissa Butcher, 'Negotiating Notting Hill'. OpenLearn, Open University Podcast, 2009; http://www.open.edu/openlearn/soci ety/politics-policy-people/sociology/negotiating-notting-hill.

36 Martin Coomer, interview with Hew Locke; http://www.timeout. com/london/art/hew-locke-interview-this-is-about-trying-to-get-to-an-essence-of-carnival.

37 Tompsett, '"London is the place for me"', p. 43.

38 Cohen, 'A polyethnic London carnival', p. 35.

39 Robin Cohen, 'A diaspora of a diaspora? The case of the Caribbean', *Social Science Information*, 31(1), 1992, pp. 193–203.

40 The phrase was popularized in the well-known work by Paul Gilroy, *The Empire Strikes Back, Race and Racism in 70s Britain*, London: Hutchinson, 1982.

41 'To create is to resist, to resist is to create.' This is the inspiring,

but exaggerated, sentiment at the end of the pamphlet that energized the 'Occupy movement'. See Stéphane Hessel, *Time for Outrage
(Indignez-vous)*, London: Charles Glass Books, p. 37.

42 Carole-Anne Upton, 'Why performance matters', *Performance Arts*,
Bristol: Intellect Books, 2013, p. 23.

Chapter 6   Constructing Heritage

1 Eric Hobsbawm and Terence Ranger (eds), *The Invention of Tradition*,
Cambridge: Cambridge University Press, 1983.

2 The full extent of the distortion of facts can be found at: http://
www.scottishhistory.com/articles/independence/braveheart.html.

3 Megan Vaughan, *Creating the Creole Island: Slavery in Eighteenth-
century Mauritius*, Durham, NC: Duke University Press, 2005,
p. 2.

4 Bernardin de Saint-Pierre, *Journey to Mauritius*, trans. and ed. Jason
Wilson, Oxford: Signal Books, 2002, pp. 122, 123 (first published in
1773).

5 Our thanks to Thomas Hylland Eriksen for this information.

6 Jawaharlal Nehru, *India's Foreign Policy: Selected Speeches, September
1946–April 1961*, Delhi: Government of India, 1961, p. 130.

7 Adele Smith Simmons, *Modern Mauritius: The Politics of Decolonization*,
Bloomington: Indiana University Press, 1982, pp. 35–44.

8 Cited in Smith Simmons, *Modern Mauritius*, p. 77.

9 We are dependent on the taxonomy provided by Rosebelle Boswell,
Le Malaise Créole: Ethnic Identity in Mauritius, New York: Berghahn
Books, 2006, pp. 46–54. We have not added, and perhaps we should,
the *Créole Ilois*, referring to the Chagos islanders who were forced
out of Diego Garcia when the British leased the island to the USA
as a military base. Most ended up in the slums of Port Louis, the
capital of Mauritius, displaced and dispossessed and prone to criminality and violence. This shocking story of colonial betrayal is told in
Laura Jeffrey, *Chagos Islanders in Mauritius and the UK*, Manchester:
Manchester University Press, 2011.

10 Patrick Eisenlohr, *Little India: Diaspora, Time and Ethnolinguistic
Belonging in Hindu Mauritius*, Berkeley: University of California Press,
2007, pp. 4–5. Though they have some similarities, Bhojpuri and
Hindi are spoken in different parts of India and use a different form

of writing. By promoting Hindi in Mauritius, the Indian government is also implicitly elevating it above the vernacular.

11 The slogan 'India Shining' was promoted by the Indian government in 2004. Some US$20 million was spent on this rebranding of the country.

12 Rosebelle Boswell, 'Heritage tourism and identity in the Mauritian villages of Chamarel and Le Morne', *Journal of Southern African Studies*, 31(2), 2005, p. 294.

13 Roger Moss, *Le Morne/Lemorn*, bi-lingual English/Kreol edition, Port Louis: Ledikasyon pu Travayer, 2000, pp. 2–4.

14 Nick Spitzer, 'Monde Creole: the cultural world of French Louisiana Creoles and the creolization of world cultures', in R. Baron and A. C. Cara (eds), *Creolization as Cultural Creativity*, Jackson: University Press of Mississippi, 2011, p. 58.

15 Gary B. Mills, *The Forgotten People: Cane River's Creoles of Colour*, Baton Rouge: Louisiana State University Press, 1977; Elizabeth Shown Mills, *Isle of Canes. A Historical Novel*, Provo, UT: MyFamily. com Inc., 2004.

16 Gary B. Mills, *The Forgotten People*, p. 45.

17 Kathleen M. Byrd, *Colonial Natchitoches: Outpost of Empires*, Bloomington, IN: Xlibris, 2008, p. 154.

18 Gary B. Mills, *The Forgotten People*, p. 194.

19 http://en.wikipedia.org/wiki/List_of_Louisiana_Creoles.

20 Robin Cohen, 'Creolization and cultural globalization: the soft sounds of fugitive power', *Globalizations*, 4(3), 2007, p. 378.

21 Richard Seale, Robert DeBlieux and Harlan Mark Guidry, *Natchitoches and Louisiana's Timeless Cane River*, Baton Rouge: Louisiana State University Press, 2002, p. 119.

22 This 'recipe' for 'Creole Gumbo', created by Josie La Cour and Michelle Pichon, is on display at the Creole Heritage Center, Northwestern State University of Louisiana. With variations it is found on serviettes (napkins) and guidebooks.

23 See http://www.lalitmauritius.org/, where the activities of Lalit are described. The site also has a useful dictionary.

24 Arnaud Carpooran, *Diksioner morisien*, Paris: Editions Bartholdi, 2005.

25 See, for example, Vijaya Teelock, *Mauritian History: From Its Beginnings to Modern Times*, Mauritius: Mahatma Gandhi Institute, 2001.

26 Boswell, 'Heritage tourism and identity', p. 294.

27 These comments derive from private correspondence with Thomas Hylland Eriksen.

28 He did not precisely propose this, but Ulf Hannerz's pioneering article, 'The world in creolization', *Africa*, 57(4), pp. 546–59, evokes this possible trajectory.

29 Peggy Levitt, *Artifacts and Allegiances: How Museums Put the Nation and the World on Display*, Oakland: University of California Press, 2015, p. 141.

30 We say this with confidence, as Robin Cohen had occasion to act as an external examiner for students at the University of Mauritius for several years.

31 The expression 'culture of poverty' was coined more than 50 years ago by Oscar Lewis, who had worked with poor families in Puerto Rico. It was taken up by Daniel Moynihan much later on to describe what he thought were dysfunctional African American families. This caused an immediate storm of protest, accusations of racism and academic critiques pointing to the wider structural causes of poverty. Certainly, we do not wish to give any comfort to policy-makers who use 'the culture of poverty' or '*le malaise Créole*' as an excuse to say 'nothing can be done' or, even worse, 'nothing should be done'. At the same time, it should be added that Oscar Lewis was rather maligned – he was trying to illuminate the coping mechanisms of the poor, not justify their poverty.

Chapter 7 Marking Identities:
The Cultural Politics of Multiple Loyalties

1 Katherine E. Browne, *Creole Economics: Caribbean Cunning under the French Flag*, Austin: University of Texas Press, 2004, p. 223.

2 William Miles, 'When is a nation "a nation"? Identity-formation within a French West Indian people (Martinique)', *Nations and Nationalism* 12(4), 2006, p. 637.

3 Richard D. E. Burton, 'The French West Indies *à l'heure de l'Europe*', in Richard D. E Burton and Fred Reno (eds), *French and West Indian: Martinique, Guadeloupe and French Guiana Today*, Basingstoke: Macmillan, 1995, p. 2.

4 It should be remembered that de Gaulle and the Free French started

their fight back against the Nazis from the colonies, a display of loyalty that de Gaulle always recognized. The Free French cause was strongly favoured by the majority of Martinicans, though a small upper class of whites (*békés*) supported the Vichy regime.

5 *Francophonie* is driven by a central organization that holds a summit every two years, and smaller network organizations that promote special ties between all 'francophones'. The notion of *francophonie* reflects the extent of France's influence over its overseas possessions and ex-colonies.

6 The most recent referendum was in 2010, when Martinicans were asked to vote on becoming an 'Overseas Collectivity', and thus having more autonomy. The proposal was massively rejected, with 79 per cent voting against the proposal on a turn-out of 55 per cent. See William Miles, 'Schizophrenic island, fifty years after Fanon: Martinique, the pent-up "paradise"', *International Journal of Francophone Studies*, 15(1), 2013, p. 24.

7 Christine Chivallon, 'Guadeloupe et Martinique en lutte contre la "profitation": du caractère nouveau d'une histoire ancienne', *Justice Spatiale/Spatial Justice*, 1, 2009, pp. 1–14; online journal: http://www.jssj.org/wp-content/uploads/2012/12/JSS1-7fr1.pdf.

8 *Békés*, the direct descendants of white colonists and slave masters, represent less than 1 percent of the inhabitants of the island, but own more than 40 per cent of the land.

9 Interviews on the island were conducted by Olivia Sheringham, whose fieldwork coincided with the French presidential elections in 2012, when there was a pronounced sense of disillusionment with mainland politics. One elderly man from the small fishing village Petite Anse remarked, 'What's the point in voting? It makes no difference. They're all the same', while another woman from Fort-de-France said, 'They come here to sweeten us up, to win our votes. But once they're in power they forget about us. They don't care about Martinique.'

10 Chivallon, 'Guadeloupe et Martinique en lutte', p. 9.

11 Richard Price, *The Convict and the Colonel*, Durham, NC: Duke University Press, 1998, p. 213.

12 Édouard Glissant, *Caribbean Discourse: Selected Essays*, trans. J. Michael Dash, Charlottesville: University Press of Virginia. 1989, p. 193 (originally published in French by Gallimard, 1981).

13 Richard Burton, 'The idea of difference in contemporary West Indian thought: négritude, antillanité, créolité', in Richard D. E Burton and Fred Reno (eds), *French and West Indian: Martinique, Guadeloupe and French Guiana Today*, Basingstoke: Macmillan, 1995, p. 140.

14 Shireen Lewis, *Race, Culture, and Identity: Francophone West African and Caribbean Literature and Theory from Négritude to Créolité*, Lanham, NJ: Lexington Books, 2006, p. xviii.

15 See Browne, *Creole Economics*, p. 92. Browne draws on the insights of Elizabeth Ezra who examines the 'colonial unconscious' and argues that beneath the surface of public discourses of assimilations, there lies 'a strong ambivalence towards colonial subjects and a latent but powerful desire for cultural separation'. See Elizabeth Ezra, *The Colonial Unconscious: Race and Culture in Interwar France*, Ithaca, NY: Cornell University Press, 2000, p. 153, cited in Browne, *Creole Economics*, p. 236.

16 Burton, 'The idea of difference in contemporary West Indian thought', p. 141.

17 Jean-Paul Sartre, 'Black Orpheus', *The Massachusetts Review*, 6, 1964, p. 18 (originally published in French by Presses universitaires de Frances, 1948), trans. J. MacCombie.

18 Mireille Rosello, 'Introduction: Aimé Césaire and the Notebook of a Return to my Native Land in the 1990s', in *Notebook of a Return to my Native Land*, trans. M. Rosello and W. Pritchard, Newcastle-upon-Tyne: Bloodaxe Books, 1995, p. 12 (originally published in French by Editions présence africaine, 1956).

19 Michel Giraud, 'Les identités antillaises entre négritude et créolité', *Cahiers des Amériques Latines*, 17, 1994, p. 145.

20 Jean Bernabé, Patrick Chamoiseau and Raphaël Confiant, *Éloge de la créolité*, Paris: Gallimard, 1989, pp. 13, 27.

21 Celia Britton, 'The créolité movement in Martinique: authenticity and/or exoticism?', presented at a conference, 'Islands and Identities: Creolization and Diaspora in Comparative Perspective', University of Oxford, 6–7 December 2012.

22 Giraud, 'Les identités antillaises'.

23 Richard Price and Sally Price, 'Shadowboxing in the mangrove', *Cultural Anthropology*, 12, 1997, p. 15; Britton, 'The créolité movement in Martinique', p. 5.

24 Édouard Glissant, *Poetics of Relation*, trans. Betsy Wing, Ann Arbor:

University of Michigan Press, 1997, p. 90 (originally published as *Poétique de la Relation (Poétique III)*, Paris: Gallimard, 1990).

25 Glissant, *Caribbean Discourse*, pp. 105–6.

26 We use the literal translation 'concretization', from the French word *béton* meaning 'concrete'. The term *'bétonisation'* is used in Martinique and Guadeloupe to refer to the 'remorseless spread of concrete in the form of hypermarkets and housing developments, *résidences secondaires*, motorways and service roads, hotels and marinas across the countryside and beaches of the two islands': Burton, 'The idea of difference in contemporary West Indian thought', p. 140.

27 Price, *The Convict and the Colonel*, p. 180; see also Patrick Chamoiseau, *Écrire en pays dominé*, Paris: Gallimard, 1997, pp. 69–70 (Olivia Sheringham's translation).

28 Renée Gosson, 'What lies beneath? Cultural excavation in neocolonial Martinique', in S. Hood-Washington, P. Rosier and H. G. Lanham (eds), *Echoes from the Poisoned Well: Global Memories of Environmental Injustice*, Lanham, MD: Rowman & Littlefield, 2006, p. 226.

29 Adlai Murdoch, 'Édouard Glissant's creolized world vision: from resistance and relation to *opacité*', *Callaloo*, 6(4), 2013, p. 881.

30 From the verb *embellir*, meaning to embellish or beautify.

31 See Aisha Khan, 'Journey to the center of the earth: the Caribbean as master symbol', *Cultural Anthropology*, 16(3), 2001, pp. 271–302.

32 Burton, 'The French West Indies *à l'heure de l'Europe*', p. 5.

33 Price and Price, 'Shadowboxing in the mangrove', p. 14; Browne, *Creole Economics*, p. 98.

34 Richard Price and Sally Price, 'Shadowboxing in the mangrove', p. 14.

35 Burton, 'The French West Indies *à l'heure de l'Europe*', p. 12.

36 Murdoch, 'Édouard Glissant's creolized world vision', p. 312.

37 Michael Dash, 'Introduction', in Glissant, *Caribbean Discourse*, p. xxv.

38 René Ménil, *Antilles déjà jadis: précédé de tracées*. Paris: Place, 1999, p. 29, cited in Murdoch, 'Édouard Glissant's creolized world vision', p. 308 (Olivia Sheringham's translation).

39 Natalia K. Bremner, 'Looking elsewhere: the construction of cultural identity in Réunion and Mauritius,' MA thesis, University of Leeds,

Department of French, School of Modern Languages and Cultures, 2010, p. 83.

40 William Miles, 'When is a nation "a nation?"', p. 649.

Chapter 8   *Encountering Difference: A Conclusion*

1 Stuart Hall, 'Living with difference: Stuart Hall in conversation with Bill Schwarz', *Soundings: A Journal of Politics and Culture*, 37, 2007, p. 155.

2 Mark Wallace, 'Introduction', in *Paul Ricoeur: Figuring the Sacred: Religion, Narrative, Imagination*, Minneapolis, MN: Fortress Press, 1995, p. 11.

3 For further discussion of creolization as a form of de-centring and de-colonizing Euro-American theory, see Shu-mei Shih and Françoise Lionnet, 'Introduction: the creolization of theory', in Françoise Lionnet and Shu-mei Shih (eds), *The Creolization of Theory*, Durham, NC: Duke University Press, 2011, pp. 1–33.

4 Michel-Rolph Trouillot, 'Culture on the edges: creolization in the plantation context', *Plantation Society in the* Americas, 5(1), 1998, p. 8.

5 C. Magbaily Fyle, 'Official and unofficial attitudes and policy towards Krio as the main lingua franca in Sierra Leone', in Richard Farndon and Graham Furniss (eds), *African Languages, Development and the State*, London: Routledge, 1994, pp. 44–54.

6 We rely here on Gananath Obeyesekere's key work, *Cannibal Talk: The Man-Eating Myth and Human Sacrifice in the South Seas*, Berkeley: University of California Press, 2005.

7 Mary Louise Pratt, *Imperial Eyes: Travel Writing and Transculturation*, London: Routledge, 2008, p. 7.

8 Robin Cohen and Olivia Sheringham, 'The salience of islands in the articulation of creolization and diaspora', *Diaspora: A Journal of Transnational Studies* 17(1), 2008, pp. 6–17 (published in 2013).

9 Ralph Crane, '"Amid the alien corn": British India as human island', in Maeve McCusker and Anthony Soares (eds), *Islanded Identities: Constructions of Postcolonial Cultural Insularity*, Amsterdam: Rodopi, 2011, p. 128.

10 Margaret J. Kartomi, 'The processes and results of musical culture

contact: a discussion of terminology and concepts', *Ethnomusicology*, 25(2), 1981, pp. 244–5.

11 Frank A. Salamone, 'Nigerian and Ghanaian popular music: two varieties of creolization', *The Journal of Popular Culture*, 32 (2), 1998, p. 22.

12 See Hélène Neveu Kringelbach and Jonathan Skinner (eds), *Dancing Cultures: Globalization, Tourism and Identity in the Anthropology of Dance*, Oxford: Berghahn, 2012.

13 One scholar suggests that Feuerbach's graphic phrase has been taken too literally and he did not quite mean it. See Melvin Cherno, 'Feuerbach's "Man is what he eats": a rectification', *Journal of the History of Ideas*, 24(3), 1963, pp. 397–406.

14 We evoke Hegel again. See Robin Cohen, 'Althusser meets Anancy: structuralism and popular protest in Ken Post's history of Jamaica', *The Sociological Review*, 30(2), 1982, pp. 345–57.

15 Ferdinand de Jong, 'Hybrid heritage', *African Arts*, Winter 2009, pp. 1–5.

16 Cheikh Anta Diop, *The African Origin of Civilization: Myth or Reality*, trans. Mercer Cook, New York: L. Hill, 1974; Martin Bernal, *Black Athena: The Afroasiatic Roots of Classical Civilization*, 3 vols, New Brunswick, NJ: Rutgers University Press (1987, 1991, 2006). There is a substantial critical literature opposing or modifying Diop's and Bernal's theses.

17 Aimé Césaire, *Notebook of a Return to My Native Land*, trans. Mireille Rosello and Annie Pritchard, Newcastle-upon-Tyne: Bloodaxe Books, 1995, pp. 89–90.

18 See Jürgen Habermas, 'The public sphere', *New German Critique*, 3, 1974, pp. 49–55, for the distinction between public and private spheres. We have added the ambivalent sphere.

19 Susanne Wessendorf, *Commonplace Diversity: Social Relations in a Super-Diverse Context*, London: Palgrave Macmillan, 2014.

20 Ben Gidley, 'Landscapes of belonging, portraits of life: researching everyday multiculture in an inner city estate', *Identities: Global Studies in Culture and Power*, 20(4), 2013, p. 367.

21 Steven Vertovec and Robin Cohen, 'Introduction', in Steven Vertovec and Robin Cohen (eds), *Conceiving Cosmopolitanism: Theory, Context And Practice*, Oxford: Oxford University Press, 2002, p. 5.

22 Paul Gilroy, *Postcolonial Melancholia*, New York: Columbia University Press, 2004, p. xv.

23 Elijah Anderson, 'The cosmopolitan canopy', *Annals of the American Academy of Political and Social Science*, 595, 2004, pp. 14–31.

24 Gilroy, *Postcolonial Melancholia*, p. xii.

25 Robin Cohen, 'Social identities, diaspora and creolization', in Kim Knott and Seán McLoughlin (eds), *Diasporas: Concepts, Identities, Intersections*, London: Zed Books, 2010, p. 73. A bold attempt to apply the concept of creolization to various European sites can be found in Encarnación Gutiérrez Rodríguez and Shirley Anne Tate (eds), *Creolizing Europe: Legacies and Transformations*, Liverpool: Liverpool University Press, 2015.

26 Mimi Sheller, 'Creolization in discourses of global culture', in Sara Ahmed, Claudia Castaneda and Anne-Marie Fortier (eds), *Uprootings/Regroundings: Questions of Home and Migration*, Oxford: Berg Publishers, 2003, p. 284.

27 Thanks to Thomas Hylland Eriksen for elaborating this point (private correspondence).

28 Hall, 'Living with difference', pp. 148–58.

29 Cited in Raphaël Confiant, Jean Bernabé and Lucien Taylor, 'Créolité bites', *Transition*, 74, 1997, p. 160.

Bibliography

A Nação (2013) 'Carnaval: "Mandingas" na verdade são Bijagós', online edition 27 January; http://www.alfa.cv/anacao_online/index.php/destaque/4119-carnaval-mandingas-na-verdade-sao-bijagos.

Abrahams, Roger D. (2003) 'Questions of criolian contagion', *Journal of American Folklore*, 116(459), 73–87.

Abrahams, Roger D., with Nick Spitzer, John F. Szwed and Robert Farris Thompson (2006) *Blues for New Orleans: Mardi Gras and America's Creole Soul*, Philadelphia: University of Pennsylvania Press.

Allen, Anita L. and Michael R. Seidl (1995) 'Cross-cultural commerce in Shakespeare's *The Merchant of Venice*', *American University International Law Review*, 10(2), 837–59.

Ancelet, Barry Jean (1996) 'Zydeco/zarico: the term and the tradition', in James H. Dorman (ed.), *Creoles of Color of the Gulf South*, Knoxville: University of Tennessee Press, 126–143.

Anderson, Benedict (1983) *Imagined Communities. Reflections on the Origin and Spread of Nationalism*, London: Verso.

Anderson, Elijah (2004) 'The cosmopolitan canopy', *Annals of the American Academy of Political and Social Science*, 595, 14–31.

Anon (2007) 'Spice routes: Cladia Roden's culinary diaspora', *New Yorker*, 5 September 2007; http://www.newyorker.com/magazine/2007/09/03/spice-routes.

Arenas, Fernando (2011) *Lusophone Africa beyond Independence*, Minneapolis: University of Minnesota Press.

Arens, William (1979) *The Man-Eating Myth: Anthropology and Anthropophagy*, New York: Oxford University Press.

Atterbury, Paul (n.d.) 'Steam and speed: industry, power & social change in nineteenth century Britain'; http://www.vam.ac.uk/content/articles/s/industry-power-and-social-change/.

Axtell, James (2001) *Natives and Newcomers: The Cultural Origins of North America*, New York: Oxford University Press.

Bakhtin, Mikhail (1984) *Rabelais and his World*, Bloomington: Indiana University Press.

Baron, Robert and Ana C. Cara (2003) 'Introduction: creolization and folklore: cultural creativity in process', *Journal of American Folklore*, 116(459), 4–8.

Benítez-Rojo, Antonio (1996) *The Repeating Island: The Caribbean and the Postmodern Perspective*, Durham, NC: Duke University Press.

Benson, Michaela and Karen O'Reilly (eds) (2009) *Lifestyle Migration: Expectations, Aspirations and Experiences*, Farnham: Ashgate.

Berg, Mette Louise and Nando Sigona (2013) 'Ethnography, diversity and urban space', *Identities: Global Studies in Culture and Power*, 20(4), 347–60.

Berger, Peter L. and Thomas Luckmann (1967) *The Social Construction of Reality: A Treatise in the Sociology of Knowledge*, New York: Anchor.

Bernabé, Jean, Patrick Chamoiseau and Raphaël Confiant (1989) *Éloge de la créolité*, Paris: Gallimard.

Bernal Martin (1987, 1991, 2006) *Black Athena: The Afroasiatic Roots of Classical Civilization*, 3 vols, New Brunswick, NJ: Rutgers University Press.

Bhabha, Homi K. (1985) 'Signs taken for wonders: questions of ambivalence and authority under a tree outside Delhi, May 1817', *Critical Inquiry*, 12(1), 144–65.

Bickerton, Derek (2008) *Bastard Tongues: A Trailblazing Linguist Finds Clues to Our Common Humanity in the World's Lowliest Languages*, New York: Hill and Wang.

Blunt, Alison and Jayani Bonnerjee (2013) 'Home, city and diaspora: Anglo–Indian and Chinese attachments to Calcutta', *Global Networks*, 13(2), 220–40.

Boswell, Rosebelle (2005) 'Heritage tourism and identity in the Mauritian villages of Chamarel and Le Morne', *Journal of Southern African Studies*, 31(2), 283–95.

Boswell, Rosebelle (2006) *Le Malaise Créole: Ethnic Identity in Mauritius*, New York: Berghahn Books.

Bradshaw, Peter (2012) 'London: the modern Babylon – review', *Guardian*, 2 August.

Brasseaux, Carl A. (1987) *The Founding of New Acadia: The Beginnings of Acadian Life in Louisiana, 1765–1803*, Baton Rouge: Louisiana State University Press.

Bremner, N. K. (2010) 'Looking elsewhere: the construction of cultural identity in Réunion and Mauritius', MA thesis, University of Leeds, Department of French, School of Modern Languages and Cultures.

Brito, Margarida (1999) *Os Instrumentos Musicais em Cabo Verde*, Praia–Mindelo, Cape Verde: Centro Cultural Português.

Britton, Celia (2012) 'The créolité movement in Martinique: authenticity and/or exoticism?' Presented at a conference 'Islands and Identities: Creolization and Diaspora in Comparative Perspective', University of Oxford, 6–7 December.

Browne, Katherine E. (2004) *Creole Economics: Caribbean Cunning under the French Flag*, Austin: University of Texas Press.

Brubaker, Rogers (2005) 'The "diaspora" diaspora', *Ethnic and Racial Studies*, 28(1), 1–19.

Burton, Richard D. E. (1985) 'Cricket, carnival and street culture in the Caribbean', *The International Journal of the History of Sport*, 2(2), 179–97.

Burton, Richard D. E. (1995) 'The French West Indies *à l'heure de l'Europe*: an overview', in Richard D. E. Burton and Fred Reno (eds), *French and West Indian: Martinique, Guadeloupe, and French Guiana Today*, Basingstoke: Macmillan, 1–19.

Burton, Richard D. E. (1995) 'The idea of difference in contemporary West Indian thought: négritude, antillanité, créolité', in Richard D. E. Burton, and Fred Reno (eds), *French and West Indian: Martinique, Guadeloupe and French Guiana Today*, Basingstoke: Macmillan, 137–66.

Butcher, Melissa (2009) 'Negotiating Notting Hill', OpenLearn, Open University Podcast; http://www.open.edu/openlearn/society/poli tics-policy-people/sociology/negotiating-notting-hill.

Byrd, Kathleen M. (2008) *Colonial Natchitoches: Outpost of Empires*, Bloomington, IN: Xlibris.

Cable, George Washington (1880) *The Grandissimes: A Story of Creole Life*, New York: Charles Scribner's Sons.

Cantle, Ted (2012) *Interculturalism: The New Era of Cohesion and Diversity*, Basingstoke: Palgrave Macmillan.

Carpooran, Arnaud (2005) *Diksioner morisien*, Paris: Editions Bartholdi.

Césaire, Aimé (1995) *Notebook of a Return to My Native Land*, trans. Mireille Rosello and Annie Pritchard, Newcastle-upon-Tyne: Bloodaxe Books.

Challinor, Elizabeth (2005) 'A history of Cape Verde: centre/periphery relations and transnational cultural flows', paper given at the International Conference on Cape Verdean Migration and Diaspora in the Centro de Estudos de Antropologia Social (ISCTE), Lisbon, 6–8 April.

Chamoiseau, Patrick (1997) *Écrire en pays dominé*. Paris: Gallimard.

Chantre, João Manuel (2011) 'Opinião: a industria do carnaval', *Expresso das Ilhas*, 11 March; http://www.expressodasilhas.sapo.cv/opiniao/item/23578-opiniao--a-industria-do-carnaval.

Chariandy, David (2006) 'Postcolonial diasporas', *Postcolonial Text*, 2(1); online journal: http://journals.sfu.ca/pocol/index.php/pct/article/view/440/159).

Cherno, Melvin (1963) 'Feuerbach's "Man is what he eats": a rectification', *Journal of the History of Ideas*, 24(3), 397–406.

Chivallon, Christine (2009) Guadeloupe et Martinique en lutte contre la 'profitation': du caractère nouveau d'une histoire ancienne, *Justice Spatiale/Spatial Justice* 1, 1–14; online journal: http://www.jssj.org/article/guadeloupe-et-martinique-en-lutte-contre-la-profitation-du-caractere-nouveau-dune-histoire-ancienne/.

Cledinnen, Inga (2005) *Dancing with Strangers: The True History of the Meeting of the British First Fleet and the Aboriginal Australians, 1788*, Edinburgh: Canongate.

Cohen, Abner. (1982) 'A polyethnic London carnival as a contested cultural performance', *Ethnic and Racial Studies*, 5(1), 23–41.

Cohen Robin (1982) 'Althusser meets Anancy: structuralism and popular protest in Ken Post's history of Jamaica', *The Sociological Review*, 30(2), 345–57.

Cohen, Robin (1992) 'A diaspora of a diaspora? The case of the Caribbean', *Social Science Information*, 31(1), 193–203.

Cohen, Robin (2007) 'Creolization and cultural globalization: the soft sounds of fugitive power', *Globalizations*, 4(3), 369–84.

Cohen, Robin (2008) *Global Diasporas: An Introduction*, 2nd edn, London: Routledge.

Cohen, Robin (2010) 'Social identities, diaspora and creolization', in Kim Knott and Seán McLoughlin (eds), *Diasporas: Concepts, Identities, Intersections*, London: Zed Books, 69–73.

Cohen, Robin and Olivia Sheringham (2013) 'The salience of islands in the articulation of creolization and diaspora', *Diaspora: A Journal of Transnational Studies*, 17(1), 6–17 (cover date 2008, published in 2013).

Collier, James Lincoln (1984) *The Making of Jazz: A Comprehensive History*, London: Macmillan.

Confiant, Raphaël, Jean Bernabé and Lucien Taylor (1997) 'Créolité bites', *Transition*, 74, 124–61.

Coomer, Martin (2014) Hew Locke interview: 'This is about trying to get to an essence of Carnival'; http://www.timeout.com/london/art/hew-locke-interview-this-is-about-trying-to-get-to-an-essence-of-carnival.

Crane, Ralph (2011) '"Amid the alien corn": British India as human island', in Maeve McCusker and Anthony Soares (eds), *Islanded Identities: Constructions of Postcolonial Cultural Insularity*, Amsterdam: Rodopi, 127–44.

Crowley, Daniel J. (1999) 'The sacred and the profane in African and African-derived carnivals', *Western Folklore*, 58(3/4), 223–28.

Darwin, Charles (1968) *On the Origin of Species by Means of Natural Selection, or, the Preservation of Favoured Races in the Struggle for Life*, Harmondsworth: Penguin, 1968 (originally published in 1859).

Darwin, Charles (1981) *The Descent of Man, and Selection in Relation to Sex*, Princeton, NJ: Princeton University Press (originally published in 1871).

Dash, J. Michael (1989) 'Introduction', in Édouard Glissant, *Caribbean Discourse: Selected Essays*, trans. J. Michael Dash, Charlottesville: University Press of Virginia (originally published in French by Gallimard, 1981), xi–xxv.

de Certeau, Michel (1984) *The Practice of Everyday Life*, trans. S. Rendall, Berkeley: University of California Press.

de Jong, Ferdinand (2009) 'Hybrid heritage', *African Arts*, Winter, 1–5.

de Saint-Pierre, Bernardin (2002) *Journey to Mauritius*, trans. and ed. Jason Wilson, Oxford: Signal Books (originally published in 1773).

Diop, Cheikh, Anta (1974) *The African Origin of Civilization: Myth or Reality*, trans. Mercer Cook, New York: L. Hill.

Dollar, Susan E. (2011) 'Ethnicity and Jim Crow: the Americanization of Louisiana's Creoles', in Michael S. Martin (ed.), *Louisiana beyond Black and White: New Interpretation of Twentieth-Century Race and Race Relations*, Lafayette: University of Louisiana at Lafayette Press.

Dominguez, Virginia (1986) *White by Definition: Social Classification in Creole Louisiana*, New Brunswick, NJ: Rutgers University Press.

Donaldson, Gary A. (1984) 'A window on slave culture: dances at Congo square in New Orleans, 1800–1862', *Journal of Negro History*, 69(2), 63–72.

Dorman, James H. (1996) *Creoles of Color of the Gulf South*, Knoxville: University of Tennessee Press.

Driessen, Henk (2005) 'Mediterranean port cities: cosmopolitanism reconsidered', *History and Anthropology*, 16(1), 129–41.

Ehrenreich, Barbara (2008) *Dancing in the Streets: A History of Collective Joy*, London: Granta Books.

Eisenlohr, Patrick (2007) *Little India: Diaspora, Time and Ethnolinguistic Belonging in Hindu Mauritius*, Berkeley: University of California Press.

Elias, Norbert (1978) *The Civilizing Process*, Vol. 1: *The History of Manners*. Oxford: Basil Blackwell.

Enwezor, Okwui, Carlos Basualdo, Ute Meta Bauer, Susanne Ghez, Sarat Maharaj, Octavio Zaya and Mark Nash (eds) (2003) *Créolité and Creolization*, Kassel: Documenta, 11.

Eriksen, Thomas Hylland (1993) 'In which sense do cultural islands exist?' *Social Anthropology* (18), 133–47.

Eriksen, Thomas Hylland (2015) 'Rebuilding the ship at sea: super-diversity, person and conduct in eastern Oslo', *Global Networks*, 15(1), 1–20.

Erikson, Erik H. (1963) *Childhood and Society*, New York: W. W. Norton (originally published in 1950).

Eze, Emmanuel Chukwudu (1967) *Race and the Enlightenment: A Reader*, Oxford: Blackwell.

Ezra, Elizabeth (2000) *The Colonial Unconscious: Race and Culture in Interwar France*, Ithaca, NY: Cornell University Press.

Fine, Robert and Robin Cohen (2002) 'Four cosmopolitan moments', in Steven Vertovec and Robin Cohen (eds), *Conceiving Cosmopolitanism: Theory, Context and Practice*, Oxford: Oxford University Press.

Folse, John D. (2005) *The Encyclopedia of Cajun and Creole Cuisine*, Gonzales, LA: Chef John Folse & Company.

Frazer, James George (1918) *Folk-lore in the Old Testament: Studies in Comparative Religion, Legend and Law*, vol. 1, London Macmillan.

Freyre, Gilberto (1964) *The Master and the Slave: A Study in the Development of Brazilian Civilization*, New York: Knopf.

Friedman, John (1986) 'The world city hypotheses', *Development and Change*, 19(2), 69–83.

Fuller, R. Reese (2011) *Angola to Zydeco: Louisiana Lives*, Jackson: University Press of Mississippi.

Furnivall, J. F. (1948) *Colonial Policy and Practice: A Comparative Study of Burma and Netherlands India*, Cambridge: Cambridge University Press.

Fyle, C. Magbaily (1994) 'Official and unofficial attitudes and policy towards Krio as the main lingua franca in Sierra Leone', in Richard Farndon and Graham Furniss (eds), *African Languages, Development and the State*, London: Routledge, 44–54.

Gidley, Ben (2013) 'Landscapes of belonging, portraits of life: researching everyday multiculture in an inner city estate', *Identities: Global Studies in Culture and Power*, 20(4), 361–76.

Gilroy, Paul (1982) *The Empire Strikes Back: Race and Racism in '70s Britain*, London: Hutchinson.

Gilroy, Paul (2005) *Postcolonial Melancholia*, New York: Columbia University Press.

Giraud, Michel (1994) 'Les identités antillaises entre négritude et créolité', *Cahiers des Amériques Latines*, 17, 141–56.

Glissant, Édouard (1989) *Caribbean Discourse: Selected Essays*, trans. J. Michael Dash, Charlottesville: University Press of Virginia (originally published in French by Gallimard, 1981).

Glissant, Édouard (1990) *Poétique de la relation*, Paris: Gallimard (*Poetics of Relation*, trans. Betsy Wing, Ann Arbor: University of Michigan Press, 1997).

Glissant, Édouard (2008) 'Creolization in the making of the Americas', *Caribbean Quarterly*, 54(1/2), 81–89.

Gonçalves, C. F. (2006) *Kab Verd Band*, Praia, Cape Verde: Instituto do Arquivo Histórico Nacional.

Gosson, R. (2006) 'What lies beneath? Cultural excavation in neocolonial Martinique', in Sylvia Hood Washington, Heather Goodall and Paul C. Rosier (eds), *Echoes from the Poisoned Well: Global Memories of Environmental Injustice*, Lanham, MD: Rowman and Littlefield/ Lexington Books, 225–43.

Gotham, Kevin Fox (2002) 'Marketing Mardi Gras: commodification, spectacle and the political economy of tourism in New Orleans', *Urban Studies*, 39(10), 1735–56.

Green, Tobias (2010) 'The evolution of creole identity in Cape Verde', in Robin Cohen and Paola Toninato (eds), *The Creolization Reader: Studies in Mixed Identities and Cultures*, London: Routledge, 157–66.

Habermas, Jürgen (1974) 'The public sphere', *New German Critique*, 3, 49–55.

Hall, Gwendolyn Midlo (1992) *Africans in Colonial Louisiana: The Development of Afro-Creole Culture in the Eighteenth Century*, Baton Rouge: Louisiana State University Press.

Hall, Stuart (2006) 'Cosmopolitan promises, multicultural realities', in Richard Scholar (ed.), *Divided Cities: The Oxford Amnesty Lectures 2003*, Oxford: Oxford University Press.

Hall, Stuart (2007) 'Living with difference. Stuart Hall in conversation with Bill Schwarz', *Soundings: A Journal of Politics and Culture*, 37, 148–58.

Hall, Stuart (2010) 'Créolité and the process of creolization', in Robin Cohen and Paola Toninato (eds), *The Creolization Reader: Studies in Mixed Identities and Cultures*, London: Routledge, 26–38.

Hannerz, Ulf (1987) 'The world in creolization', *Africa*, 57(4), 546–59.

Hannerz, Ulf (2002) 'Flows, boundaries and hybrids: keywords in transnational anthropology', working paper, Transnational Communities Programme, University of Oxford, WPTC-2K-02; http://www.transcomm.ox.ac.uk/working%20papers/hannerz.pdf.

Harvey, David (2000) 'Cosmopolitanism and the banality of geographical evils', *Public Culture*, 12(2), 524–64.

Hazan, Haim (2015) *Against Hybridity: Social Impasses in a Globalizing World*, Cambridge: Polity.

Henn, Brenna M. et al. (2011) 'Hunter–gatherer genomic diversity suggests a southern African origin for modern humans', *Proceedings of the National Academy of Sciences*, 108(13), 5154–62.

Herskovits, Melville J (1996) *The Myth of the Negro Past*, Boston, MA: Beacon Press.

Hessel, Stéphane (2011) *Time for Outrage (Indignez-vous)*, London: Charles Glass Books.

Hobsbawm, Eric and Terence Ranger (eds) (1983), *The Invention of Tradition*, Cambridge: Cambridge University Press.

Hoffman, JoAnne (2008) 'Diasporic networks, political change, and the growth of cabo-zouk music', in L. Batalha and J. Carling (eds), *Transnational Archipelago: Perspectives on Cape Verdean Migration and Diaspora*, Amsterdam: Amsterdam University Press, 205–20.

Huntington, Samuel P. (1996) *The Clash of Civilizations and the Remaking of World Order*, New York: Simon & Schuster.

İleri, Nurçin (2012) 'Rewriting the history of port cities in the light of contemporary global capitalism', *New Perspectives on Turkey*, 47, 185–209.

Inglis, Fred (2004) *Culture*, Cambridge: Polity.

ISISA (International Small Islands Study Association, 2010) http://tech.groups.yahoo.com/group/ISISA/message/468.

Jackson, Peter (1988) 'Street life: the politics of carnival', *Environment and Planning D: Society and Space*, 8, 213–27.

Jeffrey, Laura (2011) *Chagos Islanders in Mauritius and the UK*, Manchester: Manchester University Press.

Jenkins, Richard (2004) *Social Identity*, London: Routledge.

Kartomi, Margaret J. (1981) 'The processes and results of musical culture contact: a discussion of terminology and concepts', *Ethnomusicology*, 25(2), 227–49.

Kein, Sybil (ed.) (2000) *Creole: The History and Legacy of Louisiana's Free People of Color*, Baton Rouge: Louisiana State University Press.

Khan, Aisha (2001) 'Journey to the center of the earth: the Caribbean as master symbol', *Cultural Anthropology*, 16(3), 271–302.

Knott, Kim and Seán McLoughlin (eds) (2010) *Diasporas: Concepts, Identities, Intersections*, London: Zed Books.

Levitt, Peggy (2015) *Artifacts and Allegiances: How Museums Put the Nation and the World on Display*, Oakland: University of California Press.

Lewis, Shireen (2006) *Race, Culture and Identity: Francophone West African and Caribbean Literature and Theory from Négritude to Creolité*, Lanham and Oxford: Lexington Books.

Lionnet, Françoise and Shu-mei Shih (eds) (2011) *The Creolization of Theory*, Durham, NC: Duke University Press.

Lipsitz, George (1988) 'Mardi Gras Indians: carnival and counter-narrative in black New Orleans', *Cultural Critique*, 10, 99–121.

Lipsitz, George (1994) *Dangerous Crossroads: Popular Music, Postmodernism and the Poetics of Place*, London: Verso.

Lobban, Richard (1995) *Cape Verde: Crioulo Colony to Independent Nation*, Boulder, CO: Westview Press.

Marcuse, Peter and Ronald Van Kempen (eds) (2000) *Globalizing Cities: A New Spatial Order?* Oxford: Blackwell.

Martin, Denis-Constant. (2012) 'The musical heritage of slavery: from creolization to "world music"', in Bob W. White (ed.), *Music and Globalization*, Bloomington, IN: Indiana University Press.

Massey, Doreen (1993) 'Politics and space/time' *New Left Review*, 196, 65–84.

Mattern, Mark (1997) 'Let the good times unroll: music and race relations in Southwest Louisiana', *Black Music Research Journal*, 17(2), 159–68.

Mayaram, Shail (ed.) (2009) *The Other Global City*, New York: Routledge.

McCusker, Maeve (2011) 'Writing against the tide? Patrick Chamoiseau's (Is)land Imaginary', in Maeve McCusker and Anthony Soares (eds), *Islanded Identities: Constructions of Postcolonial Cultural Insularity*, Amsterdam: Rodopi, 41–61.

McCusker, Maeve and Anthony Soares (2011) 'Introduction', in Maeve McCusker and Anthony Soares (eds), *Islanded Identities: Constructions of Postcolonial Cultural Insularity*, Amsterdam: Rodopi, xi–xxvii.

Mesthrie, Rajend (2009) 'Language contact 2: pidgins, creoles and the "new Englishes"', in Rajend Mesthrie, Joan Swann, Andrea Deumert and William L. Leap (eds), *Introducing Sociolinguistics*, Edinburgh: Edinburgh University Press.

Miles, W. (2013) 'Schizophrenic island, fifty years after Fanon: Martinique, the pent-up "paradise"', *International Journal of Francophone Studies*, 15(1), 9–33.

Miles, William (2006) 'When is a nation "a nation"? Identity-formation within a French West Indian people (Martinique)', *Nations and Nationalism*, 12(4), 631–52.

Mills, Gary B. (1997) *The Forgotten People: Cane River's Creoles of Color*, Baton Rouge: Louisiana State University Press.

Moss, Roger (2000) *Le Morne/Lemorn*, Bi-lingual English/Kreol edn, Port Louis: Ledikasyon pu Travayer.

Murdoch, H. Adlai (2012) *Creolizing the Metropole: Migrant Caribbean Identities in Literature and Film*, Bloomington: University of Illinois Press.

Murdoch, H. Adlai (2013) 'Édouard Glissant's creolized world vision: from resistance and relation to *opacité*', *Callaloo*, 36(4), 875–89.

Nehru, Jawaharlal (1961) *India's Foreign Policy: Selected Speeches, September 1946–April 1961*, Delhi: Government of India.

Neveu Kringelbach, Hélène and Jonathan Skinner (eds) (2012) *Dancing Cultures: Globalization, Tourism and Identity in the Anthropology of Dance*, Oxford: Berghahn.

Obeyesekere, Gananath (2005) *Cannibal Talk: The Man-Easting Myth and Human Sacrifice in the South Seas*, Berkeley: University of California Press.

Olwig, Karen Fog (2013) 'Notions and practices of difference: an epilogue on the ethnography of diversity', *Identities: Global Studies in Culture and Power*, 20(4), 471–79.

Ortiz, Fernando (1995) *Cuban Counterpoint: Tobacco and Sugar*, Durham, NC: Duke University Press (originally published in Spanish in 1940).

Owusu, Kwesi (1986) *Struggle for Black Arts in Britain: What Can We Consider Better Than Freedom?* London: Cengage Learning.

Palmié, Stephan (2010) 'Creolization and its discontents', in Robin Cohen and Paola Toninato (eds), *The Creolization Reader: Studies in Mixed Identities and Cultures*, London: Routledge, 49–67.

Peeren, Esther (2007) 'Carnival politics and the territory of the street', *Thamyris/Intersecting*, 14, 69–82.

Pinho, Mariana (n.d.) 'Escolas brasileiras brilham no carnaval londrino de Notting Hill'; http://www.portugues.rfi.fr/geral/20140825-carnaval-de-notting-hill-tem-apresentacoes-de-escolas-brasileiras.

Pitt, David (1980) 'Sociology, islands and boundaries', *World Development*, 8(12), 1051–9.

Pratt, Mary Louise (2008) *Imperial Eyes: Travel Writing and Transculturation*, London: Routledge, 2008.

Premdas, Ralph (1996) 'Public policy and ethnic conflict', Management of Social Transformations, Discussion Paper Series No. 12, Paris: UNESCO

Price, Richard (1998) *The Convict and the Colonel*, Durham, NC: Duke University Press.

Price, Richard and Sally Price (1997) 'Shadowboxing in the Mangrove', *Cultural Anthropology*, 12, 3–36.

Rego, Márcia (2008) 'Cape Verdean tongues: speaking of a "nation" at home and abroad', in L. Batalha and J. Carling (eds), *Transnational Archipelago: Perspectives on Cape Verdean Migration and Diaspora*, Amsterdam: Amsterdam University Press, 145–59.

Rhys-Taylor, Alex (2013) 'The essences of multiculture: a sensory exploration of an inner-city street market', *Identities: Global Studies in Culture and Power*, 20(4), 393–406.

Roach, Joseph (1992) 'Mardi Gras Indians and others: genealogies of American performance', *Theatre Journal*, 44(4), 461–83.

Robinson, Jennifer (2005) *Ordinary Cities: Between Modernity and Development*, London: Routledge.

Rocha-Trindade (2012) 'Uma Celebração Catalisadora de uma Relação Intercontinental no Espaço da Diáspora Cabo-Verdiana – O Carnaval do Mindelo', paper presented at 8° Congreso Ibérico de Estudios Africanos > A ponte atlântica entre a Europa, a África e a América do Sul na época da globalização; http://www.ciea8. org/ocs/index.php?conference=CIEA2012&schedConf=pan23&pa e=paper&op=view&path%5B%5D=671.

Rodríguez, Encarnación Gutiérrez and Shirley Anne Tate (eds) (2015) *Creolizing Europe: Legacies and Transformations*, Liverpool: Liverpool University Press.

Rosello, Mireille (1995) 'Introduction: Aimé Césaire and the *Notebook of a Return to My Native Land* in the 1990s', in *Notebook of a Return to My Native Land*, trans. Mireille Rosello and Annie Pritchard, Newcastle-upon-Tyne: Bloodaxe Books, 9–19 (originally published by Editions Présence Africaine, 1956).

Rosenthal, Franz (1989) *The History of al-Tabari*, Vol. 1: *General Introduction* and *From the Creation to the Flood*, Albany: State University of New York Press.

Safran, William (1991) 'Diasporas in modern societies: myths of homeland and return', *Diaspora: A Journal of Transnational Studies*, 1(1), 83–99.

Safran, William (2005) 'The Jewish diaspora in a comparative and theoretical perspective', *Israel Studies*, 10(1), 36–60.

St Landry Parish Tourist Commission (2013) *We Live Our Culture* (tourist brochure), Opelousas: SLPTC.

Salamone, Frank A. (1998) 'Nigerian and Ghanaian popular music: two varieties of creolization', *The Journal of Popular Culture*, 32(2), 11–25.

Salopek, Paul (2013) 'Out of Eden', *National Geographic*, 224(6), December, 21–60.

Sartre, Jean Paul (1964) *Black Orpheus*, trans. J. MacCombie, in *The Massachusetts Review*, 6, 13–52 (originally published by Presses Universitaires de Frances, 1948).

Sassen, Saskia (1991) *The Global City: London, New York, Tokyo*, Princeton, NJ: Princeton University Press.

Schieffelin, Bambi B. and Elinor Ochs (eds) (1987) *Language Socialization across Cultures*, Cambridge: Cambridge University Press.

Schwartz, Leonard (2002) 'After Babel'; http://towerofbabel.com/sections/bard/thenewbabel/.

Seale, Richard, Robert DeBlieux and Harlan Mark Guidry (2002) *Natchitoches and Louisiana's Timeless Cane River*, Baton Rouge: Louisiana State University Press.

Sheller, Mimi (2003) 'Creolization in discourses of global culture', in Sara Ahmed, Claudia Castaneda and Anne-Marie Fortier (eds), *Uprootings/Regroundings: Questions of Home and Migration*, Oxford: Berg Publishers, 273–94.

Sheringham, Olivia (2012) 'A delicate dance: creolization, diaspora, and the metropolitan "pull" in the French Antilles', paper given at the Caribbean Studies Association annual conference, 28 May–1 June, Guadeloupe.

Shih, Shu-mei and Françoise Lionnet (2011) 'Introduction: the creolization of theory', in Françoise Lionnet and Shu-mei Shih (eds), *The Creolization of Theory*, Durham, NC: Duke University Press, 1–33.

Shown Mills, Elizabeth (2004) *Isle of Canes: A Historical Novel*, Provo, UT: MyFamily.com Inc.

Shrum, Wesley and John Kilburn (1996) 'Ritual disrobement at Mardi Gras: ceremonial exchange and moral order', *Social Forces*, 75(2), 423–58.

Sieber, Timothy (2005) 'Popular music and cultural identity in the Cape Verdean post-colonial diaspora', *Etnográfica*, 9(1), 123–48.

Singleton, Hubert Daniel (1998) *The Indians who Gave Us Zydeco: The Atakapas–Ishaks (a-TAK-a-paws EE-shaks) of Southwest Louisiana and Southeast Texas*, Place of publication unstated: Author.

Smith Simmons, Adele (1982) *Modern Mauritius: The Politics of Decolonization*, Bloomington: Indiana University Press.

Smith, Michael Peter (2005) 'Transnational urbanism revisited', *Journal of Ethnic and Migration Studies*, 31(2), 235–44.

Spitzer, Nicholas R. (1996) 'Mardi Gras in l'Anse de 'Prien Noir: a Creole community performance in rural French Louisiana', in James H. Dorman (ed.), *Creoles of Colour of the Gulf South*, Knoxville: University of Tennessee Press, 87–125.

Spitzer, Nick (2011) 'Monde créole: the cultural world of French Louisiana Creoles and the creolization of world cultures', in R. Baron and A. C. Cara (eds), *Creolization as Cultural Creativity*, Jackson: University Press of Mississippi, 32–68.

Stewart, Charles (1999) 'Syncretism and its synonyms: reflections on cultural mixture', *Diacritics*, 29(3), 40–62.

Stewart, Charles (ed.) (2007) *Creolization: History, Ethnography, Theory*, Walnut Creek, CA: Left Coast Press.

Sullivan, Lester (2005) 'Composers of color of nineteenth-century New Orleans', in Sybil Kein (ed.), *Creole: The History and Legacy of Louisiana's Free People of Color*, Baton Rouge: Louisiana State University Press, 71–100.

Teelock, Vijaya (2001) *Mauritian History: From Its Beginnings to Modern Times*, Mauritius: Mahatma Gandhi Institute.

Thucydides (1910) *The Peloponnesian War*, London: J. M. Dent (Thucydides on a speech delivered in 431 or 432 BC).

Tishkoff, Sarah A. et al. (2009) 'The genetic structure and history of Africans and African Americans', *Science*, 324(5930), 1035–44.

Tölölyan, Khachig (1996) 'Rethinking diaspora(s): stateless power in the transnational moment', *Diaspora: A Journal of Transnational Studies*, 5(1), 3–36.

Tompsett, Adela Ruth (2005) '"London is the place for me": performance and identity in Notting Hill Carnival', *Theatre History Studies*, 25, 43–6.

Trouillot, Michel-Rolph (1998) 'Culture on the edges: creolization in the plantation context', *Plantation Society in the* Americas, 5(1), 8–28.

Upton, Carole-Anne (2013) 'Why performance matters', *Performance Arts*, Bristol: Intellect Books.

Vale de Almeida, Miguel (2007) 'From miscegenation to Creole identity: Portuguese Colonialism, Brazil, Cape Verde', in C. Stewart (ed.), *Creolization: History, Ethnography, Theory*, Walnut Creek, CA: Left Coast Press, 108–32.

Valentine, Gill (2008) 'Living with difference: reflections on geographies of encounter', *Progress in Human Geography*, 32(3), 323–37.

Van Onselen, Charles (1976) *Chibaro: African Mine Labour in Southern Rhodesia 1900–1933*, London: Pluto Press.

Vannini, Phillip (2011) 'Constellations of ferry (im)mobility: islandness as the performance and politics of insulation and isolation', *Cultural Geographies* 18(2), 249–71.

Vaughan, Megan (2005) *Creating the Creole Island: Slavery in Eighteenth-Century Mauritius*, Durham, NC: Duke University Press.

Vergès, Françoise (2003) 'Kiltir kréol: processes and practices of créolité and creolization', in Okwui Enwezor et al. (eds), *Créolité and Creolization*, Kassel: Documenta, 11, 79–84.

Vergès, Françoise (2004) 'Postcolonial Challenges', in Nicholas Gane, *The Future of Social Theory*, New York: Continuum, 186–204.

Vergès, Françoise (2012) 'Is creolization a useful concept today?' Presentation at the conference 'Identities: Creolization and Diaspora in Comparative Perspective', University of Oxford, 6–7 December.

Vertovec, Steven (2007) 'Super-diversity and its implications', *Ethnic and Racial Studies*, 30(6), 1024–54.

Vertovec, Steven and Robin Cohen (2002) 'Introduction', in Steven Vertovec and Robin Cohen (eds), *Conceiving Cosmopolitanism: Theory, Context and Practice*, Oxford: Oxford University Press.

Vertovec, Steven and Susanne Wessendorf (eds) (2009) *The Multiculturalism Backlash: European Discourses, Policies and Practices*, London: Routledge.

Wallace, Mark (1995) 'Introduction', in Paul Ricoeur, *Figuring the Sacred: Religion, Narrative and Imagination*, Minneapolis: Fortress Press, 1–34.

Ware, Carolyn E. (2001) 'Anything to act crazy: Cajun women and Mardi Gras disguise', *Journal of American Folklore*, 114(452), 225–47.

Weiss, Toni (2001) 'The economic impact of the Mardi Gras season on the New Orleans economy and the net fiscal benefit of staging Mardi Gras for the city of New Orleans', unpublished paper prepared for the Carnival Krewe Civic Foundation, Inc., New Orleans.

Wessendorf, Susanne (2014) *Commonplace Diversity: Social Relations in a Super-Diverse Context*, London: Palgrave Macmillan.

Winford, Donald (2003) *An Introduction to Contact Linguistics*, Malden, MA: Blackwell.

Index

DATE DUE

JAN 2 6 2017			

DEMCO 38-296